Heavenly Bodies

The Realms of *La estrella de Sevilla*

Edited by
Frederick A. de Armas

Lewisburg
Bucknell University Press
London: Associated University Presses

Associated University Presses
440 Forsgate Drive
Cranbury, NJ 08512

Associated University Presses
16 Barter Street
London WC1A 2AH, England

Associated University Presses
P.O. Box 338, Port Credit
Mississauga, Ontario
Canada L5G 4L8

The paper used in this publication meets the requirements
of the American National Standard for Permanence of Paper
for Printed Library Materials Z39.48-1984.

Library of Congress Cataloging-in-Publication Data

Heavenly bodies : the realms of La estrella de Sevilla / edited by
    Frederick A. de Armas.
        p.   cm.
    Includes bibliographical references (p.   ) and index.
    ISBN 0-8387-5308-6 (alk. paper)
    1. Estrella de Sevilla.   I. De Armas, Frederick A.
PQ6458.E834   1996
862'.3—dc20   95-42784
                                                              CIP

Heavenly Bodies

Contents

Part IV. Text, Authority, and Performance

Part V. Writing

Preface

THIS volume grew out of an International Symposium on *La estrella de Sevilla* held at The Pennsylvania State University, 2–4 April 1992. At a time when this play is attracting increasing attention because of the renewed debate over its authorship, it seemed appropriate to invite leading scholars on the subject to explore the body of the text and venture into the astral, political, and literary realms of *La estrella de sevilla*.

Throughout *La estrella de Sevilla,* its eponymous heroine serves as an object of other characters' perceptions, constructions, and manipulations. King Sancho, his advisor don Arias, Sancho Ortiz, and even Estrella's brother Busto Tabera repeatedly define her from their own perspectives and on their own terms. In his contribution to this collection, James Mandrell calls attention to Estrella's resultant polyvalence, considering her functions both as "material girl" and "celestial woman" within the play's textual dynamics. In her material aspect, Estrella is Sancho's subject, a human inhabitant of Castile. Celestially speaking, the King first identifies Estrella with Saturn (141–50; Burke 1974, 144), then later in the play refers to her instead as a fixed star: "Aunque soy don Sancho el Bravo, / venero en el cielo octavo / esta Estrella de Sevilla" (vv. 958–60: "Even though I am Sancho the Brave, I venerate the Star of Seville who abides in the eighth sphere"). Thus, in the eyes of those who attempt to define her, Estrella Tabera occupies multiple realms: she partakes of generation and corruption in the sublunary spheres, but at the same time she is assigned to both the seventh and eighth ptolemaic spheres. The contributors to this volume both perceive and fashion multiple contexts for *La estrella de Sevilla,* echoing the multiplicity of realms in which she abides within the text.

Although North American *comedia* studies have granted a certain degree of canonicity to *La estrella de Sevilla,* disputes over its authorship have raised questions as to its centrality in Golden Age studies. Canonicity, then, is the first of *Estrella*'s realms to be explored. In "The Mysteries of Canonicity" I delve into the history of the play's reception. Its persistent links to historical events, which some have wanted to censor, have created a vortex of centripetal forces leading toward *Estrella*'s canonicity, as well as centrifugal forces nudging it towards marginalization. James A. Parr in turn offers his meditations on the canon itself and on the twentieth century's evolution of literary commentary, which he sees as a progression from "scholarship" to "criticism" to "theory." Parr concludes by incorporating all three of these traditions in his discussion of *Estrella*'s simultaneously unique and universal depiction of male reaction to female beauty.

Part II of this volume ventures into *La estrella de Sevilla*'s political realm(s). Grace Burton utilizes the image of Estrella's broken mirror as a metaphor for the centrality of resemblance to the play's action. Although resemblance is a system on which the feudal order is founded, that order is irrevocably shattered by the king's violence against Busto's honor. For Frank Casa, the king is the protagonist, and the text dramatizes the medieval doctrine of a monarch's dual nature. Sancho *el bravo* cannot function effectively as a king because of his failings as a man. His final recognition of wrongdoing and confession of responsibility are necessary steps in his maturation. Melveena McKendrick explores *Estrella*'s relationship to the political ideology of its time. She argues that, in depicting the tension between the interests of justice and the interests of the state, the *comedia* hints at Machievelli's presence through the compromise position of *tacitismo*. Finally, Harlan Sturm regards the play as a handbook for just monarchy, a course of instruction in the "universal values" fundamental to the sound exercise of royal power.

Part III, *Strategies,* evinces the many facets of *La estrella de Sevilla*. Whether speaking of ghosts, gazes, madness, or matter, these essays reveal the polysemic richness of the text. In "The Moor's Ghost" Catherine Connor contends that the dramatic conflicts arising from Sancho's attempted conquest of Estrella mirror the Moorish/Christian conflicts of the Reconquest. This reading draws upon the work of Edward Said and foregrounds the *comedia*'s subtle Orientalism. In "Stargazing," Anne J. Cruz offers a Lacanian interpretation of the *comedia* as playtext. The complexities of the various gazes at a performance of *Estrella,* according to Cruz, make it possible to discern revealing "ideological fissures" within the work. Daniel L. Heiple foregrounds Sancho Ortiz's "mad scene" as an ideological key to *Estrella*'s paradoxes, contextualizing this episode within the traditions of the world gone mad and of the wise madman so as to emphasize the play's dark vision of human existence. Finally, James Mandrell finds his critical inspiration in the lyrics of the postmodern Madonna for his essay "Of Material Girls and Celestial Women." Mandrell focuses on the cultural economies of exchange at work in the play, along with the manner in which they shape various characters' actions and fates. He sees Estrella as the protagonist of the work, but notes that she cannot act as an agent of self-interest in a culture where she is an important medium of exchange.

The first three essays of Part IV, *Text, Authority, and Performace,* concern themselves with the hotly contested authorship of *La estrella de Sevilla.* Carmen Hernández Valcárcel explores the intertextualities of plot, characterization, and theme between plays indisputably by Lope de Vega and *Estrella,* arguing that such commonalities confirm the traditional attribution of the play to Lope. In contrast, Alfredo Rodríguez López-Vázquez offers a statistical comparison of the mythological references in the text to those employed in other works by various candidates for *Estrella*'s authorship and, on the basis of his findings, claims *Estrella* for Andrés de Claramonte. Susan L. Fischer takes an entirely different approach, relying on Iser's theories of reader-response to bestow authority of/over *Estrella* on the *comedia*'s readers. And Anita Stoll, in her essay "Staging and Polymetry," concentrates on possible onstage realizations of *La estrella de Sevilla.* After examining the play's metrical complexities in the construction of an autotextual virtual performance, Stoll concludes with further questions concerning the challenges posed by *Estrella* as performance text.

The very prominence of writing in *La estrella de Sevilla* has led the final four contributors to focus on inscription in this *comedia.* In "Acts of Reading, Acts of Writing" Emilie Bergmann examines the failure of both spoken and written language in *Estrella,* along with women's fatal inscription in cultural systems of exchange and honor. James F. Burke discerns in this play a literary *Saturnalia* out of the classical tradition, an exemplary carnival inscribed in the text for the audience's edification. In "Shame, Writing, and Morality", Charles Oriel explores the textual opposition between inscription and orality, an opposition fundamental to the play and reflective of its many other dualities. Finally, Elias L. Rivers has graciously made available a version of one of his most influential articles on *La estrella de Sevilla,* an essay that first made us aware of the importance of writing within this *comedia.* Here, Rivers employs speech act theory to examine the role played by writing in the corruption and loss of honor, both in the specific events of *Estrella* and in a larger cultural context.

In conclusion, I would like to express my appreciation to all those who made this volume possible. My thanks to Ron Friis, Carolyn Nadeau and Christopher Weimer for their editorial assistance. I also wish to express my appreciation to those who helped me put together the Symposium: Mary Barnard, Ivy A. Corfis, and Robert Lima. I owe a special debt of gratitude to Leon Lyday for his support and encouragement. Financial assistance for the Symposium was made available by Penn State through its Institute for the Arts and Humanistic Studies and the College of Liberal Arts. A grant from the Program for Cultural Cooperation between Spain's Ministry of Culture and United States' Universities allowed us to invite a substantial number of distinguished speakers from the United States and Spain. Versions of chapters 17 and 18 have been previously published. I would like to thank Purdue University Press and the editor of *Folio* for permission to include these texts. Unless specified, all textual references to *La estrella de Sevilla* are from *Diez comedias del Siglo de Oro,* eds. José Martel and Hymen Alpern, revised by Leonard Mades (New York: Harper & Row, 1968; 2d edition). Translations of cited passages are made by the authors of the individual articles, unless noted.

Heavenly Bodies

Part I
Canonicity

1

The Mysteries of Canonicity

FREDERICK A. DE ARMAS

WHEN in the Spring of 1992 eighteen scholars arrived at Penn State University to participate in the International Symposium on *La estrella de Sevilla* (*The Star of Seville*), I did not think that the choice of this play would require any explanation. After all, it has been taught in countless courses on Golden Age Theater in the United States since it is one of ten plays included in the most commonly used anthology in American Universities, *Diez comedias del Siglo de Oro* (*Ten Plays of the Golden Age*), edited by Hymen Alpern and José Martel. I was thus surprised to hear from Melveena McKendrick that the choice was a curious one, since in Britain, *La estrella de Sevilla* is not part of the canon. In a letter, McKendrick explained that, in regard to *comedias* taught in British Universities, "there is no canon as such. Departments do not use *Diez comedias* or any other anthology for that matter (As you know, I'd never heard of *Diez comedias*) but teach whatever seems appropriate. In practice, what is appropriate is determined by the good editions available and this availability, of course, tends to be determined by shared notions of which are the 'best' plays. *La estrella*'s exposure, I suppose, suffers from the doubts over its authorship."

Although not classifying them as such, McKendrick is actually speaking of the three types of canon as defined by Alastair Fowler: the potential, the accessible, and the selective. British universities seldom choose texts at random from the potential canon (all existing *comedias*). Instead, they make their choices from the accessible canon (from good editions available at the time). The process of picking the appropriate texts from the available editions gives us the selective canon. Although it would be more difficult to pinpoint this selective canon in Britain since anthologies are not used, such a canon would no doubt emerge from a compilation of reading

15

lists from the different centers of learning. *La estrella de Sevilla* would probably not be part of the selective canon, according to McKendrick, since it "suffers from doubts over its authorship." Now, if such is the case, why did these doubts not interfere with the play's canonicity on this side of the Atlantic?

Faced with anthologizing and authorship as key questions affecting canonicity, I decided to delve into the reception of *La estrella de Sevilla* in order to better understand how a work is affected by these and other circumstances. Is *La estrella de Sevilla* a canonical play in this country simply because it was included in a popular anthology? What other elements have led to the canonization? As I began to look into this question, I took into account both centripetal forces leading toward canonicity and centrifugal forces creating a certain marginalization of *La estrella de Sevilla*. I was thus able to isolate three key moments in which there was an important shift in the canonicity of this *comedia*. The first such moment, was of course, the moment of its first staging and subsequent publication in Spain. This occurred during the second and third decades of the seventeenth century. A centripetal shift in its position in the canon occurred at the beginning of the nineteenth century, when it was adapted by Cándido María Trigueros. Although by the end of the nineteenth and beginning of the twentieth century a centrifugal movement toward the margins was created by debate over authorship, a third moment, typically American, led to the renewed canonization of *La estrella de Sevilla* with the publication of *Diez comedias*. Finally, in the 1980s the renewed concern over authorship has once again disturbed the placement of *La estrella de Sevilla* in the canon both in Spain and in the United States. In this essay I would like to explore the first three moments, omitting the most recent fluctuation since it is too early to assess its impact.

La estrella de Sevilla was not part of the canon during the seventeenth century. By this I mean that it does not seem to have been performed often nor was it printed with any great frequency. It was never mentioned critically. In fact, the play was virtually unknown from the time of its composition to the beginning of the nineteenth century.[1] The text has come down to us in two different versions. A shorter version, attributed to Lope de Vega, was published around the middle of the seventeenth century as a *suelta* (single play).[2] The long version, attributed to "Cardenio," is an *arrachement,* taken out of a volume of collected plays from the 1630s.[3] From the beginning, then, we have a series of mysteries that surround the play, including the "enigma de la autoría" ("enigma of authorship"; Rodríguez López-Vázquez 1991, 11). But perhaps the most important question concerning the play's mysteries was posed by John Hill: "On reading *La estrella de Sevilla,* a play so admirably constructed and fundamentally so moving in its tragic import as to place it in the front rank of seventeenth-century dramatic productions in Spain, one is moved inevitably to inquire into the causes of the silence that surrounds the early history of the play. Why should a play, manifestly so superior to the majority of its contemporaries, have been passed over entirely unnoticed? Was there a conspiracy of silence against it? Was it prohibited by the censor, or placed under the ban by the Inquisition?" (Reed, Dixon, Hill 1939, xxx).

I concur with Hill that the seventeenth-century silence has more to do with a political mystery than with questions of authorship. I will first investigate this enigma in the context of the seventeenth century, and then I will attempt to show how it is also a hidden motive behind the other two major canonical shifts of the play, one at the beginning of the nineteenth century and the second in the 1930s. I hope to show that canonicity or marginalization, in the case of *La estrella de Sevilla,* is very much a function of politics. Writing on the canon, John Guillory suggests that "if the history of canon-formation really were a rigorous process of exclusion, then one ought to find many works through history that were actively suppressed, actively excluded from the canon. And it should follow that we would find many of these works to be as good as the works we today consider canonical"(1990, 237). For him, such works are an exception, thus invalidating the theory of a political agenda of exclusion. Perhaps *La estrella de Sevilla* is one of these exceptions, since I hope to show that on more than one occasion it was censored and excluded from the canon.

When the question of authorship was being heatedly debated in the 1930s one of the elements brought up was a mythological allusion at the beginning of the second act. Could Lope de Vega (if he was indeed the author) have made a mistake in his mythology? Didn't this error appear in the works of Andrés de Claramonte?[4] Those arguing about authorship missed a deeper enigma. As the youthful and impetuous King Sancho IV, forgetting his duties as monarch, is about to enter Estrella's house in order to dishonor her, don Arias, his advisor, questions him: "¿Solo te aventuras?" to which the King replies: "Pues, / por qué espumosos remolcos / por manzanas paso a Colcos?" (933–35; "Upon which foaming seas am I being cast toward Colchis in quest of the apples?").[5] In other words, there seems to be no danger (no foaming seas) in the acquisition of this forbidden fruit. Yet, the reader or audience must have been jolted by the word Colchis since the *manzanas* (apples) should have been those of the Hesperides, or possibly the Biblical ones. Even though the phrase may make sense through an awareness of classical minutiae, the actual effect is one of surprise or confusion, leading the reader or spectator to consider a comparison in the midst of dramatic suspense. It would not matter that a spectator was ignorant of the fact that the Greek word *mela* refers to both sheep and apples and that classical authors would at times playfully transpose the golden apples of the Hesperides and the golden fleece at Colchis (de Armas 1979). What is important is that both myths are foregrounded by the king. If we agree with Anibal (1934), Cotarelo (1930), and Kennedy (1975) that *La estrella de Sevilla* was written in 1623, then these two mythological allusions acquire added significance since the new Spanish King, the youthful and impetuous Philip IV, was being praised as a new Hercules (conqueror of the golden apples) and a new Jason (conqueror of the golden fleece). In foregrounding this unusual allusion, the author may have been pointing to the political mystery of the *comedia*.

Once aware of this possibility, many of the elements in *La estrella de Sevilla* begin to fall in place. The play is not about Sancho IV, but is instead a critical assessment of Philip IV's first years in power. It is not my intention at this point to examine all the elements that underline such a reading.[6] I will only point to some key parallels that reinforce Ruth Lee Kennedy's intuition that *Estrella* was among the "mirrors for princes, in dramatic form, written by authors who believed with Hamlet that 'the play's the thing with which to catch the conscience of the king'" (Kennedy 1974, 55).

The *comedia* begins with the triumphal entry of Sancho IV into Sevilla. Just like the future Philip, this medieval king is the fourth of his name. This number helped to create a link between Philip and the Sun, since this celestial body resides in the fourth celestial sphere, according to Ptolemy.[7] J. H. Elliott explains: "The image of Philip as the sun was quickly taken up by the court poets and playwrights, and was to provide a central theme for the reign" (1986, 177). One of the centrifugal forces that have led to the marginalization of the play is the "astrólogo estilo" (astrological style) utilized by the author, along with the many mythological allusions that were dismissed by early critics as mere adornment. And yet, disregard for astrology and mythology may have delayed the solution to the political enigma of the play.[8]

In *La estrella de Sevilla* Sancho IV is portrayed as a sensual monarch, not interested in the architectural beauties of the city,

but only in female beauty (65–70). He asks his minister to describe
the women who stand in balconies around him. This portrayal does
not fit the medieval monarch, but it could very well be a reference
to Philip IV, whose "passion for women . . . turned him into a
jaded voluptuary well before middle age" (Lynch 1981, 68). The
seven women that surround him have been identified by James F.
Burke with the seven planets (1974, 137–56). While they mirror a
Ptolemaic universe, Sancho, standing in the middle as the Sun,
proclaims a new order, a Copernican universe. And yet, this new
order is fraught with danger, since the king believes he can shatter
all the old laws. His advisor, don Arias, will later echo this belief
by asserting to the monarch that "en el orbe español / no hay más
leyes que tu gusto" (1188–89; "In the Spanish sphere there is no
other law but your pleasure"). Arias's help in Sancho's amorous
pursuits establishes one more parallel with a contemporary situation since, as J. H. Elliott notes, the Count-Duke of Olivares,
Philip IV's minister, "was reported to be accompanying the king
on nocturnal expeditions . . . encouraging the king in 'illicit affairs'" (1986, 112). Just such an expedition in the *comedia* will lead
the king and his advisor to Estrella's house.

It is on arriving at Estrella's house that the *privado* speaks of
the king in terms of Jason and Hercules. The link between Spanish
kings and Hercules had been forged during the Middle Ages (Tate
1954) and culminates during the reign of Charles V when, according to Brown and Elliott, "the invention of the emperor's emblematic device, which was designed around the mythical columns
of Hercules, fixed the association of the ancient hero with the
modern ruler firmly in the minds of sixteenth century princes"
(1980, 157). In order to reinforce the parallel between Hercules and
the king, *La estrella de Sevilla* includes an allusion to the famous
columns (36–40). It is interesting to note that Sancho IV never
conquered Gibraltar, but Philip IV did go to that city, following his
visit to Sevilla in 1624. *La estrella de Sevilla,* then, must have been
written when news of Philip's trip to Sevilla and Gibraltar was
already circulating in Madrid (Kennedy 1975). According to Diego
Angulo Iñiguez, the city of Seville printed a commemorative coin
at this time, on which Hercules appears on one side and an image
of Philip IV on the other (1952, 73). There are at least two more
references to the Hercules myth in *La estrella de Sevilla.* The one
to Atlas, the giant who upholds the heavens and forms the second
column of Hercules, may well underline the fact that during
Philip's reign his minister Olivares was associated with Atlas, since

he helped the king with the weight of the world, the heavy burden of imperial rulership (Elliott 1986, 47).[9]

References to the myth of Jason are as important as those to Hercules. Philip IV was seen as a new Jason since he was born in April, under the sign of Aries, the sign of the ram or golden fleece acquired by Jason and the Argonauts. Not only was Philip associated with this myth because of his horoscope. As a Habsburg, he was interested in the deeds of the Argonauts since the monarchs of this dynasty belonged to the chivalric Order of the Golden Fleece.[10] The year before the composition of *La estrella de Sevilla,* Lope de Vega chose to celebrate the king's birthday with a mythological play entitled *El vellocino de oro* (*The Golden Fleece*).

While Lope's play was a great success, a second performance given on that particular evening is more problematic and may also have ties to *La estrella de Sevilla.* One of the ways in which the Conde de Villamediana's *La gloria de Niquea* (*The Glory of Niquea*) praises Philip IV is through an allusion to one of his love affairs. Francisca de Tabara, one of the ladies at the court, appears onstage seated in a cart drawn by a bull. She is "Donzella Europa, amante robo del transformado Júpiter" (1990, 1156; "Damsel Europa, amorously taken by the metamorphosed Jupiter"). The reference could not have been clearer. Francisca is the mythical Europa, abducted by Jupiter in the shape of a bull. Jupiter is none other than Philip IV, who was known to be having an affair with Francisca. According to legend, Philip had Villamediana murdered because of this Francisca Tabara. It is surely no coincidence that the author of *La estrella de Sevilla* named his heroine Estrella Tabera. Only one letter separates Tabara from Tabera. Both women trigger the murder of a powerful nobleman, Busto in the play and Villamediana at the Court.

As if to underline the importance of names in the *comedia,* the two representatives from Sevilla who receive the king are named Pedro de Guzmán and Farfán de Ribera. These are also the last names given the two women who are first described by Arias when the king arrives in Sevilla, Leonor de Ribera and Elvira de Guzmán. These are Olivares's last names. His father was Pedro de Guzmán and his mother Francisca de Ribera. Since Sevilla was the minister's home, the author of the play is clearly showing how the minister and the king transgress against family and city. *La estrella de Sevilla,* then, is a *comedia* very much like the play within the play in *Hamlet,* one with which to catch the conscience of a murderous and lustful king. No wonder this play was relegated to oblivion during its time. As a political whodunit, it pointed to

Philip IV. It also criticized his most powerful minister, his Atlas, Olivares.

John M. Hill attests that a "search of the writings of critics and chroniclers of the seventeenth and eighteenth centuries reveals not a single reference to our play" (xxxv). For almost two centuries no one noticed *Estrella*'s existence.[11] Shortly before the beginning of the nineteenth century, the pre-romantic writer Cándido María Trigueros (1736–98) unearthed one of the *sueltas* of *La estrella de Sevilla*. Believing that the play was a neglected masterpiece by Lope de Vega, he recast it so that it would conform to the neoclassical unities.[12] In the preface to his version, entitled *Sancho Ortiz de las Roelas,* Trigueros explains: "Parecióme que debía omitir todo lo que precede á la verdadera acción del drama. . . . no solo ha sido forzoso interpolar gran número de versos . . . sino también añadir escenas y desenvolver (digamoslo así) algunas excelentes situaciones que en el original estaban sino apuntadas" (1800, 7–8; "I felt I should omit all that precedes the true action of the drama. . . . not only has it been necessary to interpolate a large number of verses . . . but also to add scenes and unfold [let us put it this way] certain excellent situations that were only hinted at in the original"). Presented for the first time at the Coliseo de la Calle de la Cruz in Madrid on 22 January 1800, the *refundición* (recast) was a success and was often staged during the nineteenth century.[13] The work at once looks back at the eighteenth century through its emphasis on the unities and perfection of tragic form and looks toward the romantic movement through its characterization of star-crossed lovers and its recuperation of Medieval and Golden Age history and literature. We can only speculate as to its political importance at a time when a monarch—Carlos IV—seemed subordinate to his wife's *favorito* (favorite), Manuel Godoy. In *La estrella de Sevilla,* Sancho IV had represented Philip IV. In Trigueros's version, another monarch who is also the fourth of his name is depicted. If don Arias stood for Olivares in the original, this character stands for Godoy in the *refundición*. But the thrust of the criticism has changed in Trigueros's version. As Ermanno Caldera notes, the *refundición* reduces the *odiosità* (negativity) that surrounds the king by stressing the monarch's conflict between love and honor (1974, 42). This negative attitude is deflected toward the *privado* (favorite). At the end of the third act the king warns against heeding the counsel of an evil *privado:*

> Reyes, huid del furor,
> huid de un consejo fiero,

> sea mi exemplo el postrero:
> un error llama otro error:
> libraos bien del primero.
>
> (1800, 76).

("Kings, flee the madness, turn away from cruel counsel. Let my example be the last: one mistake calls upon another. Be rid of the first one.")

This could well be taken as advice to Charles IV against the counsels of Godoy. In his study of this *refundición,* Charles Ganelin explains that "Arias has evolved from a low-profile character in the original to the advisor who, having fostered the rule of passion, will lose royal protection and will find himself exiled from a kingdom where reason must prevail." The adviser's exile may allow the audience to envision the banishment of Manuel Godoy from the Court, as Carlos IV is seen to regain the power he has lost. Sancho IV's words in the adaptation, if spoken by another king who is also the fourth of his name, would have gladdened the hearts of his countrymen:

> Y pues vos me perdisteis
> con malos consejos, Arias, [read Godoy]
> salid luego de Castilla,
> y en vuestro destierro vaya
> el exemplo, y escarmiento
> de los que en lisonjas tratan.
>
> (1800, 113)

["Since you led me astray with evil counsel, Arias, leave now Castile and may your exile be an example and a warning to those who are persuaded by flattery."]

The success of the adaptation triggered new interest in the original, thought to be by Lope de Vega. In his biography of Lope, Lord Holland gives a summary of *La estrella de Sevilla* and also includes extracts in English verse. In France, Pierre Lebrun (1785–1873), a playwright who championed the "poetic, imaginative treatment of history in the theater,"[14] having read Holland's account, became interested in *La estrella de Sevilla.* Also aware of the version by Trigueros, he attempted to restore some of the original structure of the play. He also made Busto a part of a faction that opposes the rulership of Sancho IV. The rebels want to see the La Cerda branch of the family in power. Lebrun completed his adaptation, *Le Cid d'Andalusie (The Cid from Andalusia),* in 1823, the two-hundredth anniversary of the composition of *La estrella de Sevilla*. The original *comedia* had vanished from sight due to its political mysteries. Lebrun's version suffered a similar fate. The censors, fearing that the play was concealing a political message, one that criticized the monarchy, prevented its staging. France's ruler at that time was Louis XVIII. With the defeat of Napoleon at Waterloo, Louis XVIII strove to conciliate all parties, including the former revolutionists, through moderate policies. Unfortunately, the assassination of his nephew, the duc de Berry, in 1820 triggered a reaction from the ultraroyalists, who curbed civil liberties. The combination of murder and tyranny once again led to the play's disappearance. Lebrun's added verbal battles between the king and Busto created unease among the censors. Nor did it help his cause that the king's role was to be played by François-Joseph Talma, Napoleon's favorite actor (Rodríguez López-Vázquez 1991, 26). The censors may have also remembered that Lebrun dedicated to Napoleon one of his most famous poems, *Ode à la Grande Armée* (*Ode to the Great Army*) (1805). But the French poet and playwright did not have to wait two hundred years for his version to come to light. Two years later, Chateaubriand, minister to Louis XVIII, was able to get permission for the play to be presented. It was performed in a censored version that eliminated more than three hundred verses, "tous ceux, en général, qui avaient quelque vigueur et quelque signification" (Rodríguez López-Vázquez 1991, 25; "all those, in general, that had a certain vigor, a certain meaning"). The complete text was not published until 1844.

Throughout the nineteenth century, *La estrella de Sevilla* enjoyed critical acclaim in Spain, where Juan Eugenio Hartzenbusch not only wrote his own *refundición*[15] but also made the original play available to the public in the *Biblioteca de Autores Españoles* (*Library of Spanish Authors*) (1853). It was also popular in France, where several critical commentaries and translations were made.[16] A century when *La estrella de Sevilla* seems to enter the critical as well as the performance canon ended with Menéndez Pelayo's assertions that the play's text was corrupt and that many of its scenes had been interpolated by a third-rate playwright and plagiarist named Andrés de Claramonte. When in 1920 Foulché-Delbosc published an edition of a more complete version of the play, he clearly showed that there were no interpolations. Although Claramonte did not alter the play, neither did Lope de Vega write it. It was authored by a playwright with the pseudonym of "Cardenio." It is not my intention to describe the lengthy battles that took place over the authorship of the play. While Sturgis Leavitt attributed it to Claramonte, other critics felt that the author "must be sought among the more outstanding of Lope's contemporaries, not among the minor and comparatively obscure playwrights of the period" (Reed, Dixon, Hill 1935, xix). What is important to note, is that the play's great critical and stage successes of the nineteenth century diminished in the twentieth. It may well be that, once the play could no longer be ascribed to Lope de Vega, it lost some of its canonical appeal.

What I would like to discuss in this final section of my essay is why the play remained a canonical piece in the United States while it lost ground in other countries. It is clear that this American canonicity is directly related to the fact that the play was included in the first extensive anthology of Golden Age plays published in the United States, *Diez comedias del Siglo de Oro.* Published in 1939, this anthology has remained in print for more than fifty years, while others, such as Wardropper's and MacCurdy's, were soon out of print. Consequently, *Diez comedias* became the most commonly used text on Golden Age Theater in American schools. According to John Guillory, "the problem of canon-formation is one aspect o a much larger history of the ways in which societies have organized and regulated practices of reading and writing. . . . We are now in a position to recognize the major social institution through which this regulation is exercises: *the school.* . . . The school was assigned the general social function of distributing various kinds of knowledge, including the knowledge of *how* to read and write as well as *what* to read and write" (1990, 239). *Diez 'comedias* made it easy to know what to read and what to write about when dealing with Golden Age theater. It thus set the canon of the most read and critiqued *comedias* in this country. The inclusion of *La estrella de Sevilla* among these ten plays blocked the centrifugal forces unleashed by the debate over authorship and assured this *comedia* a place in the canon.

Twice before a canonical moment has been related to the political mysteries of the play. Following its appearance in 1623 *La estrella de Sevilla* was relegated to oblivion for its political subtext and its unveiling of a murder mystery. Two centuries later, a Spanish version criticized another king and his *privado,* while a French version was censored for its negative view of the monarchy soon after a political murder. Is there a political mystery behind the inclusion of *La estrella de Sevilla* in *Diez comedias del Siglo de Oro?*[17] Certainly, most of the plays included in the collection had been consistently included both in the accessible and selective canons. But this alone does not explain a certain propensity within the collection. In a passing remark, which I find extremely suggestive, James A. Parr explains "that the inclusion of titles typifying tyranny or other abuses of power by figures of authority in the 1939 Alpern & Martel assemblage may respond to what had obviously become an anti-democratic, totalitarian situation under Francisco Franco in Spain" (1992, 97). I would add that, together with a reaction to Franco's rule, the text may be including a warning against Hitler's tyranny and aggression. The first *comedia* in the Alpern and Martel anthology is *La Numancia,* a play about the heroic defense of a city against the overwhelming power of imperial Rome. It would not take much imagination to equate Rome with Nazi Germany. After all, the Roman Empire, through *translatio* (transference), had been relocated in the Germanic lands during the Middle Ages. Germany as heir to empire was renewing its conquests: In 1938, Austria became part of Germany while in 1939 Czechoslovakia was dismembered. After these triumphs, the example of *Numancia* can instill a desire for resistance among the smaller nations.

Cervantes's tragedy is followed in the anthology by Lope's *Fuenteovejuna.* The tyranny of a *Comendador* (knight-commander of a religious-military order) and a struggle for power at the national level can reflect both Hitler's tyranny and the Spanish civil war. *El burlador de Sevilla (The Trickster of Seville)* follows the third play in the anthology, *La estrella de Sevilla.* For those living in the shadow of the violence that led to World War II, it would not be difficult to translate Don Juan's amorous affairs into a political allegory. Don Juan, a figure akin to the devil, conquers women very much like a tyrant such as Hitler was able to conquer foreign lands. The power of evil in the form of the devil is again evoked in Mira de Amerscua's *El esclavo del demonio (The Devil's Slave),* while the power of lying, used so effectively by don Juan, reappears in Ruiz de Alarcón's *La verdad sospechosa (Suspect Truth).* These three plays thus foreground conquest, the power of evil, and the power of lies. Indeed, lies are one of the most frequently used tools of the tyrant, as in Hitler's *Anschluss,* the annexation of Austria in 1938.

Two other plays in the anthology portray tyrannical rulers. Incarceration and the use of secrecy have led Dian Fox to label Basilio in Calderón's *La vida es sueño (Life Is a Dream)* a Machiavellian ruler. In Rojas Zorrilla's *Del rey abajo ninguno (Below the King, All Men Are Peers)* don García lives in exile, fearing the tyrannical power of kings.[18] It would be difficult to discover a political subtext in Moreto's *El desdén con el desdén (Disdan for Disdain).* This work simply serves as an example of a *comedia de capa y espada* (cloak and sword play). As for Guillén de Castro's *Las mocedades del Cid* (*The Youthful Deeds of the Cid*), it serves as contrast to *La estrella de Sevilla* since in Castro's *comedia* the hero is able to marry his lady in spite of having shed her father's blood. In *La estrella de Sevilla,* on the other hand, the couple cannot be united in the end because Sancho has killed Estrella's brother.

In *La estrella de Sevilla* a tyrannical king serves as focus for the anxieties of those living in the late 1930s. Twice before, in 1623 and in 1823, this *comedia* had concealed a political mystery that included not only tyranny but also murder. Those living in the turbulent 1930s would easily remember the Night of the Long Knives when Ernst Rohm, chief of the S.A. and one of Hitler's closest companions, was shot by two S.S. guards. More than a thousand people were slain during this purge ordered by Hitler. In this third shift in its canonical status, the play is no longer censored for its attack on tyranny, but serves as an example of resistance against those who disregard liberty and law.

Although the parallels presented above offer some circumstantial evidence for the hypothesis that *La estrella de Sevilla*'s place in the American canon was attained through the political mystery it was thought to contain, the fact still remains that the centrifugal forces unleashed in 1623 and the centripetal movement toward canonicity of 1800 and 1823 are all intimately tied to politics and are often associated with murder. This *comedia* is indeed a play with which to catch the conscience of the king. Although *La estrella de Sevilla* has not yielded all its mysteries (and never will), its history stands as a guiding light for those who have fought tyranny in its myriad forms.

Notes

1. Critics are not even sure when it was published or staged for the first time. According to Emilio Cotarelo y Mori, the play was performed by the company of Cristóbal de Avendaño, who presented plays in Madrid in 1621 and again in 1623. He believes that *La estrella* was first staged in 1623 (1930, 12–24).

2. Only four separate copies are in existence. There is a copy in the British Museum, one in the Biblioteca Palatina di Parma, and two at the Biblioteca Nacional in Madrid. See Reed, Dixon, Hill, eds., (1939, x); and Alfredo Rodríguez López-Vázquez, ed., (1991, 123).

3. *La estrella de Sevilla* begins in folio 99 and ends in 120. Folios 117 and 118 are missing.

4. See, for example, Leavitt (1930 and 1931). For a summary of the debate see de Armas (1979).

5. All verse references to *La estrella de Sevilla* are to Alfredo Rodríguez López-Vázquez's edition (1991).

6. For other historical elements that support this political reading see Kennedy (1974). While this book was in press, a lengthier version of Kennedy has been published (1993). Harry Sieber has graciously made available to me proofs for his article on the subject (1994). My own arguments stress an element that has been disregarded by Kennedy and Sieber, the mythological basis for the political subtext. For a more complete account of my vision of this political mystery see de Armas (1994b).

7. On the importance of solar imagery in the play see Sturm (1969).

8. Bits and pieces of the puzzle have been emerging over time. In 1939, John M. Hill pointed to an anecdote found in Lord Holland's biography of Lope de Vega where Philip IV and Olivares, going at night to the home of the duke of Albuquerque so that the king could seduce the duke's wife, are stopped by the duke. Hill describes the parallels between this event and the beginning of the second act of *La estrella de Sevilla* (Reed, Dixon, Hill 1939, xxxii). However, Hill devotes much more attention to another theory: that the murder of Juan de Escobedo during the reign of Philip II parallels the murder of Busto in *Estrella*. Ruth Lee Kennedy (1974) has also pointed to some parallels between Sancho IV in *La estrella de Sevilla* and the historical Philip IV. See also de Armas (1994B) and Sieber.

9. Elliott cites as examples *El Fernando* (Ferdinand) by the Conde de la Roca (1632) and the *Sermones fúnebres* (Funereal Sermons) by Córdoba Ronquillo (1624).

10. The Order of the Golden Fleece was founded by Philippe le Bon, duke of Burgundy, in the fifteenth century. It was rekindled by the Spanish Emperor Charles V: "In him the Burgundian spirit lived, and through him the Spanish Court inherited an abiding interest in the ideals and literature of the Order of the Golden Fleece" (Domínguez 1979, 112).

11. A *suelta* of which two copies are extant, one at the Biblioteca Municipal in Madrid and the other at the Institut del Teatre in Barcelona, may be from the eighteenth century (Rodríguez López-Vázquez 1991, 123).

12. Triguero's successes came from *refundiciones* (recast plays) rather than from his own dramatic or poetic production. He wrote new versions of Lope's *La moza del cántaro* (The Young Woman with the Jug), *Los melindres de Belisa* (Belisa's Extravagances), *El anzuelo de Fenisa* (Fenisa's Hook) and *La esclava de su galán* (The Slave of Her Lover). See Aguilar Piñal (1987, 235–46).

13. Rodríguez López-Vázquez provides the date of the *estreno* in his edition of *La estrella de Sevilla* (1991, 23). According to Charles Ganelin the *refundición* "enjoyed performances throughout the nineteenth century that met with mixed reviews." I would like to thank Ganelin for allowing me to read the appropriate chapters in the manuscript of his book *Rewriting Theater*.

14. Howarth, 101. Lebrun was the author of several earlier plays including *Pallas* (1806), *Ulysses* (1814), and *Marie Stuart* (1820), a "very successful adaptation of Schiller's *Maria Stuart*" (Howarth 101).

15. According to Ganelin the *refundición* does not date from 1834. He cites newspapers that refer to it as an "estreno" (première) in 1852.

16. Even musical versions of the play were produced, such as the opera *L'Etoile de Séville* (The Star of Seville), with libretto by Hippolyte Lucas and music by Michael William Balfe (1845), and a *zarzuela* (musical) by Adelardo López de Ayala. The American reception was much more modest. A version made by

the actress Fanny Kemble was performed unsuccessfully in Philadelphia in 1837 (Crawford 1930). There were critical commentaries by L. de Vieil-Castel, A. de Latour, and Ernest Lafond. Eugène Baret published a translation in 1869 as part of the *Ueuvres de Lope de Vega*. A "free translation" by Eugène and Edouard Adenis was staged in 1905 (Reed, Dixon and Hill 1939, xxxvi).

17. This anthology was put together by Hymen Alpern and José Martel. Alpern, a high-school teacher in New York City, had already published several pieces on Golden Age theater when the anthology came out. He wrote articles on the *comedia* in 1923 and 1926 and edited a play by Guillén de Castro in 1926. In 1935 he published with José Martel a student edition of *Don Quijote*. This collaboration must have been successful since four years later they published *Diez comedias*.

18. Although not foregrounding the political aspect of these and other *comedias* Alpern and Martel seem to invite this kind of political parallel in a list of *proyectos*. One project included under *La Numancia* is "Estudiar la obra desde el punto de vista histórico y patriótico" (1939, 70; "Study the work from a historic and patriotic point of view"). They urge the study of "Aspectos e importancia política del tema central" in *Fuenteovejuna* (1939, 142; "Political aspects and significance of the main theme") and they ask the reader to "Contrastar el espíritu democrático con la autocracia política" in *La estrella de Sevilla* (1939, 234; "Contrast the democratic spirit with political autocracy").

2

Toward Contextualization: Canonicity, Current Criticism, Contemporary Culture

James A. Parr

I. Canonicity

The canon is a conundrum. As it is subjected to scrutiny by an increasingly alienated and politically motivated professorate, it tends to become parceled out, or partitioned into segments, reflecting special interests. But nostalgia for a simpler time when the largely lily-white, predominantly heterosexual, preponderantly old boys' club held sway is hardly an adequate response to today's icon-breaking and wholesale subversion of whatever is taken to be the dominant discourse.

While considerable sensitive commentary has appeared in recent years on the general topic of canons and canon formation—I think especially of von Hallberg's fine collection of essays by different hands, titled simply *Canons,* of Robert Scholes's recent essay on "Canonicity and Textuality," and of Henry Louis Gates's *Loose Canons*—I would focus in this section on Alastair Fowler's notion of a tripartite canon, as developed in his *Kinds of Literature.*

Fowler calls his three varieties the potential, accessible, and selective canons. They are, in fact, gradations, for the largest grouping, the potential, includes the next largest, the accessible, and it, in turn, incorporates the smallest or most selective. Following Fowler, then, we might think of a canon for the *comedia,* first, in terms of the potential canon, that is, one consisting of the total number of extant plays; second, in a considerably more limited sense, as the accessible canon, made manifest in all those works available in anthologies or editions; third, in a still more restricted sense, as the nucleus of texts that we hold up as the best (or most representative) of this particular kind of writing. This is the selective canon, and it is, of course, the one that is usually understood when we use the term "canon" without further qualification. In practice, it includes those titles which appear on graduate reading lists and on syllabi for courses on Golden Age drama at whatever level.

I would submit that there is also a "critical canon" consisting of those works which have prompted books, articles, editions, special sessions, seminars, and symposia such as this one. Although Fowler uses the term (215, 232), his comments on it are rather limited and his perspective is very different from my own. In my estimation, the critical canon occupies a nebulous area somewhere between the potential and the accessible gradations just mentioned, and it has the effect of constantly enlarging the accessible variety (via critical editions, for example), while also offering candidates for beatification and eventual election to that select core of texts revered as the best or, at least, most representative.

Where shall we situate *La estrella de Sevilla?* Clearly, it partakes of all the canonical variations catalogued above. Most important, of course, is its unquestioned status as a member of the selective canon, a status that is constantly reinforced by the critical attention it receives. Thus it is that the critical and selective canons complement and reinforce each other in what amounts to a symbiotic relationship. The more critical attention a work receives, the more certain we can be of its canonical legitimacy. The more that select status is taken for granted, the more critical attention it tends to receive. This is by no means a vicious circle, and while it may be a kind of hermeneutical circle, a more telling analogy would be to the Ouroborous, the magical serpent that forms a circle with its body in order to devour its own tail, thus quite literally feeding off itself. Perhaps this is a more adequate image for what Stanley Fish once called the self-consuming artifact. Paradoxically, this self-consumption leads not to diminution but to efflorescence, as criticism feeds canonicity, only to be nourished in turn by what it has helped create. The sum assumes dimensions that surpass the total of its constituent parts.

In the contentious environment characteristic of modern academe, there are those who would erase the concept of canon from critical discourse. Canons are said to be hierarchical and therefore undemocratic (see Scholes). Levelling and anarchy seem to be the suggested substitutes. Now it has always seemed to me that *comediantes* are not easily taken in by rhetoric. The fact that we are resistant to change may be an adaptive device that has allowed us to thrive and prosper while maintaining a sense of continuity and community. On the other hand, it seems to me that we are unusually open to change and that we somehow manage to accommodate the most heterodox notions.

The select corpus—whether defined as "best" or "most representative," or as an amalgam of these—is always already there for those of us who arrive late in the game, but we have tremendous freedom to modify that central core by proposing other candidates. We have only to show that the aspirant is meritorious. Needless to say, arguments for merit will vary according to the perspective of the critic in question, but it should be obvious to one and all that the select canon is not etched in stone. It is susceptible to modification, although the burden of proof rests always with advocates of change. In this way, there is continuity—we have at least a few texts in common that we can all talk about—while marginal titles may work their way to the center, depending upon the skills of analysis and advocacy summoned in their behalf.

It does not seem to me that the canons of the *comedia,* as I have described them, are paternalistic or WASPish or nefariously oppressive in any way. Rather, they are open and flexible; they overlap and interpenetrate; the central core is always subject to modification, and the critical canon is inhibited only by the limits of our methodologies and our imaginations. Conversely, there is no denying that the *comedia* is Eurocentric and that the bulk of it was written by Dead White European Males. There is little prospect of altering those historical facts.

Let me end this section with a word on behalf of that central core designated the select canon, as it is evidenced, for example, in Alpern and Martel's *Diez comedias* of 1939 (see Appendix). You will recall that one of those ten plays is *La estrella de Sevilla,* which had already achieved a *succès de scandale* at the hands of Sturgis Leavitt in 1931. My thesis is that canonical works like *La estrella de Sevilla* serve an instrumental function in both intellectual growth and career advancement. One is constantly tested by having to match wits with others who have been drawn to these same core texts. It is impossible to enter into and contribute to critical commentary on these much-discussed works without being challenged intellectually, more so than if one concentrates on relatively unknown authors or titles. To confront the classics, we must compete not only with previous generations of critics but also with our own by offering new perspectives and fresh insights while simultaneously juggling cutting-edge theoretical tools—all of which not only keeps us off the streets and out of mischief but is also conducive to intellectual growth and, if done particularly well, to career advancement. There can be no denying that the prizes and perquisites of the profession are more likely to accrue to those who accept the challenge of saying something significant about canonical works. They are not as likely to come to those who work, however laudably, to make the marginal central. This is meant to be not a pessimistic but simply a realistic assessment of prospects.

II. Current Criticism and Theory

I shall continue, in this section, to talk in terms more general than specific. The objective is not to give a status report on the current criticism of *La estrella de Sevilla,* but rather to present a perspective on the rush to theory, leaving you to draw inferences about its applicability to criticism of the text at hand.

Theory has by now effectively co-opted criticism, much as criticism during the 1940s, 1950s, and 1960s came largely to supplant an older historicism that drew on biographical determinism and the notion of a *Zeitgeist.* Theory itself has gone through stages since poststructuralism became ascendant around 1970, although it might be more accurate to say that poststructuralism has become an increasingly multifaceted, not to say fragmented, enterprise. Thus we have neo-Marxists, new historians, phenomenological or reader-response critics, feminists, deconstructionists, gay and lesbian approaches, speech-act theorists, and, interestingly enough, others who advocate and even announce the death of theory. I refer to Steven Knapp and Walter Benn Michaels's piece, "Against Theory," but one might also include, as representative of the anti-theory movement, John Ellis's *Against Deconstruction,* or, in a much lighter vein, Malcolm Bradbury's delightful spoof, suggestively titled *Mensonge* (Falsehood). Paul de Man was also well aware of "The Resistance to Theory," as one of his studies is titled, and he even went so far as to speak of a "Return to Philology."

Now I used the word "others" advisedly a second ago, for what stands out in postmodern critical discourse is otherness, difference, and sometimes alienation, rather than commonality, unity, and ecumenism. The more humane qualities last mentioned are the ones I would emphasize and hope to see revived. As Henry Louis Gates Jr. puts it in *Loose Canons,* the task at hand is the creation of "a civic culture that respects both differences and commonalities" (xv).

Formalism is widely felt to be impoverished nowadays, if not elitist; Eurocentrism is often deplored, even though the vast majority of the theories we manipulate come from somewhere on the Continent, probably Paris. Some say that the pantheon of Dead

White European Males must be purged in the interest of a more comprehensive and politically correct curriculum. What I am pointing to by means of a description that begins to border on caricature is the fact that discourse has become highly charged as it has come increasingly to center around identity politics, insensitivity, real and imagined abuses of power, and a hermeneutic of suspicion that questions hierarchies, like the select canon, along with the notion of the transparent text.

Whatever our individual bias, the mere fact that we expend time and energy on *La estrella de Sevilla* or any other title on the selective canon list means that we thereby celebrate the achievement of one of those Dead White European Males—whoever he was, in this case—and it is likewise inescapable that the object of our attention, the text itself, is very much a Eurocentric artifact. Those who feel the need to purge themselves might assume a patina of political correctness through a modest retracing of geographical boundaries, reviving that old saw about Africa beginning at the Pyrenees. It should thus be possible to have one's P.C. cake and eat it too, since that minor revision would place us squarely within the orbit of minority culture, thereby conferring the sweet smell of self-righteousness that seems to attend marginalization.

It does occur to me that such rhetoric may mislead both writer and audience. It is not my purpose to disavow ideology as such, or even the political unconscious, for it seems clear that there are indeed latent or overt ideological positions taken by practitioners of all critical discourse, even the most formalistic. The two Spanish authors who have influenced me most are Cervantes and Unamuno, however, which makes it difficult for me to avoid self-consciousness in expression, on the one hand, and iconoclastic questioning, on the other.

My critical credo could take the form of a paraphrase of Unamuno's essay, "Mi Religión." There, Unamuno's prickly persona manifests itself already in the second paragraph, where he speaks of "la pereza individual [que] huye de la posición crítica o escéptica" ("the indolence that leads one to avoid adopting critical or skeptical stances"). Then he proposes a perspective on skepticism:

Escéptica digo, pero tomando la voz escepticismo en su sentido etimológico y filosófico, porque escéptico no quiere decir el que duda, sino el que investiga o rebusca, por oposición al que afirma y cree haber hallado. Hay quien escudriña un problema y hay quien nos da una fórmula, acertada o no, como solución de él (255).

I say skeptical, but taking the word "skepticism" in its etymological and philosophical sense, because "skeptic" does not refer to one who doubts, but rather to one who seeks out and investigates, as opposed to someone who claims to have found [the answer]. There are those who never weary of worrying a problem and there are those who [readily] offer neat solutions to it, well-founded or not.

Following Unamuno—and the instincts of an editor—I have always found considerable diversion in questioning reductive interpretations, whether they center on poetic justice, Calderonian tragedy, proto-feminist comedy, or Marxian, Lacanian, Girardian, Derridian, or any other formulaic discourse thought to provide answers, or at least to pose all the essential questions. My own critical credo, paraphrasing Unamuno, is to search for the truth, assuming that process takes precedence over product and that the process is one of constant deferral, while simultaneously urging those who have reached some center of enlightenment to reconsider. To those who require facile all-purpose answers, "les diré que, si quieren soluciones, acudan a la tienda de enfrente, porque en la mía no se vende semejante artículo" (259) ("I shall say that, if they want answers, they should try across the street, because I don't carry that particular item").

Since I have recently committed to print an essay titled "Criticism and the *Comedia:* 20 Years Later," an updating of the "Essay on Critical Method" that appeared in *Hispania* in 1974, it seems appropriate to cite a key passage from this recent statement that summarizes my current position:

> My . . . approach has evolved into what might be called "skeptical eclecticism," implying openness to—but caution toward—the sociopolitical agendas inherent in all methods. Malcolm Read, on the other hand, takes eclecticism "to be one of the many guises of a conservatism which in a covert manner tames specific analytic models and robs them of their radical thrust" (*Visions* vii). The point is well taken, but I do not consider commitment to be a virtue in this area of endeavor. Too often it leads to an unfortunate fanaticism, an unwillingness to consider opposing evidence, and a devotion not unlike that of converts to sectarian religion. Those who have invested in some guru or some cause have done so at the expense of impartiality and, in my estimation, have simply not considered all the evidence. There is an uneasy alliance at best between commitment and the quest for truth. (155)

Allow me to recycle the final paragraph from the collected essays in which the preceding passage appears, for it clarifies my aspirations by putting a more positive spin on comments made earlier:

While there may be cause for concern over the fragmentation and conflictual nature of the enterprise (as when feminists challenge the patriarchy, Marxists oppose estheticians, and hermeneuts take on deconstructionists), the process proceeds apace, despite everything, and our best hope may be that from these dialectical encounters will come a heightened awareness of and sensitivity to the needs and desires of the many and varied players. If the study of the Humanities teaches us anything, it must be, at a bare minimum, to delight in heterogeneity and, as a consequence, to treat one another humanely, as fellow seekers after insight into the human condition. (156)

Theory is not unlike the Platonic/Derridian *pharmakon*. It is potentially a blessing but it may also be a curse. It is a blessing if it plays the role of propaedeutic to an enhanced understanding of texts, but it can be a curse if it fosters a divisive sectarianism, or if we take it to be a substitute for close reading and sound scholarship. Scholarship, criticism, and theory represent three stages along a spectrum of approaches to literature during the twentieth century; they are not mutually exclusive but inherently complementary if practiced with a modicum of reasonableness and tolerance. Interpretation remains the heart of the enterprise, buttressed on one side by scholarship and on the other by theory (see Appendix).

I once wrote a gentle caricature of the sad situation in which some of our younger colleagues find themselves these days. The allusion to Coleridge's "Ancient Mariner" should be transparent:

> One of the saddest sights in academe is that of the "postmodern mariner," bereft of moral philosophy and history but outfitted to the teeth with technique. Imagine, if you will, a novice faculty member, hoping to make permanent port but becalmed on a sea of infinite textuality and indeterminate meaning, whose waters are cluttered with the debris of floating signifiers. Framed against a horizon of shifting expectations, this neophyte navigator, having unwittingly "killed the bird that made the breeze to blow" (Coleridge, lines 93–94) charts deviously decentered discourse on a current map of misreading but remains blind to the insight that all God's creatures should be revered—even ungainly authors. (114)

Henry Louis Gates, Jr. has some pungent observations on what he calls the "style wars" that typify our love affair with theory, and he updates Oscar Wilde's quip about good Americans going to Paris when they die by inverting it to fit the current critical scene in this country: "I think in Paris, when good theories die, they go to America" (186).

If we have ignored the invitation to the table of Textuality, it may be just as well. Our inherent conservativism may have saved us considerable time and energy, for the pendulum has begun a very discernible swing back toward the more positive values of humanism and rationalism, despite the fact that the millennium looms large on the horizon. Indeed, this swing back to lucidity and liberalism may be this decade's alternative to more traditional millenarian despair. Paul Berman calls our attention to the fact that "'68 Philosophy" is very much *démodée* these days in that very same hotbed of intellectual ferment that gave us Barthes, Foucault, Derrida, Lacan, and company." As Berman puts it,

> In Paris, the '68 theories had their day, which lasted well into the late seventies and beyond. Then a new generation of writers came along, the people who were students in '68 but came into adulthood only in the calmer years that followed—writers like [Luc] Ferry, [Alain] Renaut, Pascal Bruckner, Alain Finkelkraut (and writing in English, the late J. G. Merquior), who worried about the mind-blowing ultra-radicalism of the older generation. . . . The younger writers set out to resurrect the very notions that '68 philosophy was designed to debunk—an admiration for Enlightenment reason, clarity, lucidity, and Western-style freedoms . . . the drift toward humanism was unmistakable. (10–11)

So a revitalized liberalism, free will, clear style, optimism, and other values that just yesterday seemed on the verge of extinction have staged a comeback, even in Paris. Who can say what will happen next? Authors may be restored to the place of prominence they once enjoyed in Roman Jakobson's classic communication model, their signatures may miraculously become unerased—as Barthes spins in his grave—and some authors may turn out not to be dead after all, despite Nietzsche and other prophets of extremity (see Megill).

I am guardedly optimistic about the potential futures of a literary criticism informed by both historical and new historical scholarship and by a newer kind of theory that is more tentative, more eclectic, and more tolerant.

III. Approaching Praxis: An Aspect of Contemporary Culture

Although it probably should not be so, anonymity seems to present special problems for the literary critic. For one thing, the anonymous text leaves us without the important context of the author's other works, so there is no way to focus on repeated patterns of imagery, idiosyncratic lexicon, or a peculiar use of metrical forms. For another, "bastard" texts tend to be devalued beside others whose paternity can be fixed with more certainty, specifically those claimed and published by the author in his lifetime or those for which autograph manuscripts exist.

La estrella de Sevilla is an anomaly among canonical *comedias* precisely because it continues to be taught and written about despite the impediments just mentioned. Of course, those problems miraculously resolve the moment we attribute it to Lope or someone else. But attribution, in this instance, seems a facile and unnecessary resolution to a much more intriguing anonymity. It may be better to allow this work to stand entirely on its own, as it has done very well until now. Attribution to either a major or a minor dramatist will neither enhance nor diminish its intrinsic merit.

It is a truism to say that titles of Golden Age plays are significant, for they frequently suggest a strategy for reading or viewing. Some are aphorisms (*La vida es sueño* / *Life Is a Dream*), others highlight an office or profession (*El alcalde de Zalamea* / *The Mayor of Zalamea*), while others may point to a salient characteristic, either assigned or assumed (*El burlador de Sevilla* / *The Trickster of Seville*). *La estrella de Sevilla* does not fit neatly into any of these standard patterns. Here, a proper name (Estrella) standing for an attribute (beauty) comes to suggest a dichotomy between celestial beauty, which is immutable, and its earthly counterpart, which is transitory and corruptible. There is a confirming clue to the validity of this perspective in the further juxtaposition within the title of the heavenly (*estrella*) and the mundane (*Sevilla*). Thus it is that the title announces a double focus, within the name of the main character herself *and* within her two domains, a focus that is widened within the text through the Gemini motif and through the frequent doubling of concepts—through plays on words and puns—that is so characteristic of its *pung*ent language.

Admittedly, the celestial notion of beauty will receive little attention within the action that unfolds following this suggestive title, but a point I would make is that any acquaintance at all with the Church fathers and their widely disseminated views on earthly versus heavenly beauty—of which no contemporary audience could have been innocent—should be kept in mind if we are to reach an adequate understanding of the text before us. Here, obviously, I am privileging as one potential meaning the sense it may have had during its time and place of composition. This is not, of course, to rule out other possible readings or other possible meanings.

In a recent book on Cervantes and Quevedo, George Mariscal makes the telling point that "any poststructuralism inattentive to historical problems will ultimately transform earlier cultures into false images of our own" (xii). Yet Mariscal himself is purposefully inattentive to the religious background of seventeenth-century Spanish culture, a dimension that is surely as significant in the formation of the human subject of that day as are the sociopolitical factors he chooses to foreground.

What I would bring to the fore in these comments on the cultural context is precisely that religious and philosophical background studied by a relatively innocent "old historian" like Otis H. Green—including Green's insight that Renaissance poets only pretended to believe in paganism and all its paraphernalia (astrology, in this instance), expressed as "fingen los poetas" (poets [only] pretend [to believe in such things]). At the same time, I would avoid the moralizing that sometimes accompanies attention to the philosophical and religious dimensions, as was often the case with the late, great British School.

There is an instinctive drive toward the beautiful, according to Plato and his neoplatonic followers. Coming between the ancient philosopher and his Renaissance commentators, is Augustine, who speaks in the *Confessions* (7. 23) of admiring "the beauty of bodies celestial or terrestrial." Like Plato, Augustine privileges the immutable beauty of the celestial. In *The City of God* (12. 6), he will take up a perplexing issue that seems to me central to *La estrella de Sevilla,* that is, the unsuspected relationship between beauty and the problem of evil.

How is it, he will ask, that a bodily beauty presented equally to the gaze of two men—here, Sancho el Bravo and Sancho Ortiz—will excite one of them "to desire an illicit enjoyment while the other steadfastly maintains a modest restraint of his will"? How is it, in other words, that one manifests an evil will while the other does not—or, as he phrases the question elsewhere, "How . . . can a good thing be the efficient cause of an evil will"? The answer is that it cannot; rather, it is what he calls a "deficient cause" (chap. 7), for "luxury [is not] the fault of lovely and charming objects [such as gold], but of the heart that inordinately loves sensual pleasures, to the neglect of temperance, which attaches us to objects more lovely in their spirituality, and more delectable by their incorruptibility" (chap. 8).

Sancho el Bravo is one of several material monarchs run amok, a stock character in a certain kind of *comedia*. At least he may be educable, and the lesson he needs to assimilate centers on the necessary distinction between the garden of earthly delights to which he is suddenly exposed in Seville and the storehouse of durable goods being accumulated beyond the grave. He is no Segismundo, of course, and he does not get very far on the path he needs to travel, but both the title of the text and the mirror provided by Sancho Ortiz serve to point up an itinerary and a desirable destination. The metaphorical Star of Seville is a distant and inaccessible guiding light showing the way to a "quintessential" higher plane of both beauty and the response to it, a plane that transcends the materiality and downward tug of the four earthly elements and their corresponding humors.

There is surely a semblance here of the mirror for monarchs, as Ruth Lee Kennedy contended in 1975, although it seems to me that the play is ultimately about monarchy only incidentally. Kings make fine dramatic figures, particularly in works that have a tragic dimension, but the theme of this particular text has more to do with beauty and the response to it, with power and its abuse, and with the relations between men and men (in terms of friendship and duty) and between men and women (in terms of the myth of feminine evil).

The King makes this latter dimension explicit when he blames the victim, Estrella, for inciting evil desires:

Rey.   Vuestro hermano murió; quien le dio muerte
          dicen que es Sancho Ortiz: vengaos vos della;
          y aunque él muriese así de aquesta suerte,
          vos la culpa tenéis por ser tan bella.

                                       (2134–37)

King.   Your brother is dead; they say that Sancho Ortiz
          killed him: you should seek revenge for that act;
          and although he died as I have just said,
          you are responsible because you are so beautiful.

He goes on in the same speech to connect the stimulus of beauty to the inclination arising from a more heavenly body, saying:

Rey.   si es la mujer el animal más fuerte,
          mujer, Estrella sois, y sois Estrella;
          vos vencéis, que inclináis . . .

                                         (2138–40)

> *King.*   if woman is the stronger sex (lit. "animal"),
>   you, Estrella, are a woman, *and* you are a star;
>   you are irresistible, because you predispose . . .

Sancho el Bravo exhibits a reductive and deterministic mindset, one in which *inclinar* (to predispose) and *forzar* (to determine) conveniently coalesce. Estrella's eloquent defense is reminiscent of Marcela's in *Don Quixote,* but the King will have none of it. While conceding her innocence of the act itself, he nevertheless remains convinced that her beauty remains the first cause:

> *Rey.*   Vos quedáis sin matar, porque en vos mata
>   la parte que os dio el cielo, la belleza.
>
> (2150–51)

> *King.*   You needn't act in order to kill, for your beauty,
>   with its celestial origin, takes care of that for you.

Anxiety and ambivalence exude from every phrase. He is shown to be attracted to the exceptional and unfamiliar—and, for him, Andalusia and its women are just that, exceptional and unfamiliar—yet he is also anxious and ambivalent about this brave new world and its exotic inhabitants. In *The Myth of Feminine Evil,* H. R. Hays explains this attraction-repulsion phenomenon in anthropological terms as "the double mask of mana." In view of the analysis of metaphorical twins in this play, taken by Fred de Armas (1994a) to constitute the mythic substructure, one comment by Hays is of special interest:

> We might expect that the exceptional and the unfamiliar would always be avoided or steps taken to eliminate them. An ambivalent reaction can be traced instead. Twins, which are an unusual birth, often cause anxiety. In a large number of cases one or both may be killed but they can also be considered sacred and raised to the status of heroes or gods. (35)

Estrella's comment to the King, "Nuestra hermandad envidiaba / Sevilla" ("All Seville was envious of our closeness and our similarity") (2094–95), clearly alludes to just such an ambivalent response on a large scale, that is, envy coupled with admiration. My point here is that Sancho el Bravo experiences a similar reaction to the exceptional and unfamiliar, and it results in what de Armas has called "the splitting of Gemini." Despite the elimination of one member of the pair, the ambivalence continues toward the survivor,

albeit now for different reasons, centering on beauty and the negative effects attributed to it.

Sancho el Bravo is one of a multitude of misguided lovers—from
Leriano through Calisto through Grisóstomo to Segismundo at the
palace—who respond to feminine beauty in quite different ways,
but always in a self-defeating and destructive manner. In the continuity of this myth of concern, made manifest yet again in contemporary culture, through *La estrella de Sevilla* lie aspects of both
the uniqueness and the universality of this represented action.

Appendix

Canonicity and Criticism

I

Alastair Fowler's tripartite canon:

1) potential (all *comedias*)
2) accessible (plays readily available in editions and anthologies)
3) selective (texts for classes; reading lists)

Parr's modification:

4) critical (between 1 & 2 but also informing 3)

II

Comedia Canonization by Anthology, 1939–89:   —
Alpern & Martel, *Diez Comedias* . . . (1939) (*Numancia, Fuenteovejuna,
    Estrella, Burlador, Mocedades* I, *Esclavo, Verdad, Vida es Sueño, Del
    Rey abajo, El Desdén*).
Wardropper, *Teatro español* . . . (1970)—(nine other core texts)
MacCurdy, *Spanish Drama* . . . (1971)—(twelve core texts)
Ebersole, *Selección* . . . (1973)—(lesser-known plays and authors)
Suárez-Galbán, *Antología* . . . (1989)—(ten core texts plus "Paso Sép-
    timo" ("Seventh Interlude") & "Arte Nuevo de hacer comedias" ("New
    Art of Writing Plays")

III

Concerning Criticism and Theory:

1) Communication Model (Roman Jakobson):

Addresser ---------------> Message ----------------> Addressee
(Author   ---------------> Text   -------------->   Reader)

2) Paradigm Shift in Emphasis and Orientation (Raman Selden):

Scholarship ---------->   [New] Criticism ---------->   Theory
(historical   ---------->   aesthetic--->linguistic/psychological;
                                    increasingly political)

3) Scholarship and Theory Propaedeutic to Praxis (J. Parr)

Scholarship ---------->   Interpretation   <------------   Theory
(hist. & new hist.   ---> central task   <---eclectic & tolerant)

Part II
Politics

3

The Mirror Crack'd: The Politics of Resemblance

Grace M. Burton

Michel Foucault has argued that

> up to the end of the sixteenth century, resemblance played a construc-
> tive role in the knowledge of Western Culture. It was resemblance that
> largely guided exegesis and the interpretation of texts, it was resem-
> blance that organized the play of symbols, made possible knowledge
> of things visible and invisible, and controlled the art of representing
> them. The universe was folded in upon itself. The earth echoing the
> sky, faces seeing themselves reflected in the stars, and plants holding
> within their stems the secrets that were of use to man. (1973, 19)

The mirror is the instrument of Foucault's resemblance, for "by
duplicating itself in a mirror the world abolishes the distance
proper to it; in this way it overcomes the place allotted to each
thing" (1973, 19). *La estrella de Sevilla,* however, calls into question resemblance as an organizing and unifying principle, for when
the mirrors that double and redouble the reflections and projections that bind the disparate segments of its universe together begin
to crack, words cease to reflect truth, and the monarchy ceases to
reflect honor. Truth then becomes refracted into the interplay of
truth and lie, while honor serves to sever rather than to cement
social relationships. *La estrella de Sevilla,* then, depicts the dissolution of one order and the creation of a new based not on the
tenuous bonds of resemblance, but on the interplay of independent entities.

For every character in *La estrella de Sevilla* there is a mirror
image who extends his or her presence into other spheres of action.
The play opens with King Sancho IV's entrance into Seville, the
most important city in his kingdom:

Muy agradecido estoy al cuidado de Sevilla,
y conozco que en Castilla
soberano rey ya soy.
Desde hoy reino, pues desde hoy
Sevilla me honra y ampara;
que es cosa evidente y clara
y es averiguada ley
que en ella no fuera rey
si en Sevilla no reinara.

(1–10)

[I am grateful for Seville's warm welcome for I now know that I am
the sovereign king of Castille. I reign from today, since today Seville
honors and favors me. After all, it is clear to all that the king is not
king unless he reigns in Seville.]

The king makes it clear that he who reigns in Seville also rules in
Castille. His presence in the city, then, is a manifestation of his
royal authority. Shortly after his arrival in Seville, however, the
king catches a glimpse of Estrella, the sister of Busto Tavera, a
prominent nobleman of the city. His desire to pursue this extraordinary beauty leads the king to enlist the help of Estrella's slave
Natilde, who responds, "¿Qué Estrella al Sol no se humilla?" (2.
957; "Do you mean that Estrella, a mere star, has not humbled
herself before the Sun?") when the king reveals his intention to
seduce her mistress. Natilde makes explicit what has been implicit
throughout the play: the king is a "Sol" ("Sun"), the brighest light
in Castille. But he is not the only "Sol" in Seville, for, as the King's
aide Don Arias explains, Busto Tavera "en la esfera Sevillana /
es Sol" (172–73; "is the Sun in the Sevillan sphere"). Busto and the
king are the most important figures in their respective spheres.
The nobleman's position in Seville doubles the king's place in Castille; they are mirror images who bring the microcosm of Seville
into harmony with the macrocosm of Castille.

Busto is the reflection of the king, who is himself the reflection
of God. As the alcalde don Pedro de Guzmán explains:

Dios hace los reyes, Dios
de los Saúles traslada
en los humildes Davides
las coronas soberanas.

(2836–39)

[God makes the king. The God of Saul transforms a humble David into
a sovereign lord.]

Don Pedro suggests that the king's political power mirrors God's divine authority. The human imitates the divine, and in doing so, God's sacred law acquires a human face in the person of the monarch. God communicates his authority to a king, who in turn extends his presence into the lower rungs of society through the honor code. Busto recognizes that "es el rey el que da honor" (1046; "the king confers honor"); his authority in Seville depends on the king just as the king's authority in Castille depends on God. God, king, and nobleman are analogues who occupy similar positions within different spheres of action. Resemblance, which structures the relationship between God and king, and between king and subject, thus functions in the service of cosmic order, for it is through resemblance that human beings come to understand their place within God's sacred design.

But while Busto may be the king's analogue, he is at best a partial parallel. The king, cloaked and under cover of darkness, steals surreptitiously into Busto's house one night when Busto is away: "Encubierto pienso ver / esta mujer en su casa" (465–66; "Clandestinely I intend to see this woman in her house"). The king, however, fails to reach Estrella's apartment before Busto's unexpected return from an evening of carousing. Busto and two of his companions have spent the evening enjoying what Busto calls the "dulce filosofía de amor" (898–99; "sweet philosophy of love") while the king has been at his house engaged in the same kind of nocturnal activity. Busto and the king thus share the same uncontrollable lust for women. But these mirror images are also adversaries, for the object of the king's lust is Busto's sister, a woman Busto must defend, even against the advances of the king.

The king's unscrupulous behavior fractures the system of resemblances that links subject with monarch and monarch with God. The king's presence in Busto's house offends the nobleman's sense of honor. Busto's home is his domain, and he will not allow anyone, not even the king, to usurp his authority: "En mi casa estoy / y en ella yo he de mandar" (999–1000; "This is my home, and in my home I reign"). But Busto's home is more than his castle; it is hallowed ground that he will defend at any cost:

Busto.	si pasa, ha de pasar
	por la punta desta espada;
	que aunque esta casa es sagrada,
	la tengo de profanar.
Rey.	Ten la espada.
Busto.	¿Qué es tener,

cuando el cuarto de mi hermana
desta suerte se profana?

(988–95)

Busto. You must go through the tip of this sword to get by me, for
while this house may be sacred ground, I will not hesitate to profane
it. *King.* Hold your sword. *Busto.* How can I hold my sword when my
sister's room has been so profaned?

In a cosmic order that invests meaning in resemblance, a single
action will have repercussions on a number of different levels.
Thus when the king invades Busto's house, he at once insults the
honor of a nobleman, usurps the authority of a ruler, and profanes
a sacred sanctuary.

Although Busto is quick to draw his sword when he discovers
an intruder in his home, he curbs his initial desire to take vengeance when he realizes that his adversary is in fact the King: "El
Embozado / es el Rey, no hay que dudar. / Quiérole dejar pasar"
(1049–51; "The man in disguise is undoubtedly the king. I will let
him pass"). Busto cannot confront the king directly. He instead
feigns disbelief that a monarch would do such an injustice to one
of his subjects, saying

aquí no viene el nombre
de rey con las obras, pues
es el rey el que da honor;
tú buscas mi deshonor.

(1044–46)

[Your deeds are not befitting of your title, for while the king
confers honor, you confer dishonor.]

When the king violates the sanctity of Busto's home, he ceases
to act in accordance with his position as king. As the ruling monarch, he is the fount of honor in society, yet he himself has acted
dishonorably. His lecherous behavior has opened a gap between
the monarch and the man, a gap Busto will exploit to expose the
inherent instability of a cosmic order predicated on resemblance.[1]

Busto uses words as mirrors in his initial encounter with the
king. Shortly after his arrival in Seville, the king learns that one
of his most valient generals has died, and two noblemen, Don Gonzalo de Ulloa and Don Fernán de Medina, have come to petition
the king for a promotion to fill the vacancy. The noblemen have
come to the Alcázar both to make their verbal arguments to the

king and to present written petitions that list their accomplishments on the battlefield:

Don Gonzalo.	este memorial os dejo.
Don Fernán.	Y yo el mío, que es espejo
	del cristal de mi valor,
	donde se verá mi cara
	limpia, perfecta y leal.
Don Gonzalo.	También el mío es cristal
	que hace mi justicia clara.

(270–76)

Don Gonzalo. I leave you this petition. *Don Fernán.* And I leave you mine. It is the mirror image of my valor in which you can see reflected my face, pure, perfect, and loyal. *Don Gonzalo.* Mine is also a mirror that makes manifest my just claim.

Both Don Gonzalo and Don Fernán suggest that these petitions are a true and accurate representation of their loyalty and bravery. Deeds done on the battlefield are doubled and redoubled in the word, a mirror whose reflections make present past glories. When the king asks Busto if he would consider the promotion, Busto responds that he would like nothing more than to honor those who deserve:

Busto.	Sólo quiero (y la razón
	y la justicia lo quieren)
	darles a los que sirvieren
	debida satisfacción.
Rey.	Basta; que me avergonzáis
	con vuestros buenos consejos.
Busto.	Son mis verdades espejos;
	y así, en ellas os miráis.

(392–400)

Busto. Reason and justice demand, and therefore I do wish to honor those who have served you well.
King. Enough. You shame me with your good advice.
Busto. My truths are mirrors in which you should see yourself reflected.

Like Don Gonzalo and Don Fernán, Busto claims that his words are mirrors; but while the noblemen insist that their petitions reflect the reality of their lives, Busto insists that the king should see himself reflected in the truth of his words. Busto suggests that his words have political import because they reflect truths that then redound on the king. Truth and the monarchy have become mirror images thanks to the unifying principle of resemblance.

When the king violates the sanctity of Busto's home, he severs the link between words and truth. Words cease to reflect reality; they instead fracture truth into the interplay of truth and lie. Busto, for example, suspects that Estrella's slave Natilde has conspired with the king to dishonor him, but he cannot level the accusation until he has ascertained the truth. He therefore constructs an elaborate ruse in which he feigns having more knowledge than he actually has:

> (Esta me vende, que está
> avergonzada y humilde.
> La verdad he de sacar
> con una mentira cierta.)
> Aquí os tengo de matar:
> todo el caso me ha contado
> el Rey.
>
> (1119–26)

[This maid's shame and humility betrays the fact that she has betrayed me. I will extract the truth from her with a certain lie. I am going to kill you here and now, for the king has told me everything.]

When Busto allows Natilde to believe that the king has already told him about her complicity in his dishonor, she quickly confirms that she has allowed the king access to Busto's house in exchange for her freedom. Busto's lie thus functions in the service of truth; it is a "cierta mentira," a certain lie which in turn makes certain all of his suspicions.

Busto uses a similar strategy in his conversation with the king immediately after he discovers the monarch in his home. Busto, who continues to show respect for the monarchy even as he shows his contempt for the monarch, must speak obliquely if he is to speak the truth:

> Pasa, cualquiera que seas,
> y otra vez al Rey no infames,
> ni el Rey, villano, te llames
> cuando haces hazañas feas.
>   Mira que el Rey, mi señor
> del Africa horror y espanto,

es cristianísimo y santo,
y ofendes tanto valor.

(1061–68)

[Come out, whoever you are, and do not insult the king's good name
again. You cannot call yourself a king, peasant, when you do such vile
deeds. The king, my lord, horror and terror of Africa, is a sainted
Christian. How dare you offend his valor.]

Busto, who speaks as though the king were not even there, asserts
that the "villano" before him could not be the king because a monarch would never have committed so vile an act as to enter his
house uninvited. He predicates his speech on a lie, a lie that nevertheless conveys a very real truth: the king has brought dishonor
both to himself and to the monarchy; he has abdicated his responsibilities as king; and he has emptied his title of any meaning. Busto's
words, then, no longer serve resemblance. They no longer function
as mirrors, or reflectors of truth; they have become prisms that
fracture reality into the interplay of truth and nontruth.

If, as Foucault says, resemblance is the means through which
"things scattered through the universe can answer one another"
(1973, 19), refraction is the means through which such resemblances are broken down into component parts that, once sepa-
rated, can never be reunited. The king, for example, has
understood all too well the meaning of Busto's "equívocas razones"
(1171; "ambiguous words"); and although he wants to take his revenge, he cannot do so publically. His aide Don Arias suggests
that he enlist the help of Sancho Ortiz, a prominent nobleman in
Seville, and mirror image of King Sancho. In his initial exchange
with the king, for example, Sancho Ortiz acknowledges that God,
king, and nobleman relate as analogues:

Rey.   Pues decid: ¿qué veis en mí?
Sancho.   La majestad, y el valor,
            y al fin, una imagen veo
         de Dios, pues le imita el Rey;
         y después dél, en vos creo,
         y a vuestra cesára ley,
         gran señor, aquí me empleo.

(1440–46)

King. Tell me, what do you see when you look at me?
Sancho. Majesty and valor. I see the image of God, for the king must
imitate God. Therefore I believe in you and your law as I believe in
Him. My lord, I come to serve.

Sancho Ortiz is a nobleman whose honor binds him to the monarch, himself the living image of God. But Sancho Ortiz mirrors the King in other ways as well. Not only do the nobleman and the monarch share the same name—Sancho—but they also have the same demeanor. Don Arias, for example, characterizes his majesty as

> El Rey don Sancho, a quien llaman
> por su invicta fortaleza
> *el Bravo* el vulgo, y los moros,
> porque de su nombre tiemblan,
> el Fuerte, y sus altas obras
> el Sacro.
>
> (781–86)

[The peasants call the king, don Sancho, the Valient for his fortitude. The Moors, who call him Powerful because they tremble at the very mention of his name, call him Sacred in honor of his grand deeds.]

Don Arias suggests that the king has earned his reputation on the battlefield. He is Valiant, Powerful, and Sacred, defender of the Faith and scourge of the Moors. This same Don Arias later describes Sancho Ortiz in similar terms, saying that he is

> el Cid andaluz, después.
> Este le dará la muerte,
> señor, con facilidad,
> que es bravo, robusto, y fuerte.
>
> (1219–22)

[He is an Andalusian Cid. He will execute [Busto] because he is valiant, brave and powerful.]

Don Arias implies that Sancho Ortiz is the right man to carry out the king's wishes because he is most like the king himself. The king need not exact his own revenge; he need not commit yet another dishonorable act; his analogue will do it for him.

But if Sancho Ortiz is the mirror image of the king, he is also the mirror image of Estrella. At the end of Act 2, Estrella is in her room talking to her maid Teodora while preparing herself for the arrival of Sancho Ortiz, when the mirror she is holding shatters as it falls to the ground:

> Bien hizo, porque imagina
> que aguardo el cristal, Teodora,

en que mis ojos se miran;
y pues tal espejo aguardo,
quiébrese el espejo, amiga;
que no quiero que con él,
éste de espejo me sirva.

(1906–16)

[I'm glad it broke. I am waiting for another mirror, Teodora, one in whom I can see my own image, and since I am waiting for such a mirror, let the other one break. I no longer have any need of it since I now have him (Sancho Ortiz)]

Estrella says that she no longer has any need of her looking glass because she will be able to see herself reflected in another mirror, her beloved Sancho Ortiz. Estrella has no existence of her own; she has become linked with every other member of society through the multiple reflections and projections made possible through resemblance.

The play of resemblances binds the king, Sancho Ortiz, and Estrella together: Estrella is the mirror image of Sancho Ortiz, who is in turn the mirror image of he king. But Sancho Ortiz knows that this harmonious situation will soon break apart because of his inability to serve both his king and his lady at the same time: "Mas no puedo con mi honor / cumplir, si a mi amor acudo" (1721–22; "I cannot fulfill my duties as an honorable man if I choose to serve love"). If he keeps his word to the king and kills Busto, he will lose Estrella forever; but if he lets Busto go free, he will have acted dishonorably. Sancho Ortiz's predicament illustrates the precarious nature of a cosmic order predicated on resemblance. The universe remains unified only so long as every element in the world mirrors every other element; the moment one mirror breaks, however, the whole system collapses. The king forces Sancho Ortiz to choose between his loyaly to the monarchy and his love for Estrella. He forces Sancho Ortiz to break one of the mirrors that binds these three characters together. In doing so, he fractures resemblance into its component parts and casts them out into a world now devoid of a unifying principle.

In the end, Sancho Ortiz reluctantly decides that he must serve his king. When the two *alcaldes mayores* arrive at Estrella's door with the news that he has killed her brother, Estrella responds, "¡Mi hermano es muerto, y le ha muerto / Sancho Ortiz! ¡El quien divida / tres almas de un corazón! (1975–77; "My brother is dead and Sancho Ortiz has killed him. In doing so, he has broken a single heart in three"). Estrella suggests that Sancho Ortiz has destroyed the system of resemblances that once structured all social relationships. The same death that forever separates her from her brother, the sun to her star ("[Busto] es el Sol. si Estrella es su hermana" [173; "Busto must be the sun if Estrella is his sister"],[2] will also separate her from her lover, the mirror in which she had once seen herself reflected. When, in the last scene of the play, the king attempts to reunite her with Sancho Ortiz, the lovers refuse the match for lack of "conformidad" (3000; "conformity"):

> *Estrella.* jamás podremos hallarla
> viviendo juntos.
> *Sancho.*   Lo mesmo
> digo yo, y por esta causa
> de la palabra te absuelvo.
> *Estrella.* Yo te absuelvo la palabra;
> que ver siempre al homicida
> de mi hermano en mesa y cama
> me ha de dar pena.
>
> (3001–8)

> *Estrella.* We will never find such conformity if we live together.
> *Sancho.* I agree. I therefore free you from your obligation to marry.
> *Estrella.* I do the same, for it would be too painful to see my brother's killer at my table and in my bed.

Sancho Ortiz and Estrella are no longer mirror images. Busto's death has fractured the world of resemblances that once bound them together. If Estrella had once invited Sancho Ortiz into her home, she now refuses to see him either at her table or in her bed. They have ceased to relate as analogues who move in perfect harmony and have become independent entities who, once scattered, will never, as Foucault says, "answer one another" again.

A mirror image is both an excess and an absence, an excess because it doubles an originary presence and an absence because it is virtual, not real. It is there and not there at the same time. Sancho Ortiz, for example, is a mirror image who doubles the king's presence in Seville, yet lacks the royal claim to absolute power. He has no real authority to kill Busto; he commits the deed only as a service to the king. But while his authority may be virtual, his actions—and their consequences—are very real.

Sancho Ortiz is a virtual monarch who puts an absent monarch's words into action. Sancho IV's word is law in Castille; but while don Arias suggests that such laws are simply a manifestation of the king's pleasure ("No hay más leyes que tu gusto" [1189; "There are no other laws than your pleasure"], Sancho Ortiz makes it clear that they are words that have acquired the force of action: "vuestras palabras cobran / valor que los montes labra, / y ellas cuanto dicen obran" (1562–64; "your word have the strength to make mountains, for the act of saying makes it so"). When the king asks Sancho Ortiz to act on his behalf, however, he severs the link between word and deed and fractures the law into the interplay of excess and absence. Sancho IV commissions Sancho Ortiz to execute Busto for *lèse majesté:* "Sancho Ortiz, luego por mí / y en mi nombre dalde muerte" (2. 1549–50; "Sancho Ortiz, execute him in my name"). The king proposes and Sancho Ortiz disposes. Don Arias nevertheless identifies Busto's death at the hands of Sancho Ortiz as a "temerario exceso" (1852; "fearful excess"), which leads to a "temeraria confusión" (3. 1994; "fearful confusion") when Sancho Ortiz refuses to say why he has killed. Sancho Ortiz knows that his murderous deed is an excess that threatens to undermine social stability; as such it is a crime punishable by law: "Prendedme, llevadme preso; / que es bien que el que mata muera" (1853–54; "Arrest me, make me your prisoner. It is right that he who kills should himself be put to death"). The king, however, feels more threatened by the nobleman's silence, the absence that serves to undermine royal authority: "Callando quiere vencerme" (2654; "He will defeat me with his silence"). A social structure predicated on the unity of word and deed has become fragmented into its component parts, murder and silence, excess and absence. Sancho IV asks Sancho Ortiz to do his bidding, but in doing so he forfeits his claim to absolute authority. When the king allows his subjects to put his words into action, he loses his privileged position in society and becomes subject to his subjects' reading of those words.

The king relies on the written word to conduct the affairs of state. At the end of Act 1, for example, don Arias dismisses two courtiers from the palace because the king has other business: "quiere el Rey escrebir" (902; "the king desires to write"). When the king hands Sancho Ortiz a document that would exonerate the nobleman of Busto's death, however, Sancho Ortiz rips it to pieces, saying that "desacredita / vuestra palabra el papel" (1575–76; "such documents undermine your word"). Sancho Ortiz recognizes that such documents are excesses ("los papeles sobran" [1566; "documents are a surplus"] that threaten to undermine the king's authority; he nevertheless decides to obey the letter of the law even after he discovers that he has agreed to kill Busto. The king never utters the name of the traitor; he hands Sancho Ortiz a piece of paper which the nobleman reads only after he is out of the king's pres-

ence: "Al que muerte habéis de dar / es, Sancho, a Busto Tavera"
(1691–92, 1709–10, 1729–30; "Sancho, the one you are to execute
is Busto Tavera"). Sancho Ortiz reads the letter left by an absent
king not once, but three times. In the process he becomes a virtual
monarch, but only after his almost obsessive repetition of the
king's words has emptied him of his own individual—and separate—identity. Sancho Ortiz's initial reading of the king's letter
leaves him in a state of shock and disbelief. After his audience
with the king, he receives a letter from Estrella in which she announces that Busto has finally given the lovers permission to
marry. His joy quickly turns to anguish, however, when he opens
the king's letter and discovers that the man he has agreed to execute is his future brother-in-law (1693–1704). The second time he
reads the king's letter, Sancho Ortiz considers the injustice of the
situation from the point of view of a lover who will lose his beloved
should he decide to carry out the king's wishes:

> Que al Rey la palabra he dado . . .
> de matar a mi cuñado,
> y a su hermana he de perder . . .
> Sancho Ortiz, no puede ser.
> Viva Busto. —Mas no es justo
> que al honor contraste el gusto:
> muera Busto, Busto muera.—
> Mas detente, mano fiera;
> viva Busto, viva Busto.
>
>   (1712–20)

[I promised the king that I would kill my brother-in-law. As a result, I
am sure to lose his sister. Sancho Ortiz, this cannot be. Let Busto live.
But it is not right that honor should oppose desire, so Busto must die.
But wait. Restrain your violent hand. Busto must live. Let Busto live.]

Sancho Ortiz initially reacts more as Estrella's betrothed than as
the king's analogue. He soon realizes, however, that he is both;
and while the lover may wish to preserve Busto's life ("viva Busto,
viva Busto"), the nobleman demands his death ("muera Busto,
Busto muera"). Sancho Ortiz's final reading of the letter, however,
serves to remind him that fealty must take precedence over passion. He is a nobleman who must fulfill his social obligations even
at the expense of his own happiness:

> aunque me cueste disgusto
> acuidir al Rey es justo:

Busto muera, Busto muera,
pues ya no hay quien decir quiera:
"viva Busto, viva Busto."

(1756–60)

[As horrible as it may be, it is only right that I serve my king. Busto must die, for there is no longer anyone left to say "let Busto live."]

The lover who would seek to preserve Busto's life has disappeared; Sancho Ortiz's obsessive and excessive repetition of the king's words has purged him of his individual identity and transformed him into a virtual king; it has emptied him of his private self and left him with nothing but his honor.

Sancho Ortiz understands this loss of self as a madness that compels him to act. The king has decreed that Busto must die. Sancho Ortiz is the king's analogue and he will carry out the king's directive, but he does so only because he can do no less: "El exceso/ del Rey me ha quitado el seso, / y es el resistirme en vano" (1812–14; "The king's excesses have deprived me of my good sense. I can no longer restrain myself"). The king has robbed Sancho Ortiz of his good sense and left him with nothing but his honor, a form of insanity that leads him to kill Busto and remain silent about the king's complicity in the matter.[3] Farfán de Ribera and don Pedro de Guzmán, the two *alcalde mayores* responsible for maintaining civil order, incarcerate Sancho Ortiz for a crime obviously committed by a madman.[4] While in prison, Sancho Ortiz has a delirious conversation with Honor himself, in which Honor chides the nobleman for having acted honorably:

—Honor, un necio y honrado
viene a ser criado vuestro,
por no exceder vuestras leyes.
—Mal, amigo, lo habéis hecho,
porque el verdadero honor
consiste ya en no tenerlo

. . . .

¿Qué hicisteis? —Quise cumplir
una palabra. —Riendo
me estoy: ¿palabra cumplís?
Parecéisme majadero;
que es ya el no cumplir palabras
bizarría en este tiempo.

(2478–83, 2488–93)

[—Honor, an honorable man and a foolish one has obeyed your laws
and become your servant. —You acted foolishly, friend. Real honor
consists in not having honor. What did you do? —I tried to keep my
word. —I'm laughing now. You kept your word? How foolish. Nowadays not keeping your word is the sign of valor.]

Honor, which structures all social relationships, is fundamental to
a world order predicated on resemblance. It is a mirror, a "cristal
puro" (743; "a glass mirror")[5] which doubles the king's presence
in the noblemen who serve him. Sancho Ortiz tells Honor that in
keeping his word and killing Busto he has acted in just such a
kingly fashion. But if, as Honor says in reply, the only honorable
men in society—that is, the only ones who uphold the status quo—
are those who lack honor, then in acting honorably Sancho Ortiz
succeeds only in perverting a world order he had sought to
preserve.

When Sancho Ortiz agrees to execute an as yet unknown traitor,
he asks only that the king grant him permission to marry whomever
he pleases: "yo os voy luego a obedecer; / y sólo por premio os
pido / para esposa la mujer / que yo eligiere" (1584–87; "I will go
and carry out your wishes. I only ask that you allow me to marry
whomever I please"). When Sancho Ortiz kills Busto, however, he
renders the king powerless to fulfill his end of the bargain. As the
king explains:

> El cumplió lo prometido.
> En confusión vengo a verme
> por no podelle cumplir
> la palabra que enojado
> le di.
>
> (2656–60)

[He did what he promised to do. I am now in a state of confusion
because I find myself unable to keep a promise I made while angry.]

The king has lost the capacity to act. His inability to bring about
the marriage of Sancho Ortiz and Estrella manifests an inability
to govern. The king's words cease to function as actions once he
loses the ability to enact them into law. Sancho Ortiz's honor, then,
serves revolutionary ends. Honor, which compels the nobleman to
act in the king's stead and thus precludes the king from acting for
himself, undermines the king's authority and effects a radically
new relationship between king and subject.[6]

The king is aware that he has put himself in a precarious political position. His decision to have Busto killed has serious repercussions in Seville, in Castilla, indeed, in all of Christendom:

> Pues, ¿he de decir que yo
> darle muerte mandé,
> y que tal crueldad usé
> con quien jamás me ofendió?
>   ¿El Cabildo de Sevilla,
> viendo que la causa fuí,
> Arias, qué dirá de mí?
> ¿Y qué se dirá en Castilla,
> cuando don Alonso en ella
> me está llamando tirano,
> y el Pontífice romano
> con censuras me atropella?
>
> . . . .
> ¿Qué he de hacer?
>
> (2682–93, 2699)

[Am I supposed to admit that I ordered the execution, that I treated an innocent man so cruelly? What will the Council of Seville say when they discover that I was the cause of his death? And what will they say about me in Castille? After all, don Alonso is already calling me a tyrant and the Pope in Rome overruns me with his censure. . . . What am I to do?]

The king structures this speech around the interplay of word and deed, "decir" and "hacer." He worries what the City Council of Seville, the pretender don Alonso in Castille, and the Pope in Rome will say when thay discover that he is responsible for the death of an innocent man. His fear that one of these three will undermine his position as king leads him to ask the final desperate question, "¿Qué he de hacer?" But the king can do nothing to reassert himself as the absolute monarch once he allows others to put his words into action. Sancho Ortiz's deeds mirror the king's words; both are excesses that give rise to confusion. The king exonerates Sancho Ortiz with written documents, "papeles rompidos" (2938; "shredded paper") that "dan confusas las palabras" (2939; "render words confusing"), while Sancho Ortiz commits a crime, a "temerario exceso" (1852; "fearful excess") that leads to "temeraria confusión" (3. 1994; "fearful confusion"). This confusion is absence, the necessary consequence of excess. Both Sancho Ortiz's silence and the king's inaction empty the monarchy of its authority. The king no longer enjoys absolute power; he must solicit the help of his subjects if he is to reestablish order in Seville.

The king knows that Sancho Ortiz is an innocent man who will die at the hands of an executioner unless he can persuade the two *alcaldes mayores,* Farfán and don Pedro, to pardon him. As the king explains to Farfán: "sólo os pido que miráis, / pues sois padres de la patria, / su justicia, y la clemencia / muchas veces la aventaja" (2808–11; "since you are the guardians of this country, I ask you to be vigilant about justice. And remember, clemency often works in justice's favor"). Negotiation has replaced proclamation as the means by which the king executes the royal prerogative. A self-satisfied king exclaims "bien negocié" (2886; "I negotiated well") after his audience with the alcaldes. Farfán, however, responds to the king's request by reminding the monarch of his obligations to God. Human justice must reflect, not pervert, divine law:

> Estas varas representana
> Vuestra Alteza; y si tratan
> mal vuestra planta divina,
> ofenden a vuestra estampa.
> Derechas miran a Dios,
> y si se doblan y bajan,
> miran al hombre, y de Dios,
> en torciéndose, se apartan.
>
> (2820–27)

[These staffs represent Your Highness, and if they mistreat your divine feet, they necessarily offend your person. When pointing upward, they see God, but if they double over and look downward, they see only man, and in so twisting, they turn away from God.]

In a world order predicated on resemblance, Farfán and don Pedro could serve their God, their King, and their people at the same time because their role as vassal would be in perfect harmony with their role as *alcalde.* The king, however, asks them to turn their staffs of justice away from divine perfection and toward human frailty. Don Pedro complains that the king has become the "causa de nuestras causas" (3. 2831), a blasphemous pun that suggests that the monarch, the mirror image of God, the "cause of all causes," has become the source of social unrest, the "cause of our complaints."[7] Resemblance has failed to structure the nobles' relationship with the king and the king's relationship with God, for, when the king ceases to function as the mirror image of God, honor, the mirror that links the king to his subjects, fractures Farfán and don Pedro into their component parts, vassal and *alcalde.* They can serve either the king or the people; they cannot do both. As don Pedro explains to the king, "Como a vasallos nos manda, / mas como alcaldes mayores, / no pidas injustas causas; / que aquello es estar sin ellas, / y aquesto es estar con varas" (2915–19; "We are your vassals, and you command us. But we are also civil authorities, and you have no right to ask us to commit an unjust act, for while the vassal may lack the staff of justice, the civil authority does not.")

Don Pedro and Farfán change the power relations in society when they choose to discharge their duties as *alcaldes*. They, the representatives of the people of Seville, compel the king to submit to the will of his subjects. Their refusal to pardon Sancho Ortiz forces the king to accept responsibility for Busto's death: "Sevilla / matadme a mí, que fuí causa / desta muerte" (2968–70; "Put me to death, Seville, for it was I who caused his death"). The king fears for his life until Farfán absolves him of any wrongdoing: "Sevilla se desagravia; / que pues mandasteis matalle, / sin duda os daría causa" (2979–81; "Seville is no longer offended. If you had him killed, without doubt you had cause"). The stability of the monarchy now resides not in the person of the king, but in the judgment of the *alcaldes*. The king is still king, but he has lost his claim to absolute power; his word cannot be enacted into law unless it is first ratified by the people. When, in the final scene of the play, Sancho Ortiz asks for Estrella's hand in marriage, the king tries to reassert his authority:

Rey.	Estrella, ésta es mi palabra.
	Rey soy, y debo cumplirla:
	¿qué me respondéis?
Estrella.	Que se haga
	vuestro gusto. Suya soy.
Sancho.	Yo soy suyo.
Rey.	¿Qué os falta?
Sancho.	La conformidad.

(2995–99)

King. Estrella, I am king. I gave my word and I should keep it. What have you to say?
Estrella. Do what you will. I am still your subject.
Sancho. I, too, am your subject.
King. Then what is missing?
Sancho. Conformity.

The king knows that he cannot bring about the marriage without the consent of both parties. His leading question, "¿qué me respondéis?" is a tacit acknowledgment that he cannot govern without the support of the people. And while both Estrella and Sancho Ortiz recognize the king as king, the monarch can no longer impose his will on them; it is they who now impose their will on him.

La estrella de Sevilla depicts the political implications of the dissolution of cosmic order predicated on resemblance. When the king violates the sanctity of Busto's home, he fractures the system of resemblance that links God, king, and subject. Words then cease to convey truth; they instead fracture truth into its component parts, truth and lie. Honor then fractures society; it forces Sancho Ortiz to choose between his king and his beloved. Once resemblance breaks down, its various parts become independent entities that become the foundation of a new order. In the very last scene of the play the king says, "Toda esta gente me espanta" (3021; "These people instill fear"). The king will have a new relationship with his subjects after what has happened in Seville; he will never again enjoy the same privileged position he had once held. In a fractured society, political power depends on the favor of the people, not on the prerogative of the king.

Notes

1. McCrary (1971) says that "[a]s head of state, the prince . . . had two bodies: the body natural or personal, and the body corporate or mystical, i.e., the office" (506). He goes on to argue that the author of *La estrella de Sevilla* dramatizes "the development of royal consciousness and conscience from that of a self-centered individuality to the fullness of the mystique which kingship embodies" (507). McCrary thus sees the split between the monarch and the man as a necessary step in the education of a young monarch. I will contend, however, that it signals a radically new definition of kingship.

2. Frederick de Armas (1980) has a similiar view. He describes the relationship between Busto and Estrella, and between Estrella and Sancho Ortiz, in mythological and astrological terms, saying that they are two sets of twins, both guided by the zodiacal sign of Gemini.

3. De Armas (1979) also sees the relationship between honor and madness, but he only hints at the possible ramifications for society: "Sancho in his madness is also poisoned by the question of honor—not so much honra but honor. He suspects, but does not want to admit that in doing what he should, in abiding by the higher ideal (honor) as opposed to love, he has facilitated the King's dishonor of Estrella, his would-be wife, even though the monarch should be the one that confers honor on his subjects" (8).

4. Farfán says that Sancho Ortiz "ha perdido el seso" (2. 1866) ("has lost his mind"), while don Pedro says simply, "Loco está" (2. 1871) ("he is mad").

5. The word "cristal" ("glass") is always associated with a mirror in this play. Fernán, for example, calls his petition the "espejo / del cristal de mi valor" (271–72; "the mirror of my valor"). Don Gonzalo calls his petition a "cristal / que hace mi justicia clara" (275–76; "a mirror, which makes manifest my just claim"). Es-

trella explicitly links the two, saying that Sancho Ortiz has become the mirror in which she sees herself: "aguardo el cristal, Teodora, / en que mis ojos se miran; y pues tal espejo aguardo, / quiébrese el espejo, amiga" ("I am waiting for the mirror, Teodora, in whom I see my own image, and since I am waiting for such a mirror, let the other one break").

6. Elias Rivers (1980) disagrees, saying that "*La Estrella de Sevilla* is a moving dramatic defense of the system of personal honor" (116). Rivers, who bases his argument in speech-act theory, says that the play depicts the conflict between an "oral society's system of honor and shame, and modern society's dependence upon written documents as substitutes for speech acts" (115). He concludes that the honor system triumphs over the written document when Sancho Ortiz succeeds in making the king understand that he "has an unwritten obligation to come to his defense orally and in public" (115). I would argue that the king loses the capacity to speak any kind of performative utterance once he loses the ability to act. He has lost the capacity to do things with words; saying so can no longer make it so.

7. Alpern and Martel (1968) read the line as the "cause of our complaints" (227), but the verse is also a reference to Saint Thomas Aquinas (1972), whose second proof for the existence of God posits God as the First Cause, the cause of all subsequent causes: "In the sensible world we find causes in an order of succession; we never see, nor could we, anything causing itself, for then it would have to pre-exist itself, and this is impossible. Any such succession of causes must begin somewhere, for in it a primary cause influences an intermediate, and the intermediate a last (whether the intermediate be one or many). Now, if you eliminate a cause, you also eliminate its effects, so that you cannot have a last cause or an intermediate one without having a first cause. Without an origin to the series of causes, and hence a primary cause, no intermediate causes would function and therefore no last effect, but the facts seem to contradict this. We must therefore suppose a First Cause, which all call God" (123).

4

The Centrality and Function of King Sancho

FRANK P. CASA

INVESTIGATIONS on the role of the king in the *comedia* have amply established the importance of this personage for the theater of the Golden Age (Crapotta 1984, Díez Borque 1976, Fox 1986, Lauer 1987, Young 1979). While we cannot discuss on this occasion the many dramatic purposes of the royal figure, we can explore the ramifications of his function for *La estrella de Sevilla*. This play is particularly useful for our discussion because it is a virtual storehouse of themes dealing with kingship. Among the topics that are to be found are: the contradiction between divine kingship and erring humanity, the conflict between king and noble, the dispensing of justice, the royal audience, the education of the prince, the assumption of royal responsibility, the recognition of the sacred duties of the king, the relationship between prince and subjects. All of these topoi are employed in the play in order to explore the question of the nature of monarchy that passionately interested theoreticians and that was translated into an equally absorbing theme for Golden Age dramatists: the ambiguity inherent in the "gemina persona", the intriguing contradiction implicit in the dual nature of the king, the monarch edged with divinity who is also a man beset by human frailties.[1]

The king's role in a comedia can be roughly divided into two types. When the king is the protagonist of the play, the action focuses either on the fulfillment of his duties as a monarch, such as in Moreto's *La fuerza de la ley* (*The Power of the Law*) or on the duality implicit in his equivocal nature as king and as man as in Lope's *El rey don Pedro en Madrid* (*King Don Pedro in Madrid*); if his role is complementary or marginal to another plot, he is presented, mostly at the end of the action, as the legitimizing figure for the play's resolution as in *Fuenteovejuna, Peribáñez, El alcalde de Zalamea* (*The Mayor of Zalamea*). In the second case, the characterization of the king is often cursory if at all existent. The plot requires only that the king appear as the upholder of justice. This kingly attribute is often accepted as a given, without previous preparation or even in contradiction with an earlier characterization of the monarch. *El caballero de Olmedo* (*The Knight from Olmedo*), for example, presents a weak king dominated by his minister only to be transformed into an unbending upholder of justice at the end of the play. In other plays, the monarch's commitment to justice is established through the use of an audience, a scene in which the disposition that the king makes of his subjects' claims certifies his competence and gives absolute proof of his righteousness (Casa 1986).

In plays belonging to the first type, the figure of the monarch is placed in conflict with his human nature, and the final confirmation of his royal substance comes about only after he has given evidence of his capacity to control his human instincts, as in *La vida es sueño*. In these cases, the playwright normally unfolds an ironic opposition between the theoretical privileges of royalty, nearly always based on the concept of the divine rights of the monarch, and the less august behavior of the man. It is precisely on this contrast that the author of our play focuses to develop his themes.

Generally, personages in honor dramas are used by the playwright to furnish an exemplification of human conduct that exists principally within the imagined or idealized society of the play. In order to capture and awe the public, dramatists create circumstances of extreme complexity peopled with personages who are intensely self-aware and who are confronted by alternatives that affect both their estimation of themselves and their place within their social order. For dramatic purposes, they are placed in a situation in which they are obliged to make decisions of an absolute nature: the choice between dignity and ignominy, honor and life, fidelity and betrayal. The structure of these plays inexorably directs the attention of the spectator toward a central conflict that allows for no attenuation, no modification, and therefore no compromise. The personages are circumscribed by a narrow range of possibilities and they are forced to act within a limited number of parameters: religion, fealty to the liege lord, honor, and love. These four pillars of the *comedia* provide the moral imperatives of this fictional society and all decisions by the protagonists are affected by the unflinching and absolute obedience that they demand (Casa 1983).

The inevitably harsh consequences that ensue have been variously interpreted by critics either as illustrative of aberrations in the character of the protagonists, as an implicit condemnation of a society that forces them upon this path, or as illustrative of individuals' ignorance of the complexity of their circumstances and acting upon flawed and partial knowledge (Dunn 1960; Stroud 1990). Whatever explanation we may offer, it is in the nature of the *comedia* to construct situations in which extreme circumstances are posited, in order to explore the outer limits of human capabilities. Conceptually, it is akin to the kind of game that requires one to make hypothetical and extreme choices: which books are to be saved if all the rest have to be destroyed or what would you do if you had to choose between the life of your mother and that of your son, and so forth. It is an earnest game that reveals not so much the psychological makeup of the person involved but his personal values or feelings. As a consequence, analyses that do not take into consideration the rules of this dramatic game invariably lead us to the conclusion that we are dealing with deeply disturbed personalities. If a person is forced to choose between the death of his mother or that of his son, can he be accused of cruelty when he finally makes his decision? Or to use a related example, what conclusions can we derive about the moral, and not political, make-up of Agamemnon when he sacrifices his daughter Iphigineia at Aulis in order to ensure the auspicious departure of the Greek host for Troy?

In his recent book, Matthew Stroud rejects the concept of a unitary dramatic conflict that informs the criticism of the wife-killer plays, and he suggests the application of a multilayered response (21). The proposal is not without merit and, if we were to apply it in dealing with the famous example of *El médico de su honra* (*The Surgeon of His Honor*), we could choose any combination of the following explanations: we can blame society for having structured itself along the lines of honor/non-honor, Gutierre for observing this moral code, King Pedro for his weakness in not controlling his half-brother and future murderer, Enrique for not being able to control his passion, or Mencía for trying to find refuge in deception. If we follow this path, we will face a complex network of motivations that makes an absolute judgement on the moral responsibility of the protagonist impossible.[2] However appealing and even logical this view may be, it can only be held at the expense of the dramatic intensity of the play. Golden Age dramas, notwithstanding the thematic relevance of their subplots, are normally shaped by an overriding conflict that unfolds either between opposing forces or between opposing tendencies within the protagonists.[3] Whatever is gained in seeing these plays as reflectors of a fragmented social and spiritual reality is lost in giving up the emotional and ethical experience of seeing personages struggle against the dilemmas that face them. In the case of *La estrella de Sevilla* there is no doubt that its fundamental dramatic scheme is based on an unequivocal and dominant theme—whether or not Sancho deserves to be a king—a theme that is developed by a series of illustrative episodes which lead first to a crisis and then to an ironic resolution.

The writer of this celebrated play uses this basic device of the *comedia* to create a dramatic conflict that places all of the personages within a cycle of mutually exclusive positions that in turn leads to an impasse which requires an extraordinary act of self-abasement in order to resolve it. It is for this reason that the king must be considered not only crucial to the play but also its protagonist. Once the exposition of the play has taken place, it becomes clear that the monarch not only originates the crisis but constitutes the thematic focus of the play. Indeed, it can be stated that all the other personages are accessories to his drama.

A cursory look at the rest of the personages makes this manifest. Busto is literally removed from the action once he affirms with his death the unquestioned primacy of honor over obedience to the monarch. Apropos, his behavior toward the king helps to establish conclusively a sometime controversial topic, the place that these two values—honor and obedience to the monarch—have within the *comedia*. As far as the rest of the personages are concerned, once Estrella unfolds her honorableness and steadfastness in confronting the king, her dramatic function is limited to a plea for justice, an action that is more crucial to the monarch's educational process than to her own development. Sancho Ortiz is relegated to a passive, although highly symbolic, role once he has demonstrated the integrity of his word by choosing obedience to the king over both love and friendship. As we can see, none of these principal characters remains at the center of the play. The attention reverts to the king because he is the initiator of the action, the instigator of the dramatic knot, and the eventual resolver of the conflict.[4]

La estrella de Sevilla begins with a stark proposition—that, in order to deserve being king in Castile, Sancho must prove himself worthy of this title in Seville (9–10). The very formulation of the issue calls forth the need for a dramatic treatment that can only be expressed in terms of a test or trial. The dramatic conflict necessary to illuminate this theme of the play could be expressed in the form of a struggle against an external force, as for example in *El mejor alcalde el rey* (*The Best Judge Is the King*), in which the challenge by the rural nobleman must be met and overcome by the king; or it could be represented as an internal strife in which the king struggles against himself. Our dramatist prefers the latter as the more persuasive of the two alternatives. The passions that bring about internal dissension traditionally employed by the *comedia* are arrogance, ambition, violence, and, of course, lust, that perennial prop of the *comedia*. The dramatist's choice for our play is immediately evident when we witness the review of the Sevillian women in the first scene,[5] whose purpose is to establish that the king is ruled by sexual obsession. In the code of the *comedia*, a man incapable of steadfast and faithful love to one woman is automatically suspect.[6] He is a person in whom passion dominates, manifestly unable to control his impulses and therefore of potential danger to his society. In a private man this disposition brings about personal and even social disorder but in a public man, and especially the king, unchecked lust may lead to the unraveling of the kingdom.

The connection between sexual excesses and bad government is long established in Western political thought. It appears in Thucydides (6. 54), Aristotle (*Politics* 10. 1311a, 1314b), and Machiavelli (*Discorsi* 3. 26), and they all converge on the idea that tyranny often expresses itself through sexual violence and libertinage. Stephanie Jed finds that Aristotle converts this thought into a political formula: "one of the primary reasons that tyrants are ruined is that they offend the honor of their male subjects by raping and violating their wives and breaking up their marriages" (1989, 3). Sexual violence is frequently used as the act that brings about social and political changes: the abduction of Helen brings about the destruction of Troy, the rape of Lucretia the fall of the monarchy and the establishment of the Roman Republic, and in the *comedia* the attempted rape of Laurencia brings about Fuenteovejuna's rebellion and the establishment of a new order.[7]

When the king rejects all the light-skinned, blond women of Seville because he finds them unexciting, he is, at the same time, rejecting the prototype of the ethereal woman, the blond, angelical woman of the neoplatonists, and the source of spiritual love. And in seeking a dark beauty, the emblem of the passionate woman, he is revealing his bondage to sexual impulses. Thus Sancho begins his test of worthiness on very precarious grounds—which makes him at least suspect, if it does not disqualify him altogether. The highly stylized nature of the *comedia* permits us, even after this short scene, to formulate the dramatic conflict: can Sancho maintain his position as king in light of his moral shortcomings? Will he be able to pass the test that he himself has proposed: to reign in Castile he must be worthy of Seville. This, then, is the thematic purpose of the author, and the rest of the play unfolds events on the basis of whose significance this judgment is to be rendered.

Subsequent scenes further emphasize the king's weaknesses, already implicit in the scene of the review of women, and build up a negative characterization until Sancho is literally immobilized by his actions. The series of scenes that develop the theme provide a moral profile of Sancho that demonstrates his failure as a king. It is for this reason that the monarch must be placed in a sequence of situations in which kingly virtues can be judged: fairness, justice, respect of his subjects, obedience to the law of the land, an awareness of his divine mandate, the honoring of his word. This exemplification acquires an emphatic delineation with the use of one of the emblematic scenes connected to kingship, the royal audience. The audience is the dramatic device that the *comedia* employs to show the king in the exercise of his primary function, the dispensing of justice. It is here that the monarch is judged for his sense of fairness, his capacity to comprehend human nature, and his ability to render God's justice on earth—the principal role of the monarch as the vicar of Christ. If a king fails in this, he will have failed in his most sacred duty and he will render clear his incapacity to govern.[8]

We must become totally aware of the sacramental nature of this responsibility before we are able to weigh correctly the importance of the next scene and the depth of his error. Sancho, in order to curry favor with Busto and for the most base of reasons, treats this duty, invested with the highest social and religious significance, in a frivolous manner. He is not only ready to accommodate his judgment to the circumstances, but he is also willing to let Busto render the judgement. He is then, symbolically, divesting himself of a God-given duty, and in so doing he desecrates both the order of things and the will of God. This dereliction of responsibility horrifies Busto who, unlike Sancho, is aware of its implication. Indeed, Busto's behavior at this and at other moments is designed specifically to make evident the gulf that exists between the theoretical nature of the king, represented by Busto's religious awe of the monarch (278–88), and Sancho's behavior. When in the attempted violation scene Busto reminds the monarch that he ceases to be a king when he does not act as such, he is reminding us that in reality Sancho has long ceased being one. The king's exhilaration in relishing the ease with which his prerogatives allow him to enter

Estrella's bedroom—"divina cosa es reinar" (929; "To rule is a divine thing")—reveals in a moment of deep irony the monarch's inability to fathom the true meaning of his words. This total unawareness of the scope of his divinely appointed role is the clearest indication of his incapacity to govern. And when he decides to take vengeance upon Busto for killing the slave Natilde, an action that is designed to protest against the attempted dishonor to his home, King Sancho foregoes definitely all pretensions as the giver of justice, the single most important attribute of kingship. In giving vent to both anger and vengeance, without considering his responsibility for the events, he shows a lack of that other kingly requisite for good government, prudence.[9] King Sancho has now lost both his capacities to govern the kingdom and to control himself. Indeed, his insistence on giving Sancho de las Roelas a written document that upholds the bargain the two have struck is an indication of a deep uncertainty regarding the self. He no longer trusts the absoluteness of his word, and it is Sancho who has to remind him that the king's word is good enough to seal the bond. The king, prey first to lust and then to vengeance, falls immediately into the pit of injustice and in so doing loses his essential and irreplaceable quality as monarch. The death of Busto, the unjust imprisonment of Sancho, and Estrella's need to plead for justice represent the king's separation from his divinely appointed duty. Having lost his purpose, he is no longer able act on his own volition. If he is to find the road to self-knowledge and salvation, it will have to be shown by those persons who have maintained their integrity.

King Sancho's incapacity to act is a direct result of his fall from grace. Having demonstrated his unworthiness as a monarch, he no longer possesses the moral force to impose his will. Indeed, he is incapable of generating the steps necessary to regain control over events. Although he had promised Sancho his protection by giving his word (1565–67), he is now speechless. He seems to be unable to use his own voice to exculpate Sancho de las Roelas and prefers that others speak for him. His words have lost *valor*—that is, both valor and value—and he is lessened not only as monarch but also as man. Sancho has fulfilled his obligation: "que tienen los Sevillanos / las palabras en las manos," (1846–47; "Sevillans keep their words with their deeds"). His word has been honored with the exercise of his hands, and since he has rejected the king's "palabra de papel" (1576; "word of paper"), only the live, human voice of the monarch can reestablish the lost equilibrium.

As I have indicated earlier, the *comedia* ties an unyielding dramatic knot to create a situation that cannot be resolved by accommodation. Compromise is impossible because conflicts are not based on personal choices that can be altered but on absolute principles that cannot be sacrificed without diminution of the self.[10] It is for this reason that the only way out of an impasse in the *comedia* is to follow the situation to its logical and often cruel and destructive consequences. At this stage of the action, there is an absolute deadlock: a murder has been committed not only against a highly placed individual but also against the city of Seville (2352–55). Sancho Ortiz refuses to talk and implies quite clearly that the responsibility for an explanation resides in another person. The king is being pressured to do justice but he is unwilling or unable to act. The city demands satisfaction because Sancho Ortiz, having "spoken" with his hands, remains silent. The solution in both moral and political terms can only come from the monarch, a solution that can bring only personal shame and political difficulties for him (2682–99). Having arrived at this juncture, can the king find the moral strength to redeem himself as a man and as a monarch? It is clear now that the dramatist has chosen to develop the theme not on the basis of physical courage but on the protagonist's capacity to redeem himself from a moral flaw. This choice will have a heavy influence on the nature of the ending of the play.

The way out of the dilemma is curiously complex. It begins with Sancho Ortiz's steadfastness in his resolve to keep silent the reason for the assassination. Once again, and just as in the case of Busto, the king sees reflected in the conduct of his subjects those virtues that he himself should have shown. It is through the moral examples of his victims that he begins the recovery of his own dignity. Unlike Segismundo in *La vida es sueño,* who could read only arrogance and pride in the flight of eagles (1048–57), King Sancho comes, although reluctantly, to understand the meaning of the examples of greatness put before him. The second step is to be found in Estrella's plea for justice. The defenseless woman who appears before the monarch to plead for justice is a staple of the *comedia* and it carries with it a particular charge. The rendering of justice to the woman without recourse is offered as the ultimate test of the king's capacity for fairness. Without protection, unable to defend herself, she is left at the mercy of the powerful. When a woman appears before the king to ask for his protection, she is coming to the last authority on earth, after which there is nothing but an appeal to the divinity, that same divinity which graced this particular human being with the task of being its representative on earth. This is a most critical moment for the king. It is at this juncture that he must recognize his responsibility if he is to be redeemed at all. There is a moment of weakness when the king, still hesitating to assume his responsibility, blames Estrella's beauty for his error,[11] but, when the fiery noblewoman leaves the palace, the king cannot but reflect upon his circumstances. In recognizing his obligation, he takes the decision that will bring about the resolution of the conflict:

> Yo incité a Sancho Ortiz: voy a libralle;
> que amor que pisa púrpura de reyes,
> a su gusto, no más, promulga leyes.

(2171–73)

> [I incited Sancho Ortiz and I will free him;
> because love which treads on royal purple,
> needs only its will to engender laws.]

The decision, however, is not easily taken because, as I have said, it involves a high risk for the monarch. He worries about the political impact that his admission will have both in Seville and in Castile and, once again, he seeks a way out by attempting to manipulate events. His advisor suggests exile for Sancho Ortiz, a solution he hopes can be seen as a punishment for the assassin and a reparation for the city, plus an advantageous marriage for Estrella. However, this accommodation goes totally against the moral foundations of the play and its protagonists.[12] At various times in the play, we have already witnessed definite rejections of compromise on the part of Busto, Sancho Ortiz, and Estrella. It is an arrangement that cannot be accepted by anyone, but, in considering it, the king reveals his essentially flawed character. There is yet another foreshadowing of this impossibility to arrive at an accommodation in Sancho Ortiz's refusal to be freed by Estrella: he will not countenance anything short of complete exoneration. Nor are the city counselors any less committed to the maintenance of their honor for they draw an indelible distinction between personal allegiance to the king and their responsibility as *alcaldes*—a precious delineation between the personal and the official nature of man that King Sancho is not able to make.

We have, then, a clear example of the *comedia*'s unwillingness to provide circumstantial solutions to its dilemmas as well as of its tendency to solve the dramatic conflict along the inflexible lines of its initial proposition. Having lost all possibility of arriving at an accommodation, the king has only one way out—to take full responsibility for the crime. When he finally confesses publicly his role in the murder, he satisfies the Sevillans' demand for the proper affixing of culpability. Considering that there has been a murder and that the lives of both Sancho Ortiz and Estrella have been devastated, the mere acknowledging of his error on the part of the king seems not totally satisfactory. That the king should make amends for his egregious abuse of authority with so little censure seems disturbingly unbalanced. Indeed, if viewed from a modern or democratic perspective, it is undeniably so. However, once again, we must revert to the deliberately symbolic nature of many endings in *comedias* if we are to find this solution acceptable. A look back at some well-known plays will reveal that endings characterized by ambiguity are not infrequent: Segismundo's treatment of the rebel soldier, the Catholic Kings' circumstantial judgement in *Fuenteovejuna,* King Pedro's acceptance of the murder of Mencía, the Duke of Ferrara's murder of Casandra and Federico. In *La estrella de Sevilla* the king's shortcomings as a man and as a monarch can be resolved only by means of a personal awareness of his errors, a self-knowledge that is the prelude to good government. In the *comedia*, the criticism and punishment of a legitimate king who has gravely erred does not normally include the possibility of deposition or assassination. Many monarchs are killed, as Robert Lauer has shown, but generally the redressing of kingly errors follows what can only be viewed as a conversion, brought about by the recognition and acceptance of his errors or crimes. In *La estrella de Sevilla,* King Sancho has to come to a realization of his faults on a personal level—"¡ Cómo estoy arrepentido / don Arias de mi flaqueza!" (2727–29; "How much I regret, don Arias, my weakness")—because he needs first of all to correct himself as a human being. He has to accept the fact that his weaknesses as a man obstruct the discharge of his duties as a king, and only when he has come to that awareness and accepted its consequences can he resume his role as a king. The admission of his transgressions paves the way for the recognition of his error, and the public confession serves as the cleansing mechanism that will lead him to behavior befitting a king.[13]

It is important to note that the play does not end with a false appearance of unconditional harmony. There is, as in other dramas, no happy pairing of disparate couples implying a return to social accord. The irrevocable deed of murder weighs heavily upon the ending, and an awareness of its dreadful implications casts a pall upon the lives of all the protagonists. What the ending does is to re-establish a social equilibrium whose precariousness indicates both the destructive nature of the past experience and the newly acquired vulnerability of the chastised king.

Notes

1. The fundamental work on this subject is Kantorowicz's book (1957). For an application of his research in Golden Age Drama see McCrary (1971).

2. The concept of diffusion of responsibility was first advanced by Alexander Parker (1962).

3. John Lyon (1983, 23) draws a difference between the structure of drama based on conflicting forces in the traditional mode and modern drama, where individuality and conflict are replaced by rhythm, patterns, and images.

4. McCrary (1971) had already affirmed the centrality of the king in the play but he chose to see in him an example of the *sparagmos,* the sacrificial victim who takes upon himself the collective guilt of the people.

5. The review of women as an example of unchecked lust is present in many plays, notably *Fuenteovejuna* and *El burlador de Sevilla.*

6. The neoplatonic idea that love should be directed only toward the loved person and should be the result of mutual knowledge and acceptance of the persons involved informs the representation of love in the *comedia.* All deviation from this standard is viewed as an error (Castiglione 1969, book 4).

7. Stephanie Jed (1989, 27) speaks of the long-held view that passions are seen as inimical to liberty and as promoters of tyranny: "In this sense, passions, inasmuch as they are conceived as inimical to liberty, come to be associated with tyranny."

8. "Realmente, después de la religión, entre las demás virtudes propias de los reyes y necesarias para el buen gobierno y conservación de sus reinos y estados, la que resplandece como lucero de la mañana entre las estrellas, es la virtud de la justicia, que con igualdad da a cada uno lo que es suyo y pertenece" (Salazar 1945, 92; "Truly, after religion, among the virtues that are proper to kings and are necessary to good governance and to the preservation of their kingdoms and lands, the one that shines like the morning star among other stars, is the virtue of justice, which gives with equality to each what is his and what belongs to him").

9. For the development of the concept of prudence in the Renaissance, Garver (1987) and Eulogio Palacios (1957).

10. The undesirability or even impossibility of compromise in matters of import is clearly shown in Guillén de Castro's *Mocedades del Cid,* where Count Lozano refuses to apologize because the action would diminish him without returning the lost honor to the Cid's father (Juliá Martínez, ed., 1925–27, 2, 178).

11. The theme of the woman's beauty as responsibile for the misdeeds of men is an important one in the *comedia.* For a discussion of this topic see Casa (1988); see also Gravdal (1991).

12. *Fuenteovejuna* is an example of a play in which the original dramatic lines of the play are perverted to effect a social purpose. For a discussion of this subject see Pring-Mill (1962).

13. Illegitimate or tyrannical kings are often deposed and killed (Lauer 1987). In cases where censure of a legitimate king is called for, the punishment takes the form of an implicit apology or, in extreme cases, a self-imposed punishment. The best example I know is to be found in Guillén de Castro's *El amor constante* (The Constant Love), where the king pays for his errors through conversion and

self-imposed death: "Sea así; que tal estoy / y tal me contemplo aquí, / que aun para matarme a mí / licencia también te doy." ("And so be it; for when I look at myself and see me in such a state that I give you permission to kill me"; Juliá Martínez 1925–27, ed., 1, 44). The technique is also used in French theater: "Conversion of the king afforded the best solution of all, whether it was accredited to the sovereign's magnanimity or Heaven, which "est toujours pour les Rois" ("which always favors the kings"; Baudin 1941, 84).

5

In the Wake of Machiavelli—*Razón de Estado,* Morality, and the Individual

MELVEENA MCKENDRICK

For all its medieval setting, the dramatic business of *La estrella de Sevilla* places it at the very heart of the two greatest political issues of the age in which it was written. One of these issues was absolutism: the monarch's relationship to the law—whether his will was supreme whatever the interests of the state—was the subject of passionate concern and debate in western Europe. The other issue was the connected but larger and even more controversial matter of the relationship between the political and the ethical spheres, a question forced upon the new national monarchies of Europe by the views on political expediency expressed by Machiavelli in his influential treatise *Il principe (The Prince)*(1513).[1] Machiavelli argued that the virtues could legitimately yield to the best interests of the ruler or the community, that a morally reprehensible course of action could be justifiably undertaken for political ends—a view vehemently rejected by Erasmus in his *The Education of a Christian Prince,* which insisted that justice must never be sacrificed even to life, realm, or religion. As far as Spain was concerned, Stradling (1988, 14) points out that the arguments for royal absolutism as propounded by Bodin were rejected in Spain at the end of the sixteenth century, along with the practice of reason of state, and that the assertion of the divine right of kings made in England by the Scots William Barclay and James VI would have struck Spanish thinkers as both barbarous and blasphemous. He goes on: "Their objections were clear: to cynicism, they opposed ethical idealism and to absolutism, a constitutional legalism. Surprising as it may be for the English mentality to discover such round Whig principles with deep roots in Spanish thought, they were in fact the fundamental assumptions of political philosophy under the Philips." Such a statement was long overdue. In spite of the fact that the Spanish monarchy enjoyed a degree of continuity and solidity unknown elsewhere in western Europe and constituted a formidable machine of government in which political power for practical purposes resided with the prince,[2] Spain's contemporary political philosophers were unanimous in their rejection of absolute power and in their assertion that it is only the tyrant who knows no law but his own will.[3]

Where the question of reason of state is concerned, Spanish thinking did in fact shift its ground surreptitiously with the passage of time. In Spain as elsewhere in the sixteenth century, Machiavelli's privileging of politics at the expense of ethics and what was seen as his demotion of religion to the status of instrument of state earned him the reputation of devil incarnate and his philosophy the opprobrium of full-blown atheism. Spanish humanists and Jesuits condemned his godlessness, which ensured his works a place on the papal Index of prohibited books of 1557, and Counter-Reformation theorists in general then attacked reason of state and its defenders, coupling Luther and Machiavelli as the two founding fathers of the impious modern state.[4] In 1595 in his *Tratado de la religión y virtudes que debe tener el príncipe cristiano* (*Treatise on the Faith and Virtues Essential in a Christian Prince*) Pedro de Rivadeneyra launched Spain's first full-scale attack on Machiavellianism and the reason of state, to be followed by, among others, Mariana (1599), Márquez (1612), Santa María (1615), López Bravo (1616), Claudio Clemente with his tellingly named *Maquiavelo degollado* (*Machiavelli Decapitated*, 1628),[5] Salvador de Mallea (1646), and Blázquez Mayorales (1646)—not to forget Quevedo's virulent onslaught in *Política de Dios y gobierno de Christo* (*The Politics of God and the Governance of Christ*) (1617, pub. 1635).[6] Full-blown Machiavellianism never did acquire any self-confessed converts in Spain, as one might expect, although a very few commentators such as Antonio Pérez and Arias Montano are sometimes regarded as almost openly Machiavellian.[7] Even in Spain, however, the uncomfortable conviction grew that the simple equivalences of the past could no longer cope with the political complexities of the modern world. Christian virtue was essential in a prince, but it was now perceived to be no longer enough; to be a good prince, the prince needed to be more than good.

As interest in the concept of statecraft grew, therefore, the idea of reason of state began to slough its association with the Italian anti-Christ and to acquire a more acceptable image. Many purportedly anti-Machiavellian tracts are themselves testimony to the in-roads Machiavelli had made on political thinking. The simulations and fraud that Spain connected with Machiavelli and with what became known as false reason of state were still unequivocally refuted—the sphere of the political could never function independently of morality—but their place was taken by an ethical version of reason of state connected with the convenient notion of strategic concealment or dissimulation—a stance considered entirely suited to the awe-inspiring remoteness of majesty increasingly cultivated by the Spanish crown.

Those searching for such a compromise solution drew authoritative support from the contemporary intellectual enthusiasm—which went back to Luis Vives—for the classical historian Tacitus, who was regarded by foes and followers alike as weaving into his writings the very essence of statecraft. They established a seam of thought, known as *tacitismo*,[8] that enshrined history, along with nature and psychology, as a flexible and pragmatic model for the political life of the nation, in opposition to the rigidity of Machia-vellian theory. *Tacitismo* naturally did not go uncriticized by the religious ethicists—it took its authority after all from a pagan and did not privilege moral exemplariness at all, let alone Christian principle. Many of its opponents did not bother to differentiate between Machiavelli and the *políticos*[9] on the one hand and the *tacitistas* on the other—Salas de Barbadillo mentions Tacitus, Machiavelli, and Bodin all in the same breath in his *Coronas del Parnaso (Crowns of Parnassus, 1635)*[10]—and some writers no doubt did use Tacitus as a camouflage for Machiavellian senti-ments. But by 1640 the Christian ideal of the prince had ineluctably become a politico-Christian ideal, as the title of Saavedra Fajardo's treatise *Idea de un príncipe político-cristiano (Concept of a Politi-cal Christian Prince)* shows. In this, the best-known political work of seventeenth-century Spain, an erudite, cultured, and admirably reasonable diplomat set out views that, grounded as they are in historical example and personal observation and experience, en-capsulate the *tacitismo* that permitted Spanish intellectuals to rec-oncile Machiavellian theory with Christian principle: political imperatives must be held in balance with ethical considerations. The *aprobación* (official approval) written by Fray Pedro de Cuenca y Cárdenas, which praises the erudition with which "la razón de estado se adorna" ("reason of state is adorned")in the treatise, is a vivid indication that the concept of "reason of state" had been sanitized and that even in Spain entrenched thinking had moved on; in the forty-five years between the publication of

Rivadeneyra's *Tratado de la religion y virtudes que debe tener el principo cristiano,* with its reference to "la falsa y perniciosa razón de estado" ("false and pernicious reason of state", 455), and Saavedra's *Idea de un príncipe político-cristiano* the idea that the good governance of the state required more than the application of Christian principles had been assimilated into Spanish thought.

La estrella de Sevilla's nineteenth-century critics, or rather the critics of the refundición of the play by Cándido María Trigueros *Sancho Ortiz de las Roelas,* were reduced to moral outrage by the behaviour of don Sancho, the man who undertakes to kill on the order of his king without knowing whom and exactly why. One of them, Alberto Lista, observed: "Para hacer interesante a Ortiz sería necesario que su manera de sentir fuese conforme a la razón o a los afectos comunes de los hombres o, por lo menos, una preocupación propia de la época a que se refiere la acción del drama" ("To make Ortiz interesting his thinking would have to accord with reason or with common human feeling, or at least with some concern of the period to which the action refers").[11] It is not clear why Lista regarded thirteenth-century concerns as more interesting or valid than seventeenth-century concerns—it is another example, perhaps, of the antiimperialist sentiment Golden Age theater fell foul of in the nineteenth century—but of course the *comedia* was not in the business of dramatizing the historical problems of the distant past (except in so far as they had any bearing on the present). It habitually projected seventeenth-century preoccupations about kingship upon the Middle Ages. Medieval dynastic leaders were judged against Renaissance ideas of the king as the embodiment of the state and found wanting. But the comparison, paradoxically, produced in the process a critique of contemporary monarchy as well: the superimposition of contemporary ideals upon a previous age was an enabling stratagem that allowed misgiving about contemporary realities to be aired.

In the context of traditional perceptions of kingship *La estrella de Sevilla* can be seen, and no doubt was seen by the politically unaware in the audience, in terms of personal loyalty and obedience to the monarch, honor, keeping the faith, and so on. But in the context of contemporary Spain and Europe the play takes on a much wider political dimension—not merely the question of absolutism, of the king's will being paramount whatever the circumstances, but of the ethical problems created by giving priority to the principle of political necessity. The state, that is, the king—for the theory of state was at the time inseparable from the figure of the prince—comes before all else. To neglect this dimension of the play seems to me to miss the hard thrust of its contemporary relevance and to misconceive, as did Lista and other nineteenth-century critics, the full nature of its dramatic impact. Trigueros himself put his finger on the powerful appeal exerted by the play when he placed Sancho's dilemma at the heart of the suspense it generates: "¿Executará Sancho Ortiz su encargo? ¿Descubrirá al rey? ¿Cuál será su suerte?" ("Will Sancho Ortiz carry out his task? Will he expose the King? What will happen to him?"). This dilemma is precisely that created by the pull of the opposing values of loyalty to the king—invoked here in the name of political necessity—and individual conscience, between the good of the republic and Christian ethics. I use Renaissance terminology because of course traditionally in Western Europe there would, in theory at least, have been no problem: kingship was firmly grounded in Christian principle. It was, as I have already observed, the writings of Machiavelli that forced Europe to contemplate the prospect of the autonomization and secularization of political activity. In practice dynastic and personal loyalty to a prince would obviously have been a complicating factor, but significantly it is the idea of lèse majesté, an offence against the king as the embodiment of the state, that instantly overcomes Sancho's reluctance to kill an unknown man and that is of course deliberately invoked by the king knowing it will have this effect.

The story of the play is a blatant and brutally simple formulation of the dilemma posed by the part to be played by ethics in politics, but herein I think lies its impact and its lasting grip on our imagination. For the pull of opposing allegiances is one we all instinctively recognize. The claims made upon human loyalty by nation or leader have traditionally made of spying, treason, military desertion, draft evasion, cowardice in battle, heinous crimes or at least shameful acts and have created appalling dilemmas for individuals caught in the crossfire of their loyalty to the nation and their loyalty to their own consciences or to those they love. The fact that the state wields punitive powers is a complication that inevitably reinforces its claims, but of course society in complicity with the state employs no less effective psychological weapons in the control of individual behaviour—weapons such as shame, humiliation, dishonor. Kings have always exerted a special influence upon the behaviour of the individual, as the anthropologist Julian Pitt-Rivers (1977, 15) has pointed out: "The respect felt for the monarch possesses something of the same power to render sacred as the reverence felt for the Divine: in paying this respect, we abnegate our right to question and bind ourselves to accept what might otherwise appear to us wrong. The arbitrary nature of sacred power extends beyond the frontiers of religion." This special feeling is precisely what is at work in *La estrella de Sevilla,* what the king cynically and shamelessly exploits in order to conceal, in the name of political necessity, behavior inappropriate in a prince.

In the play the use of *force majeur* and the privileging of reason of state lead to a human tragedy that offends against natural law—man's instinctive, God-given sense of what is reasonable and just. The ending, overturning as it does *comedia* convention and normal audience expectation—love after all as we know conquers all—may in itself be taken as a strong invitation to disapproval and dissent. Its very title, rather than perversely suggesting a thematic bias toward Estrella that is at odds with the centrality of Sancho's dilemma, as Trigueros thought—which is why he suppressed act 1 and part of act 2 and renamed the play in his refundición—images the way in which the play concentrates the political and moral tensions to maximize their tragic effect. For it is in Estrella that the clash between two opposing sets of values achieves full human impact—her lover kills her brother and she as a consequence necessarily loses both. Hers is arguably the most poignant dilemma in the play, after all: Busto is killed, Sancho kills on the order of his king, but it is Estrella who voluntarily renounces an impossible happiness, to be haunted for the rest of her life by the ghost of what might have been.[12] Yet the handling of this issue in the play is not, I think, without its complexities. Indeed, one of the compelling things about it is precisely the way in which it seems to reflect both the convictions and the uncertainties of contemporary Spanish thought on the matter of how the reason-of-state argument related to Christian ideas of good and evil.

Central to the play's formulation of the problem is the question of the prince's two identities: not the contemporary conception of the monarch as being human by nature and divine by grace—this was not an idea promoted by Spanish political philosophy—nor the bizarre English concept of the king's two bodies, the body natural and the body politic, for which Spanish political thought offered no exact parallel either terminologically or conceptually,[13] but the play between the private and the public person based on the perception that the king was human by nature but suprahuman by role. The unsuitability of the individual man for the public role, the delegation of power, royal youth and inexperience, the conflict between personal desires and princely responsibility, all are recurrent themes in the comedia, inspired to a large extent of course by contemporary concerns about Spain's own monarchs. King San-

cho el Bravo presents the familiar figure of a redoubtable leader
and warrior betrayed by his sexual drive—the conversation he
initiates with his despicable sidekick don Arias, which reviews
Seville's pretty women as if they were mares at a horse fair, sets
the tone of his behavior at the very beginning of the play, creating
expectations of unkingliness soon confirmed by the way in which
he distorts justice, judgment, liberality, and prudence in his campaign to suborn and dishonor a loyal and worthy subject. This
behavior reaches the very nadir of cynicism when, about to buy
his way into Estrella's bed, he declares "Divina cosa es reynar"
(2. 929; "It is divine to be a king"); at that point of blasphemous
irony he loses all claim to respect. The real problem posed by *La
estrella de Sevilla* seems to me, however, to be rather knottier than
the dichotomy presented by the private person within the public
figure. It is whether in the last analysis it is actually possible to
distinguish in a king between the personal and the public, between
the individual and the state he embodies.

The play at first sight seems to argue a strong and convincing
case against reason of state and for morality. It does this by
exposing reason of state as the all-too-convenient instrument of
vice. The king trades on the loyalty Sancho owes him, a proper act
only if he himself were behaving as a king should. But of course
it is the king himself who puts the interests of the state at risk in
the first place. In his passion for Estrella he scorns all thought of
reputation (473–74). He invokes the principle of political necessity
initially in order to legitimate behavior aimed not at protecting the
kingdom from some political danger beyond his control, but at
concealing his own sexual unruliness and exacting personal revenge upon the man who dared thwart him (1103–4). He has lost
sight of the fact that power must be subject to voluntary restraints
if tyranny is to be avoided, as Sancho points out:

> Que si un brazo poderoso
> no se vence en lo que puede
> siempre será riguroso.
>
> 1492–94

[For if a powerful arm does not restrain itself in what it can do, it will
always be harsh.]

To Bustos's observation that the King's law ought not to trample
on justice, Sancho realistically and prophetically replies:

> Si el Rey la quiere torçer
> ¿quién fuerça le podrá hazer,
> aviendo interés o gusto?
>
> 648–50

[Should the King wish to bend it [the law], who can oppose him when interest or pleasure is at stake?]

The assumption here of a coincidence of public authority and private will is buttressed by the conventional notion that a king can never give offense—a notion that largely determines the play-king's behavior. Mariana and other theorists of the day, however, pointing to the realities of history, warned princes against the legitimate anger of the people—an anger we see at work, of course, in Busto Tabera.[14] Saavedra Fajardo (*Empresa* 8), approaching the same problem by a different route, advised kings never to revenge offenses directed at them personally rather than at the throne, so that they would not incite hatred by invoking the enormous power at their disposal in order to deal with them—which is exactly what our play-king does. The fact that the word *ley* seems to be used indiscriminatedly in the play to denote now the king's will, now the idea of codified rules of government, is in itself an interesting indicator of the fusion of man and role in the minds of the characters (1751–54, for example). The confusion within the king himself between his two personae is encapsulated very nicely in the confrontation scene with Busto, but it lies at the heart of the entire play and is indeed articulated by the king himself at one point:

> y aunque más me resistí,
> las naturales acciones
> con que hombre nací
> del decoro me sacaron
> que pide mi Magestad.
>
> 1172–76

[And although I resisted as hard as I could, the natural impulses with which I was born a man robbed me of the decorum demanded by my rank.]

Busto is fully conscious of the respect owed a king: when the King bids him rise he remarks,

> Bien estoy ansí
> que, si el Rey se ha de tratar

como a santo en el altar
digno lugar escogi.

289–92

[I am fine where I am, for if a King is to be treated like a saint on the altar I chose a worthy place.]

This is one of many references to kings and kingship in the play, from Busto, Sancho, Estrella, the alcaldes, and Clarindo, that serve as lessons in what King Sancho ought to be and is not.[15] But Busto is at the same time resolute in refusing to allow the king's will to prevail whatever the cost. Once the king has infringed his sphere of responsibility—"En mi casa estoy / y en ella yo he de mandar" (999–1000; "I am in my own house and in it I shall give the orders")—he at least is in no doubt as to the absolute necessity to oppose vice even in a monarch. In order to send him a message that Seville will not tolerate tyrants, he is prepared to place the king's reputation at risk, publicizing his disreputable behavior by means of poor Natilde's hanged body with the royal warrant in its grasp—an act the king fears might incite a rebellion against him.

The reason-of-state argument essentially comes into play on two crucial occasions. First, Busto Tabera must be killed and killed secretly in order to keep the whole affair quiet and protect the king's reputation;[16] in the light of the king's subsequent worries about an uprising in Seville, to this motive is then by implication added the need to guarantee public order. Relevant to this is the problematical matter of whether Busto's rash act really does put the state at risk, that is, constitute lèse majesté, as the king maintains, or whether this is merely another piece of cynical manipulation on the king's part. The technical point is probably arguable, but dramatically the king's responsibility for all that has thus far happened, his petty impulse to revenge (which ends up conflating the ideas of dishonor and lèse-majesté) for what he considers Busto's impertinent resistance, and his intention to deceive Sancho, all undoubtedly affect the audience's perception of the situation and make death seem a punishment inappropriate to the crime. It is not insignificant, however, as we shall see, that, once Sancho is apprised of the supposed nature of the crime, his automatic acceptance of the idea of a secret execution is entirely logical—if the crime is treason, then the king's dishonor would only compound it.[17]

Later on, and for the same reasons, the king cannot keep his word and own up to his responsibility for Busto's murder in order

to save Sancho. This time the king spells out the possible consequences if his behavior were to become known: he would be de-
nounced as a tyrant by his deposed father (Alfonso X) and lose
the Pope's support in his struggle to contest his young nephew's
claim to the throne. The ill-considered behavior that has dragged
the king from the start into a mire of dishonesty, cunning, and
evasion thus culminates in the worst sin of all—not the murder,
which can be rationalized as execution—but the unwillingness to
keep faith. Just as Sancho is bound by his word to kill Busto, even
when he knows who his target is, so the king—his word being
law—is all the more committed to come to Sancho's aid. Keeping
faith is more important than a man's life. Even the repellent don
Arias, the fox to King Sancho's lion,[18] who urges him on to crime,
draws the line at reneging on a solemn promise (2660–81). The
king's reluctance to grasp this nettle, the revelation that he made a
promise he seems to have had little thought of keeping, his shabby
opportunistic attempts to the very last to achieve the same end
by other means serve finally to render contemptible an already
disreputable royal character.[19]

Morality and honor, of course, prescribe very different behavior
from reason of state. They rule out in the first place the aggressive
sexual behavior that knowingly insults the integrity and jeopardizes
the reputation and the happiness of two scions of a noble family.
But even allowing for the fact that kings are men and make mis-
takes, they subsequently proscribe the murder of an innocent man,
the deceitful maneuvers and subterfuges adopted to cover it up,
and the blatant evasion of responsibility that puts another man's
life at risk—all actions taken in the name of what must be, that is,
in the name of political necessity.

This ignoble behavior in a king and, as I suggested earlier, the
blighted lives of the three young people caught up in it strongly
signal the dangers inherent in a political principle that ignores morality. The play's resolution convinces us that good ends do not
justify evil means, that "no se ha de hacer lo injusto / porque fue
razón de estado", as the Count points out to the King in Lope's
La inocente sangre (*Innocent Blood* 1604–12, probably datable to
1604–8).[20] There is, however, one intractable element in this resolution. The king is eventually forced by circumstances to admit that
the order to kill Busto Tabera came from him. And in the event
the step he found so difficult to take has absolutely no consequences for himself. Why? Because it is automatically assumed by
Farfán de Ribera and seemingly all other uninformed recipients of
the news that, if he ordered Busto's execution, it must have been

with good reason. No questions are asked and Busto goes to his grave branded as at worst a traitor, at best a criminal. Sancho's confident assertion to the king—"y gana más el que muere / a trayción que el que le mata" (1578–79; "he who dies betrayed gains more than he who kills him")—may be a telling epitaph for the play, but of course within the action it is sadly not true. Only the king himself, don Arias, Estrella, don Sancho and the audience are left in possession of the fact that Busto was killed for doing what all good heads of family were expected to do, trying to protect his family's reputation. His misfortune was in having in his king an adversary who would or could brook no opposition. Is this another of the play's poignant dimensions? Is it a a further subversion of absolutist behaviour? Or is it, in addition perhaps to both these two, the manifestation of a genuine hesitation over the problem of identifying the point where personal responsibility ends and the public good begins, where morality necessarily gives way to political necessity? The king has revealed enough to keep his word, free Sancho, and satisfy his subjects. To reveal more would have exonerated Busto, but only at the price of tarnishing the king's own reputation.

The crucial question is whether the personal conduct of a king and therefore his reputation constitute a reason of state sufficiently pressing to justify the murder and disgrace of an innocent man. Again, since the king is the only true begetter of the situation, we might be tempted to answer no, but there is a pronounced ambivalence in the play regarding this matter. One of the points made by this and other kingship plays is that the private persona cannot ultimately be dissociated from the public—the private has to reflect the public role precisely because the public role is affected by the private. The fact that the king himself has put his reputation at risk is not only deeply reprehensible but damaging to the state; once that act has been committed, however, the protection of his reputation can only be in the interests of the state. And we must not underestimate what is at issue here. The idea of reputation, the idea that the image of a monarch or a nation is important not only to an appearance of strength but to a nation's actual strength and health, was a largely new, key factor in seventeenth-century political thought. Saavedra Fajardo explained it with his usual clarity:

> Los imperios se conservan con su misma autoridad y reputación. En empezando a perderla, empiezan a caer, sin que baste el poder a sustentallos; antes apresura la caída su misma grandeza. Nadie se atreve

a una coluna derecha; en declinando, el más débil intenta derriballa; porque la misma inclinación convida al impulso; y, en cayendo, no hay brazos que basten a levantalle. Un acto sólo derriba la reputación, y muchos no la pueden restaurar . . . y así, en no estando la corona fija sobre esta coluna derecha de la reputación, dará en tierra.[21]

[Empires are maintained by their own authority and reputation. If they begin to lose them they begin to falter, and might alone is insufficient to maintain them; rather does their greatness accelerate the fall. Nobody challenges an upright column; when it starts to decay, the weakest attempts to bring it down, because its very inclination invites such a response; and when it falls, there are no arms strong enough to raise it. A single action demolishes reputation, and many cannot restore it . . . and so, should the crown not be firmly planted upon this upright column of reputation, it will fall to the ground.]

The sacrifice of Busto's reputation is, by this measure, a sacrifice well made. On 22 May 1508 Fernando el católico wrote a letter to his nephew the Conde de Ribagorza, then Viceroy of Naples, reprimanding him for not responding to a papal brief that infringed upon his royal authority by hanging the clerk who delivered it. One hundred and thirteen years later, the self-same Quevedo who in his *Política de Dios* inveighs so violently against reason of state and its founder and denounces Tacitus as a *bellaco* makes the following observation in an apologia to the letter: "La conservación de la jurisdicción y reputación ni ha de considerar dudas, ni tener respetos, ni detenerse en elegir medios" ("The preservation of jurisdiction and reputation must take no cognizance of doubts, must heed no considerations, and must not pause to decide on means").[22] Such would seem to be the unpalatable logic of the play's final unravelling. Since the king embodies the state, the protection of his image—whatever the reality—necessarily constitutes reason of state, and this is precisely why Rivadeneyra and others so distrusted it—leave ethics out of politics and there are no constraints on behavior inappropriate to either man or king. Ultimately the play arrives at a rather uneasy compromise position. Busto's death was not only unnecessary—it was not the only way out consistent with the good of the kingdom—but against justice, the very foundation stone of all successful government—"la madre y ama de los imperios" ("mother and soul of empires"), in López Bravo's words[23]—and the first duty of those responsible for it, as Farfán sternly points out (2906–14). Whether Busto's attempt to publicize the king's behavior constitutes lèse majesté or not, the decision to have him killed is taken by the king at don Arias's instigation before the sight of Natilde's corpse incites the king to fury. The murder itself and the deceitful measures adopted to conceal the king's responsibility, therefore, on the evidence of the text and the response it invites, pass beyond the bounds of morality into the terrain of false reason of state. At the end, on the other hand, the king's economy with the truth would seem to constitute no more than the silence, the dissimulation, that did come to be regarded as expedient in the handling of political matters. The King's exhortation to Sancho, "obrad, y callemos" (1606), before the event may not be acceptable, but secrecy after the event is.

In the 1570s, several decades before *La estrella de Sevilla* was written, the Escobedo affair had implicated that most catholic of kings, Philip II, in a reason-of-state scandal that outraged the misinformed and caused great anguish to Philip himself when he discovered that he had been manipulated by his treacherous adviser Antonio Pérez (to whom don Arias bears more than a passing resemblance). The incident undoubtedly contributed to the bad name that the principle of reason of state was then acquiring in Spain. *La estrella de Sevilla* can, I think, be seen as a measure of the ground the idea of political necessity had gained in the intervening years. Here we have a king who is his own enemy, who himself creates a situation whereby the state has to be protected from the consequences of his actions by means of subterfuge and deceit and at the cost of innocent lives, and who yet gets away with it. His lamentable conduct is resoundingly condemned: Sancho's remark as he is taken off to prison makes nonsense of the Maravallian contention that the play promotes absolute rule, however tyrannical and unjust:[24]

> Yo si atropello
> mi gusto, guardo la ley:
> esto, señor, es ser Rey, (i.e., what ought to happen)
> y esto, señor, es no sello (i.e., what is happening)

$$(1871-74)$$

[If I trample on my inclinations at least I observe the law; this, sir, is to be a king, and this, sir, is not to be one.]

But the cloak of silence publicly drawn over the true extent of his misbehavior is, because he is a king—that is, for the sake of the state—implicitly legitimated. For Spain's seventeenth-century theorists the specter of tyranny was equalled only by the specter of tyrannicide—a certain, not merely a probable, promoter of political instability and civil strife. The potency of the play's tragedy lies in its depiction of the sacrifice of individual destinies in the name of a higher cause, in the name of a concept of nationhood that transcends any particular human manifestation of it, however weak, however corrupt. The king was wrong: long live the king. For all that renowned Renaissance individualism defined by Burckhard,[25] man was still in the seventeenth century defined primarily in relation to family, state, and religion, his personal self but an aspect of his public identity. The idea that the individual is a totality and the measure of all things is a modern one; during the ancien regime the individual was still subsumed in the social identity. The individual served society, not society the individual.[26]

By normal standards *La estrella de Sevilla* should be a bad play: the verse is at times wretched, the imagery forced and heavy-handed, the dialogue repetitive, the seaming clumsy. Yet it is redeemed by a superbly compelling story, by an extremely well-developed feel for the telling dramatic scene, and by a magnificent sense of tragedy that exactly establishes the fine balance between sympathy, outrage, and reluctant acceptance which is necessary to tragedy's emotional complexity. The story is the story of the clash, played out within the parameters of individual lives, between two opposing value systems held in tension by the need to sustain the social and political system. That absolutism breeds opposition; that reason of state misapplied leads to injustice and tragedy; that a kingdom cannot be properly ruled by the wishes of its sovereign alone;[27] that virtue and integrity must form the basis of just and effective government; that blind obedience to a ruler's will is dangerous—all these are amply demonstrated. But so too is the need to allow political necessity to dictate when required in the interests of the state. The compromise arrived at in *La estrella de Sevilla* is no more and no less than the compromise that political thought in Spain was evolving in *tacitismo*. In the wake of Machiavelli, the role of morality in the political sphere would nowhere in Western Europe ever be the same again.

Notes

1. See the edition by Skinner and Price (1988); chapters 14–21 were the chapters that attracted most attention, chapter 18, "How Rulers Should Keep Their Promises", being the most discussed and the most notorious.

2. In theory it rested with the abstract notion of the republic.

3. For the differences, however, in their understanding of the king's relationship to divine, natural, civil and customary law, see Velasco (1925); Maravall (1944 and 1975); Hamilton (1963); Abellán (1979 and 1988).

4. See Quentin Skinner (1978, 2. 143).

5. The original Latin version, *Machiavelisimus jugulatus,* was published in 1628, the Spanish translation in 1637.

6. See the edition by J. O. Crosby (1966, 173).

7. For Machiavelli see, for example, Skinner (1978); and, more specifically, Sydney Anglo (1969). For Machiavellianism in Spain see Velasco (1925); Maravall (1944, 1975); Abellán (1979, 1988); J. A. Fernández-Santamaría (1983).

8. For *tacitismo* see Maravall (1944, 1975); Francisco Sanmartín Boncompte (1951); E. Tierno Galván (1971); André Joucl-Ruau (1977); J. A. Fernández-Santamaría (1983); Abellán (1988). Blázquez Mayoralgo called Tacitus the father of the *políticos* and Machiavelli their captain (Fernández-Santamaría, 77n.23). Among the *tactistas* (open and closet) are normally included Alamos de Barrientos, Narbona, Setanti, Ceballos, Ramírez de Prado, Mártir Rizo, Antonio de Herrera, Antonio de Fuertes y Biota, Saavedra Fajardo, and Gracián.

9. *Políticos* was the name given political commentators thought to be influenced by the political atheism of Machiavelli; *estadistas* was normally the neutral term used for those versed in the theory of state.

10. See Maravall (1975, 95).

11. See Menéndez y Pelayo's *Observaciones preliminares* to the play in *Obras de Lope de Vega,* Real Academia Española, 9. liii.

12. She is sacrificed on the altar of political imperatives no less than Inés in that other deeply tragic dramatization of the reason of state principle, Luis Vélez de Guevara's *Reinar después de morir (Queen after Death).*

13. For the concept of the king's two bodies, see Maitland (1936, 104–27) and Ernst Kantorowicz (1957).

14. *Del rey y de la institución de la dignidad real* 1. 6. 112.

15. The confrontation between the king and Busto in Busto's house in act 2 is a prime example, with Busto using the technique of "decir sin decir" ("saying without saying"), reprimanding the king indirectly by pretending not to have recognized him and maintaining he cannot be the king because kings behave differently. Sancho the man is confronted with the idea and the reality of Sancho the king (lines 1061–64), and at one point Busto adoptes the *tú* form of address to hammer his point home (a man who conducts himself thus cannot be a king), before reverting to *vos* out of respect for the intruder's real station. Sancho's remarks to the king when he learns what is required of him similarly constitute a clear lesson in kingship; so too do his arguments, when in prison, for not revealing his motives.

16. "Matarle públicamente / Arias, es yerro mayor (2. 1190–91; "To kill him in public, Arias, would be a great mistake"); and later to Sancho, "deve a mi honor importar / matarle de aquesta manera" (2. 1510–11; "it must be crucial to my honour to kill him thus."

17. We are still compelled to wonder why the king, if secrecy were so important, tried to press upon Sancho a cédula accepting responsibility.

18. I refer here, of course, to the qualities of the lion and the fox seen by Machiavelli as being essential to the effective prince (*Il principe* 18).

19. Little wonder that in Restoration France the first performance of Pierre Lebrun's *Le Cid d'Andalousie,* which was partly based on *La estrella de Sevilla,* was delayed because the French authorities objected to its portrayal of royal misbehavior; in seventeenth-century Spain such portrayals were only too familiar. See Menéndez y Pelayo's *Observaciones preliminares* lxvii.

20. *Obras de Lope de Vega, Biblioteca de Autores Españoles* (Madrid, 1860)

4. 51. 367b. In fact the count is being tactful—in punishing the wrong men the king is obeying personal feelings of grief and outrage at the murder of a favorite, not pursuing the good of the state. But it shows how "razón de estado" had unfavorable connotations still at this stage.

21. *Empresa* 31. 81. One has only to think of the way in which modern money markets respond to the slightest indication of a withdrawal of confidence to understand his line of reasoning.

22. "Advertencias disculpando los desabrimientos desta carta"; Del Rey don Fernando el Católico al Primer Virrey de Nápoles (1958, 704a).

23. *De rege et regendi ratione* (1616 and 1627), translated by Antonio Pérez Rodríguez as *Del Rey y de la raçón de governar,* (Mechoulan 1977, 114).

24. See the section written by Maravall, Blecua, and Salomon in Wardropper (1983), 270.

25. *The Civilization of the Renaissance in Italy* 98–119.

26. For a discussion of the individual and individualism in relation to society see Louis Dumont, *Homo Hierarchicus* (1980).

27. Cf. the king himself in act 3: "que amor que pisa púrpura de Reyes, / a su gusto, no más, promulga leyes") (2172–73; "for love which tramples the royal purple promulgates laws only to its own taste"). Gregorio López Madera in his *Excelencias de la monarquía y reino de España (Excellencies of the Monarchy and Kingdom of Spain,* Madrid, 1625) went so far as to equate the princely exercise of will with tyranny, effectively turning the reason of state argument against the prince: "No consiste en otra cosa la propia tiranía que en hacer los príncipes su propia voluntad, sin sujetarse a la razón y derecho" ("tyranny itself consists of nothing other than princes acting in accordance with their own will, without submitting to reason and justice"; folio 17, quoted by Abellán 1988, 67). The prince cannot act as if he were independent of and above the state.

6
Historical and Textual Underpinnings
HARLAN STURM

ONE might very possibly say, especially after the present volume, that *La estrella de Sevilla*[1] has been honored by more intense criticism than is normally accorded a Golden Age drama of doubtful authorship, leading one to wonder what has attracted the attention of so many critics through the years. As students of Golden Age drama, we first come into contact with the play because it has become part of a canon. Spanish studies has tended not to question canon as much as other disciplines but it is now becoming one of the emerging issues in Hispanic literary criticism. The play's inclusion in *Diez comedias del Siglo de Oro* insured wide coverage in 1939, and most who studied the play in the United States read it in the 1967 edition, which has now been reprinted. What is it in the play that inspires in such intense critical dialogue? The play has been variously appreciated for its form as one of the best examples of lopesque tragedy, for its symbolism (even Foulché-Delbosc [1920] includes an index to "astrológico estilo" ["astrological style"]), as well as for its symbolical subtlety (McCrary 1971, De Armas 1979, and Burke 1974), and recently, Teresa Soufas (1992) discusses the mise en scène of the play, focusing on visualization and dramaturgy.

The basic archeology of the play was done, of course in 1920 by Foulché-Delbosc, fine-tuned by H. Thomas in Oxford in 1923. It was chosen for the Austral series in Buenos Aires and for the Colección Ercilla in Santiago de Chile in 1938, roughly the time of the first edition of *Diez comedias,* where it is referred to as "a marvelously constructed and technically perfect example of the *capa y espada* genre" (x). It was also edited by Frank Otis Reed and Esther M. Dixon, and published with an introduction by John M. Hill in 1938. The focus of its earlier inclusions is characteristic of the times, where how it represents a *genre* would be central to the reasoning. We owe something to its disputed authorship for the canonization, since it was that question which caused Sturgis Leavitt to bring the play under close scrutiny in 1931.

Second only to the question of author would be the need to classify its genre, a question treated by many who asked and answered the question of how does this play match up with our conception of what a Lope play ought to be. Or, as in Brooks (1955) and others, what is its relationship to tragedy—a relationship that is not always easy given the parameters of other European dramas? Alexander Parker (1959), of course, discusses the relationship of Golden Age Drama to the dramatic forms of other European cultures, and his five principles are still arguably one of the best generalizations of dramatic form for the period.

The play itself shows dramatic force, passion, and well-crafted internal dilemmas. Put in terms far too simplistic for this group, it is a form of *de regimine principum,* involving a study of duty and honor on the part of the king, Sancho IV, the son of Alfonso el Sabio. The fact that a version of Guido della Colonna's *De regimine principum (On the Education of Princes)* is included in the *Biblioteca de autores españoles* edition of *Castigos y documentos del Rey Don Sancho (Teaching and Documents of King Sancho)* is an interesting irony, but probably only that. One might ask why Sancho IV is the subject of this particular play, as well as "why Seville?" There are three historical ingredients essential to the development of the play. It is true that the early stage of the career of Sancho IV did indeed involve Seville and that his character was known to be brash and that he had a definite temper, earning his nickname early in his life, much before he became king:

> El Rey don Sancho, a quien llaman
> por su invicta fortaleza
> *el Bravo* el vulgo, y los moros,
> porque de su nombre tiemblan,
> el Fuerte, y sus altas obras
> el Sacro y Augusto César.
>
> (781–786)

[King Don Sancho, whom the people call "brash" for his invincible strength, and the Moors, trembling at his name call "the strong," whose deeds show him to be a sacred and august Caesar.]

Covarrubias (1610) says that when "bravo" refers to a man "cuando es valiente, o enojado, o cuando sale muy galán y bizarro" ("when one is valiant or enraged, or when excessively gallant"), showing the complexity of the terminology and leaving many interpretations.

In history, Sancho, the son of Alfonso X, became king through his bold actions, while taking on his father and confronting situations he saw as the result of a father's inactions. He reigned for only a short time, from 1284 until his death in 1295. Alfonso had tried to disinherit Sancho, instead giving the throne to Alfonso de la Cerda, creating vassal kingdoms at Seville and Murcia for Juan and Jaime,[2] but Sancho ignored this upon the death of his father and quickly consolidated power. It was Alfonso who was in Seville when he died, thus the lines, "conozco que en Castilla / soberano rey ya soy. / Desde hoy reino, pues desde hoy / Sevilla me honra y ampara" (3–6; I learn that in Castile / I am now sovereign king. / From today I reign, and from today / Seville honors me and becomes my home"—3–6 if I read them correctly—have a certain amount of irony for the historian. But Seville was the center of his early political machinations, and he held court in that city from 1284. It was in Seville that his wife, María de Molina, gave birth to Fernando, the future king.

The marriage with María de Molina was the subject of a long dispute with the Pope. As one history has it: "Cautivo del amor que con justa razón profesaba a la Reina, no bajó la cabeza ante la autoridad del Papa Martino IV, que le requirió y amonestó para que se apartase de doña María por ser aquel matrimonio incestuoso" ("Captivated by love which he professed to the Queen, he did not bow his head even to the authority of the Pope, Martin IV, who admonished him to leave doña María since the marriage was incestuous" (*Historia General* 1893, 140). The epoch of Sancho IV and María de Molina is extremely well documented, and Mercedes Gaibrois de Ballesteros (1922) has given us the three-volume *Historia del reinado de Sancho IV de Castilla (History of the Reign of King Sancho IV of Castile)*, as well as the intriguing and complete *María de Molina: Tres Veces Reina (María de Molina: Three Times a Queen)* (1939). María de Molina and Sancho are buried together, their marriage endured even the attempts by the Pope to get it annulled, and their children inherited the throne. This conflict is brought out near the end of the play when Sancho (the king), showing a transition in his awareness of right and wrong, worries aloud how his wrongful doings in Seville will seem to others:

> Y qué se dirá en Castilla,
> cuando don Alonso en ella
> me está llamando tirano,

> y el Pontífice romano
> con censuras me atropella?

> (2689–93)

[And what will they say in Castile / when Alonso / is calling me a tyrant / and the Roman Pontiff / censures me?]

A constant, then, in the characterization of Sancho IV in history both medieval and contemporary is that love and passion play a part in his personal makeup. Very early on he marries Maria de Molina, a marriage that endures in spite of the Pope's efforts to cause the marriage to be annulled. Mercedes Gaibrois de Ballesteros (1939, 21) quotes Paul Groussac, who says that his only positive personality trait is having loved such an admirable woman. "C'est le seul côté sympathique du roi 'feroce' d'avoir aimé pasionnément et jusqu'à la fin cette admirable femme" ("The only good thing the ferocious king ever did was to love passionately and to the end that admirable woman.")

The real history is one thing, however exciting and worthy of study. But perhaps more important for a play in the seventeenth century is the understanding then current. History written by moderns would not have been in the hands of the dramatist, much less the audience, and a complete reconstruction of the period would not be possible. The audience of the seventeenth century, would, however, have had access to popular lore, and certainly to the *romancero,* which is really the great mine from which the drama of the period gets its historical mythology. Sancho's character as a brash young man is put into hyperbole, and one anonymous ballad has Alfonso as the narrative voice lamenting the treason of his son:

> Yo salí de la mi tierra
> para ir a Dios servir,
> Y perdí lo que havía
> desde mayo hasta abril. . . .
> pues los amigos que habia
> no me osan ayudar;
> que por medio de don Sancho
> desamparado me han.

> (*Romancero General* 949. 25)

[I left my land / to serve God / and I lost what I had / between may and April . . . The Friends I had / don't dare help me / for they have abandoned me / for fear of don Sancho.]

Another, recognizing the weakness of Alfonso, says, "Aquese infante Don Sancho / Hizo lo que no debía / Alzóse contra su padre / Que Alfonso el Sabio decían" ("That prince don Sancho / did what he should not have done. / He rose up against his father / who was named Alfonso the Wise" (*Romancero general* 25). This same ballad (950, "Aquese infante Don Sancho") goes on to recount the battle with the moorish king Aben Yuza, who says at one point:

> —Voluntad grande me viene
> De ir, y hacerlo quería.
> A ayudar a ese buen Rey
> Que su mal hijo afligia:
> Todo el reino le ha quitado
> Sola le queda Sevilla.—
>
>   (*Romancero general* 25–26)

[I had a strong desire / to go and do what I wanted / to help that good King / whose evil son afflicted him. / He has taken his whole kingdom from him, / leaving him only Seville.]

Alfonso recovers much of the land taken by Sancho, which is the topic of that ballad.[3] The conflict between father and son is the subject of several of the *romances* dealing with the epoch of Alfonso X, making him a tragic figure and illustrating Sancho's character as brash, impetuous, and generally in need of some intervention. In one ballad, (*Romancero general* 952. 26–27) Sancho is rumored to be dying, and Alfonso is not sad at all, but only distraught because now he will not have time to get back the land his son Sancho has taken from him. The demise of Sancho turns out to have been prematurely reported in this ballad, and it is Alfonso who dies and is buried in Seville next to his father, Fernando el Santo. Sancho's good qualities are also in ballad form. In "Don Sancho reina en Castilla" (Don Sancho Reigns in Castile) we see him referred to as "el buen rey ganó a Tarifa, / De los moros le ha ganado" ("The good King won Tarifa, / taking it from the Moors"; (*Romancero general* 955. 30). Were only the negative characterizations surviving and not the fact that he played a crucial role in the reinitiation of the reconquest, he would not be all that worthy of the dramatic redemption the play gives him.

At any rate, the ingredients are present both in the thirteenth-century history as well as in the subsequent mythology found in ballad material. Seville plays a part, Sancho's character plays a part, and love plays a large part. Certainly, the cosmic conflict of the period, and the reconquest, gives the dramatic action an important backdrop.

The stage, so to speak, is set: character is strong, role is important. So the conflict between character and role, based on the duality of the king politically, as much as on the dual personality of Sancho the historical figure, becomes central in the dramatic development of the thesis of this play. On the duality of the roles he has been given to play, Sancho the man describes Sancho the King, responding to the question "Pues decid: ¿qué veis en mí?" (1440; "What do you see in me?"):

> La majestad, y el valor,
>   y al fin, una imagen veo,
> de Dios, pues le imita el Rey;
> y después dél, en vos creo,
> y a vuestra cesárea ley,
> gran señor, aquí me empleo.

(1441–46)

[Majesty and valor, / and ultimately, I see an image / of God, since the King is an imitation of Him, / and after Him, / I believe in you, / and in your imperial law / I here am employed.]

This is the scene where the two Sanchos meet for the first time, scene 11 in the second act. The duality is made visual, dramatized, by the subtle use of text, which, especially in the last act, underlines the dual nature of the Sancho IV and the internalization of the conflict within Sancho Ortiz. It is the visualization of his nature as a man and his nature as a king, as Kantorowicz (1957) explains it, that occasions this dual role playing.

One of the principal ways this drama objectifies the conflict produced by Sancho the king when he upsets the natural order of Seville through following his passions is the use of the written word and the role, as it were, of *papel*.[4] In his passion for Estrella, the king first promises to give poor Natilde a *cédula,* a written document (845)—the word is related to English "schedule"—that promises her freedom from slavery if she helps him approach the beautiful Estrella. The first act ends with a powerful and suggestive scene, with don Arias clearing the chamber so the king can sit down to write: "A recoger, caballeros; que quiere el Rey escrebir" ("Let's go out, gentlemen, for the King wants to write"). We are left with the evil irony of don Arias and Sancho drooling over the delicious Natilde, signing the paper that will cause her death rather than her freedom. For continuity and reinforcement, the second

act begins with the king handing over the *papel* to Natilde granting
her freedom in exchange for the favor, and it is this scene that is the
occasion for the famous line "Divina cosa es reinar" (929; "What a
divine thing it is to reign!"). Natilde, caught in the act, tries to use
the *papel* as her excuse. "En dándome este papel, / entró el Rey,
y tú tras él." (1150–51; "In giving me this paper, / the King entered,
and you after him"). When Natilde is found hanged, she has a
papel in her hand: "La esclavilla / con el papel en las manos!"
(1240–41; "The slave girl / with a paper in her hands!"). The dramatic force in the opsis of the scene cannot fail to impress for its
revelation of cause and effect. It is clear that Natilde is the first
"wound that speaks" of the drama, and one that begins the unfolding of the dramatic action. It is at this point that the King is at
his lowest point, morally and dramatically, and he vows to kill
everyone involved. "Se ha de arder / hoy con su Estrella Sevilla"
(1258–59; "Seville will burn / today with its Star!). Values have
been turned upside down.

Busto, having met the king in Estrella's room, confronts her with
the possibility of wrongdoing. She asks, "What have I done?" in a
manner befitting the textual underpinning of the work: "En las
manos de algún hombre / ¿viste algún papel escrito / de la mía?"
(1288–90; "Did you find a clandestine note in the hands of some
man, written by my hand?").

The main section dealing with the *papeles* begins in the tenth
scene in the second act, when the king comes out with two *papeles,*
the ones that will seal the fate of nearly all the characters in the
drama. One asks Sancho to kill Busto, and the other exonerates
him from doing it. Sancho Ortiz destroys one, preferring to act on
his word:

> ¡Yo cédula! ¡Yo papel!
> . . . .
> dandome aquí la palabra,
> señor, los papeles sobran.
> A la palabra remito
> la cédula que me dais
> con que a vengaros me incito,
> porque donde vos estáis
> es excusado lo escrito.
>
> . . . .
> . . . desacredita
> vuestra palabra el papel.
> Sin papel, señor aquí
> nos obligamos los dos.

. . . .
Si es así, no hay que hacer
cédulas.
                        (1558, 1565–71, 1575–78, 1582–83)

[For me, a document! A piece of paper! / Giving me here your word /
Lord, papers are not necessary. / I put your word over the document
you give me / by which I seek to avenge you, / because wherever you
are, / writing is not necessary. . . . Your paper discredits your word. /
Without paper, Lord, we are here together bound.] If this is so, we do
not need to prepare documents."

In effect, Sancho suggests another arrangement. Rather than a
piece of paper releasing him from responsibility, which he feels the
king would do out of duty and honor anyway, he wants in payment
the hand of the woman of his choice. He asks, as it were, for
the stars.

The transmission of knowledge in the play is all written. Elias
Rivers (1983) has studied the use of text in the play, and Charles
Oriel's (1989) dissertation *Writing and Inscription in Golden Age
Drama,* which includes this play with others in a study of the use
of the written word, has recently been published. Sancho, while
holding in his hands a paper naming Busto as the man he is to kill,
receives another *papel,* this one from Estrella, granting him his
wish, her hand, by Busto. Scenes 12 and 13, an actor's dream,
juxtapose extreme happiness and extreme sadness, both brought
about by the *papeles.*

Decilde que bien pudiera
dar papel; mas me afrento
de que papeles me pida
habiendo visto rompellos.

                                    (2318–21)

[Tell him that he might well / ask for written proof, but I'm offended /
that he's asking for papers / since he saw me tear them up.]

What Sancho is saying, and what seems to be one of the main
themes of the play as it develops its relationship to the written
text, is that there comes a time when *la escritura* no longer suffices.
Sancho is forcing the king to learn from experience and to abandon
his "letters": "Que los versos son cansados / cuando no tienen
provecho" (2194–95; "Words are tired / when they have no effect").
In his "mad" scene, thinking he is in hell, he says, "si el infierno

es, cómo escribanos no vemos?" (2416; "If we are in Hell, why
are there no scribes here?"). Rivers (1983, 85) sees this in terms
of a battle between written and oral traditions: "It would seem that
writing in itself poses a threat to the traditional oral system of
honor and shame." He concludes that writing is a "shameful act"
in the play. Sancho obliges the king to turn the written word into
the spoken word, saying: "Rey soy en cumplir la mía" (2315; "I
am King in honoring my word"). It is Arias who now refers to
Sancho Ortiz as a "bravo esfuerzo" (2360) as they become more
as one: "que conozca que en Sevilla / también ser reyes sabemos"
(2336–37; "May he know that in Seville / we also know how to be
Kings"). The extent of the lesson learned by Sancho IV is seen in
"Falso mi intento imagino; / también si dejo morir / a Sancho Ortiz,
es bajeza. / ¿Qué he de hacer?" (2697–2700; "My intent has been
in error. / If I let Sancho Ortiz die, it is wrong. / What am I to
do?"). He recognizes the scope of his transgression and is resolved
to make it right.

We have in *La estrella de Sevilla* a play that instructs a king in
the universal values—values that involve his treatment of people,
domination over his passions, and the need to have the smaller
matters in the kingdom set right in order to make things right in
the kingdom itself. It instructs him in the relationship of the part
to the whole, of microcosm to macrocosm, of his own role in harmony and disharmony—factors recognized as constants in Golden
Age drama by critics from Spitzer (1934) on, and this play is one of
the better examples of them. I would agree with González-Marcos
(1982, 2), that Sancho Ortiz is the principal protagonist of the play,
rather than Estrella, and that "la última lección de *La estrella de
Sevilla*, es una lección *jurídica* si bien como la ley se base en la
moral," although we might differ on some of the symbolic devices
operating in the play.

Sancho Ortiz has been used in a textual battle between an historical nickname, a sense of passion, and a secure place in history
for Sancho IV ("el Bravo"). But he instructs the king when he
denies the *cédula*. He has been a champion in a battle where *palabra* defeats *papel,* where the former has the force of experience
and the latter is vacuous.

On the gap between that which is said and that which is written
Sancho himself presents an interesting comment. He has, of
course, left his own written text for us, in the *Castigos y documentos del Rey don Sancho,* which includes several admonitions
in the form of advice to his son. Although his eighteenth chapter,

"que te guardes de non facer pesar a Dios en pecados de fornicio," is formulaic and perhaps biblical, chapter 27 is more to the point:

> para mientes é comide mucho sobre ello la palabra que dijeres ante que la digas; ca tal es la palabra del home, desque sale por la boca, como la saeta desde sale de la ballesta." (142)

> [Pay attention and think long about the words you say before you say them, for such is the word of the man, that after it leaves his mouth, it travels like an arrow from a bow.]

Notes

1. See O'Callaghan (1975, 381) and Rubio (1970, 46–56).
2. This ballad is said to be from Sepúlveda's *Romances nuevamente sacados* and carries with it designation of author, Lorenzo de Sepúlveda.
3. See Sturm (1970) for a discussion of the two Sanchos.

Part III
Strategies

7

The Moor's Ghost: The Orientalist Subtext at Play in the Play

Catherine Connor (Swietlicki)

In the present study I attempt to tease out several threads of the social and material culture intextuated in the warp and woof of *La estrella de Sevilla,* but the subtextual strand that I will follow most closely is one that can be called Orientalist. My working definition of Orientalism is derived, of course, from the generative study on the topic by Edward Said. Briefly, in Said's terms, Orientalism is several interdependent things: 1) it is the academic study of any aspect of Oriental society and culture; 2) it is a "style of thought based on an ontological and epistemological distinction made between 'the Orient' and (most of the time) 'the Occident'"; and 3) it is "a Western style for dominating, restructuring, and having authority over the Orient" (1979, 2–3). All three Orientalist elements are expressed implicitly or explicitly in numerous early modern Spanish texts representing a wide variety of literary genres.

However, in comparison with the Orientalist tendencies of other Europeans, Spanish Orientalism is colored by the Spaniards' own private and public neurosis. I employ a psychoanalytic shorthand to describe the myriad sociocultural and interpsychic complexities springing from centuries of *convivencia* and confrontation that chronicled the Christian and Moorish experience in Spain. The Spaniard is simultaneously the Christian self and the Moorish other (or the Moorish self and the Christian other): sharing the same physical space and, in many cases, the same blood, and yet simultaneously producing antibodies resistant to one's own otherness. A crisis of subjectivity—a process of simultaneously valorizing and marginalizing varied components of one's identity—plays out paradoxically in the cultural artifacts of Spanish history. Spanish historiography is peppered by accounts of Christian ambivalence and ambiguity toward the Moor and the Morisco: almost always an enemy, often an ally, frequently a valued employee or vassal, sometimes a suspicious intruder, an immoral presence to be expelled or processed and condemned by the Inquisition, and very often an exotic other to be treasured and esteemed but always contained in its proper place like a prized museum piece. The literary record also offers abundant examples of the ambiguous process of sociocultural assimilation: the cult of the noble Moor, of the sentimental Moor, the Abencerraje and Jarifa, or the Cervantine creations of a Christianized Zoraida and an affable yet cunning Ricote are just a few examples.[1] Literary texts can help us to realize more clearly that distinctions between Occident and Orient are creations not only of physical geographic space but also of imaginative geographies, of interior and subjective space. Perhaps Africa *does* begin at the Pyrenees. Spain has been, after all, Western Europe's buffer zone against the Moslem world. It has been the frontier, the marginal space where notions of boundary and identity become most rigidly constructed and most easily blurred. Simultaneously conflicting tendencies support the parallel valorization and marginalization of the otherness on the opposite side of the border.

Nonetheless, with regard to critical studies on *La estrella de Sevilla,* the Orientalist subtext has remained an absent presence. I take courage to pursue this absent presence from Toni Morrison who, with reference to a similar cultural phenomenon in mainstream American literature, has spoken about "ghosts in the machine" (1989, 12–13). The erasure of the Afro-American presence from nineteenth-century American literature—accomplished by the "intellectual feats" she describes—is not unlike the disregard that has been required to erase the Moorish presence from the Spanish social structures inscribed within the *La estrella de Sevilla.* By no means do I wish to deny the value of critical readings focusing on any of a wide variety of elements that might be studied in this dramatic text. However, I do believe with regard to this play that we can go beyond discussing topics such as honor, tyranny, and the divine right of kings in the purely Occidental framework within which "Spanish society" is monologically constructed.[2] My efforts to uncover the residues of Spanish Orientalism in this play are animated by contemporary theoretical concerns not unlike those informing other current studies on *La estrella de Sevilla:* gender questions, subjectivity, discursive practices, canonicity, and other related issues.

A sympathetic reading of my particular approach requires a willingness to track the irrepressible traces of Moorish cultural otherness within the dominant cultures of medieval and early modern Spain and a desire to pursue a shadow presence of the Moor in the text. There are occasions in *La estrella de Sevilla,* however, when the intextuation of a Moorish past and of the Orientalist history of Spain are rather clearly manifested by the interplay of thirteenth- and seventeenth-century dramatic and historic narratives. In those instances, the play is similar to the Giralda of the cathedral of Seville—that monument to Christian hegemony superimposed over Moslem mosque and minaret where muezzin once called the faithful to prayer and where Moorish astronomers/astrologers gazed at the stars.[3] As with the Giralda, so too in *La estrella de Sevilla* questions of identity, power, knowledge, ethics, and religion are salient. Above all, as with the Giralda, there is in *La estrella* a sense of placeness, of physical presence, and of location, that traces an Orientalist blueprint in the text.

The significance of physical space is apparent in the first verses of the *comedia,* when we are made abundantly aware that Castile has come to Seville in the material presence of King Sancho IV and his court (1–50).[4] Christian and Occidental hegemony are reasserted on what has long been Moslem and Oriental soil. But where are the Moorish traces in the Seville that had been conquered less than forty years before by Sancho's grandfather, Fernando III? Where can we find evidence of the Castilian colonization of Moorish Seville and of the inner and subjective colonization of Islamic identity by Christian cultural ascendancy? Seventeenth-century Castilian dominance would appear to be reconstructing a Christianized and Castilianized facade over the play's late-thirteenth-century setting and to be erasing the conspicuous presence of the Moor from what would have been his former dwelling place. The play would appear to allow the conquering culture a self-congratulatory reassurance that the national Christian identity is intact, however superficially. The text of *La estrella de Sevilla,* for example, makes reference to several post-Reconquest architectural landmarks that did not exist in 1284: San Marcos (944), Nuestra Señora de las Cuevas (1320), and even the Alcázar, where a large percentage of the dialogue among monarch and subjects takes place.[5] At first glance, it seems that problems of Moorish otherness and the national identity crisis might have been swept under the Persian carpets. Nevertheless, not all cover-ups are successful (nor are they necessarily intentional): deceptive lumps in the carpeting hint at what lies underneath. The Alcázar of Seville, an emblem of Christian hegemony, was built upon the site of an ancient Moorish fortress, a location that conjures up Orientalist notions of despotic

Islamic rulers and of hedonistic Eastern potentates relishing every imaginable pleasure amid sumptuous surroundings.[6] Questions of tyrannical rule, the *injusto*, and of pleasure or *gusto* haunt the Alcázar. Perhaps it is not so coincidental that the playwright of *La estrella de Sevilla* elected this exotic Andalusian setting for a *comedia* that deals so centrally with hegemonic struggle and conflicts between personal pleasure and the obligations of honor.[7] Even the cherished matter of honor itself—a topic speculated by *comedia* scholars to have been more a dramatic convention than an essential ingredient of everyday life in the seventeenth century—is somehow more vibrantly and "authentically" depicted in the exotic Sevillian setting. Sense of place permeates the text's consideration of questions of nobility, and the ghost of the noble Moor haunts the dramatist's descriptions of the Sevillian aristocracy. Although they are Christians, as denizens of the southern tier of Spain the Sevillians embody many of the traits conventionally attributed to the phantom Moor. "Toda esta gente me espanta" (3021; "All these people astonish me"), the King declares with reference to the brave and noble determination of the Sevillians. However, his Orientalist discourse also indicates that the Sevillians incarnate the composite identities of the Christian knight and the noble Moor. "No he visto gente / más gentil ni más cristiana / que la desta ciudad" (2774–76; "I have not seen people more noble or more Christian than those of this city") he says. The Sevillian noblemen Bustos and Sancho Ortiz are especially exemplary of the synthesis of cultural values. Speaking of them the King exclaims:

> No se habrá visto en el mundo
> tales dos hombres jamás.
> Cuando su valor confundo
> me van apurando más.
>
> (2028–31)

[The world will never see two such men. When I compare their valor, they go on confusing me more.]

Sancho Ortiz manifests the very essence of "El Cid andaluz" (1219; "the Andalusian Cid"), "bravo, robusto y fuerte" (1222; "fierce, robust, and strong"). With similarly Cid-like signifiers, Bustos is also depicted by his friend Sancho as the "más noble caballero / que trujo arnés, ciñó espada, / lanza empuñó, enlazó yelmo" (2265–69; "the noblest knight that ever bore arms, girded on sword, brandished lance, or laced helmet"). Curiously, it is another Sancho, who in theory, as the Castilian king, should be exemplifying all the noble virtues of the Cid. Indeed, this other Sancho is described as the personification of the ferocious warrior-king who so valiantly had fought and defeated the rival otherness of Islam, the king "a quien llaman / por su invicta fortaleza / el Bravo el vulgo, y los moros, / porque de su nombre tiemblan" (781–84, "called Brave by the people for his undaunted courage and Fierce by the Moors because they tremble at his name"). In this manner King Sancho's Christian essence is constructed in opposition to the Moor. Nevertheless, it is obvious that the fierce Castilian king lacks the chivalric gentility he so admires in the Sevillians, the Christian inhabitants of the land of the noble Moor and their apparent inheritors of Moorish integrity.

As the twin Sanchos act out their confused struggle of cultural and personal values, one begins to ask what is Castilian and what is Sevillian?[8] How is each "othered" by the other? Who is the most noble Moor? Who is the most Christian? Simply put, one finds in *La estrella de Sevilla* remnants of the Spanish national identity crisis hatched during the first encounters with Islamic otherness, reared in the struggles for Reconquest, and theoretically exterminated by the Christian victory. The hegemonic struggle among sociocultural and political forces is now recast as a shadow dance, a spectral representation on the interior stage of subjectivity. The contest of chivalric values is played out in Seville on the site of former encounters with the Moor and all his admired/despised otherness. The issues of monarchical rights, aristocratic privilege, and imperialist colonization spar in an arena haunted by old cultural conflicts and more recent regional rivalries. Thirteenth- and seventeenth-century historical narratives become inextricably entwined with issues of characterization and dramatic narration in *La estrella de Sevilla.*

Shadows of the old conflict between Christian and Moor, and the new one between Castile and Andalusia, are recast when King Sancho acts out his own version of Reconquest in Seville. From the outset of the *La estrella de Sevilla,* matters of geography and hegemony are foregrounded when King Sancho announces

> Mi corte tendrá su asiento
> en ella, y no es maravilla
> que la corte de Castilla
> de asiento en Sevilla esté;
> que en Castilla reinaré
> mientras reinare en Sevilla.

(14–20)

[My court shall have its seat in *her,* nor is it strange that the court of
Castile should have its seat in Seville.]

What I find particularly fascinating in these verses and in the
scenes that follow are the nuances of Orientalism that color the
account of the King's arrival and—above all—the inflections of
Orientalist discourse that modulate the tone of play's central conflicts. It is "en ella" (15; "in her")—*in Seville* the beautiful, in
Seville the feminized, the exotic and Oriental—that imperial victory is relived and Sancho IV's personal conquest is plotted out.
The King is clearly captivated by Seville's "riqueza y su lealtad"
(27; "wealth and loyalty"). In the sumptuous surroundings of the
feminized Seville his desires quicken and his ego swells. With gra-
cious salutations and noble humility the *alcaldes* tender their city
before him—their demonstrations of loyalty and submission to hierarchy paralleling the relationship of females to males in their
patriarchal society. The effects of the *alcaldes* rendering homage
to him, and of the city's majestic milieu, spawn in the King an
image of Seville temptingly displayed before his covetous eye.
When don Arias inquires of him, "¿Qué te parece, señor, / de
Sevilla?" (51–52; "What do you think, my lord, of Seville?"), King
Sancho responds, "Parecido / me ha tan bien, que hoy he sido /
sólo rey" (53–55; "I think she has treated me so well that only
today am I really King"). It is she, Seville, who finally makes him
feel like a complete king in dominion over his property. But delight
in his kingly power over Seville is accompanied by lascivious desires like those of an Oriental potentate gazing at his harem. He
quickly turns the discussion from the "ciudad tan rica y bella"
where "viviendo despacio en ella / más despacio admirará" (58–60;
"the longer one lives in a city so rich and fair, the more he will
feel her charm") to examining Oriental Seville personified in the
lovely ladies of the city—"las divinas bellezas" (64; "the divinely
beautiful women").

King Sancho participates in the Occident's tendency to describe
the Orient as feminine, fertile, sensuous, and abundant in the symbol of the harem.[9] Seville becomes a seraglio of beautiful noble
women proffered for the listener's or the reader's imaginative gaze.
The king and don Arias enumerate the Sevillian lovelies by name,
objectifying and dissecting them for more detailed contemplation.
Although they are all Christian women, the Oriental allusions in
the play facilitate their comparison and categorization in a sensuous and erotic context or, as the King puts it, "al apetito del hombre" (120; "pleasurable to masculine desire"). In contrast with

other early-modern Spanish texts containing passages praising no-
blewomen—such as we find in *La Diana,* for example—there is in
the King's appraisal no treatment of the Sevillian ladies' noble
lineage, honor, and dignity.[10] They are highly objectified and, in
fact, commodified as so much "mármol y azófar" or "ébano" (124,
144; "marble and brass," "ebony"). The *sevillanas* are shown to be
as resplendent as the exotic world colonized by Occidental Castile
in conquered Andalusia in medieval times. Moreover, the ladies
are treated metaphorically as a valued medium of exchange and,
by implication, as the object of imperialistic rapacity in later eras
of colonization and money-based economies. Abundant wordplay
surrounding "blanca y rubia" with regard to appearance (121, 123)
and "blancas" (86, 89, 129) referring to coins typifies the discourse
of acquisition and exchange in which the Sevillian women—especially Estrella—are constructed. The commodification of women
in this play is underscored by the discourse of Spanish hegemony
inscribed in varied references to the two historic periods intertex-
tually conjoined within *La estrella de Sevilla.* It bears reminding
that the site of the play, the rich port of Seville, was a coveted
jewel under medieval Moorish dominion and that it became the
fertile harbor through which the riches of the New World—the new
Orient conquered by the heirs of the Reconquest—were made to
flow into Spain in the following centuries.[11]

Of course the treatment of women as objects, as media of exchange, is an anthropological trope as well as a literary one.[12] However, I believe the presentation of that convention in *La estrella
de Sevilla* is complemented by several Orientalist undertones col-
oring the text. In the Sevillian context the wordplay with "blancas"
(coins called "whites", "blondes") takes on additional Orientalist
tinges because the fair "rubias" are not the preferred object of
desire for the Castilian king recently come to rule in exoticized
Andalusia. In his words, a blonde "con rayos de nieve / poca ala-
banza se debe / si en vez de abrasar, enfría" (76–78; "with her
frigid glances merits little praise if she chills rather than inflames").
King Sancho has little interest in the "blancas" associated with the
Northern Germanic cold: "Que andaba / muy prolijo el alemán"—
as he puts it when denying any real attraction for the blonde Dona
Elvira de Guzmán (83–84; "the German in her was too conspicuous").[13] Rather it is the local color—that of *las morenas,* and particularly one stunning brunette—that most fires his passion. For
the King, in this sensuously exotic setting it is Estrella, the "mo-
rena" dressed in black who "vivica y enciende" with her dark
beauty (130, 160; "brunette," "enlivens and enkindles").

There are in the King's comparison of *blancas* and *morenas* reverberations of traditional verses sung about the relative values of *toledanas* and *sevillanas*—poems comparing the northern and southern women, Castilians and Sevillians.[14] As in the *cancionero* poems, similar verses in *La estrella de Sevilla* are not just about the comparison of fair and dark beauties. Comparative valorizations of the feminine are veiled by the many tensions between North and South—geographic, sociopolitical and cultural-economic— materialized in the rivalry between two early modern seats of power, Toledo and Seville. Similarly in *La estrella de Sevilla,* the pairings of Castile and Seville and of *blancas* and *morenas* subtly suggest hegemonic struggles represented as conflicts for posses- sion of the feminine. In the play, however, the Orientalist discourse is more apparent. The struggle to possess or to control possession of the most sensuously beautiful woman in Orientalized Seville is central to the play's conflicts. Estrella becomes the fertile ground for a new version of the Reconquest, for dramatic and sociohistori- cal contention between regional and cultural values, embodying simultaneously the crisis of national unity and a subjective cultural identity crisis. Estrella *is* Sevilla; *she* is the site and target of the Christian and Castilian king's colonization efforts throughout the play.[15]

King Sancho's plot of conquest is tinged by traces of his Orien- talist admiration for and his dominion over exotic Andalusia. He sees himself metaphorically transformed into an Eastern magus in pursuit of the bright star he longs to possess. Characterizing his actions territorially and hegemonically, he declares "diga Castilla / lo que quisiere entender; / que rey mago quiero ser / de la Estrella de Sevilla" (473–76; "let Castile say what it might like to under- stand; I want to be like the Magi Kings in pursuit of the Star of Seville").[16] Sancho IV wants to possess her, to master the star, and—by implication—to control the secret knowledge and power denoted in the name Estrella, a name reminiscent of the Orient's special position with regard to astrology and astronomy. Complex astrological imagery pervades the play, although it is important to note that explicit references to the Oriental sources of such astrological knowledge in *La estrella de Sevilla* are not apparent.[17] A memory has been erased, the memory of the enormous debt owed by Castilian and all Western astrology to Arabic texts such as the *Picatrix,* translated during the time of Alfonso the Wise and his son Sancho.[18] In the play's seventeenth-century representation of courtly astrological discourse, Castilian power is associated with knowledge of the stars and heavenly powers. The Oriental sources

of such wisdom have been obscured by Western cultural colonization of astrology, by absorption within the Greco-Roman sphere
of influence.

A similar ghost presence of the Oriental can be traced to verses
depicting Sancho Ortiz's delirious flight into the underworld. He
sings his woes in a guilt-tripping scene theatrically staged with
musicians and vivid descriptions reminiscent of Baroque texts on
sociospiritual disillusionment such as *El diablo cojuelo* (*The Limp-
ing Devil*).[19] More formative intertexts recreated in the scene, are
of course, the medieval and the Dantesque. Embedded at a still
more deep intertextual level in those scenes are examples drawn
from Mohammed's underworld journey as adapted by Dante for
the *Inferno*.[20] Dante's debt to the Islamic world was not openly
recognized in the early modern period, and it is difficult to say
whether any of the spectators or readers from the period would
have sensed the Orientalist subtext in the scene. However, the
delirium or flight scene was definitely too exotic for later Spanish
dramatists and playgoers. Hartzenbush, for example, erased it
from his recasting of the *La estrella de Sevilla*.[21] Nevertheless, I
think that the staging of Sancho's flight of delirium within the 1634
play is reminiscent—by its very theatricality—of what Edward
Said has called the Orientalist tendency to represent the East in a
closed setting and to exoticize it in literature (1979, 63).[22]

I have characterized the conflicts of *La estrella de Sevilla* as
representing issues of Reconquest and colonization of the geographic space that is Seville and of the internal geographic space
of subjectivity. The contest in the play for dominion in Seville
and for possession of Estrella is Orientalized by the specter of
Moorish/Christian tension. The major complications and resolutions of the play are constructed within the framework of the larger
struggle to advance and maintain Christian-Castilian territorial
expansion. The King wants to enjoy his rule in Seville, in part,
through the conquest of Estrella, the city personified. To achieve
that end, his first weapon is the prestige and power synonymous
with a strategic military command post on the Moorish frontier.
By offering Estrella's brother Bustos that honored position, King
Sancho hopes to buy off Bustos, to conquer him with favor, to
displace him from the conflict by coopting his loyalty and by spatially marginalizing him on the frontier.

The Moorish/Christian conflict and the implied tensions between
North and South are also evident in the play's resolutions. As the
cruelties of the King's attempted conquests in Seville become more
apparent, and his personal dilemmas more precarious, the territo-

rial inflections of the conflict are foregrounded. "¿Y qué se dirá de mí en Castilla?" (2689; "And what will they say about me in Castile?"), he asks don Arias, in the face of Castilian threats to his hegemony, which are piling onto his Sevillian preoccupations. King Sancho's attempts to settle his problems are territorially represented. The borderlands are the solution to the Sancho Ortiz quandary: by exiling the "Cid andaluz" to the boundary between Christendom and Islam, the King also honors him. But events surrounding that paradoxical "destierro y premio" (2891; "exiling and honoring") of Sancho are yet another enigma of inner and outer geography in the play. Sancho Ortiz appears to embody identities of the noble Moor, the sentimental Moor, the idealized Christian knight of the thirteenth century, and the monomaniacally honorable knight called into question by changing standards of the seventeenth century. Such images of Orientalized noble Sevillians—of Sancho, the Alcaldes, the "noble gente de Sevilla" (2983; "noble people of Seville"), and of Estrella—remain morally superior to their Castilian king, the supposed exemplar of chivalric Christian nobility. Nevertheless, Castilian hegemony triumphs in the end when the king's resolution of Estrella's predicament is territorially represented. Seville's own star is ultimately colonized by King Sancho's marrying her to a Castilian grandee of his court and by transforming her Sevillian beauty into Castilian property.

The most extreme example of colonization and of the misappropriation of human property in *La estrella de Sevilla* is the case of the slave Natilde. She is marked by her name and her speech as a non-Negroid Moslem: the type of slave most commonly found in medieval Spain.[23] It is that identity and social position which make Natilde the most othered and Orientalized character of the play. Curiously, however, when she attempts to claim through a writ of manumission and an act of betrayal what Christian males of Seville's aristocracy consider their birthright—their freedom to act as subjects and agents—Natilde is stereotypically treated as the deceitful Moslem other. In this sense she represents a negatively Orientalized otherness at odds with the admired image of the noble Moor, with an otherness dominant Christian males could appropriate for themselves. For that reason it is highly ironic when she who appears to be the most othered and most marginalized by Castilian Christian values is simultaneously valorized by that society's leaders. When the king and don Arias believe that Natilde has worked her magic for them and opened the door to Estrella's seduction they proclaim that "La esclavilla / es extremada. Castilla / estatuas la ha de labrar" (906–8; "the little slave girl is wonderful. Castile should erect statues in her honor"). By transforming the other's vice into virtue, they have exposed the degenerate condition of their own Christian identities. Ironically, in a Moslem slave, in this other, in this mere supplement to the central plot of the text, and in slavery—a prestigious practice in seventeenth-century Spain—we encounter one of the central issues of *La estrella de Sevilla:* agency versus hegemonic control. Although the existence of Natilde seems to add a sense of placeness appropriate to the seventeenth-century Sevillian setting, the Orientalism intextuated in the matter of Natilde's freedom is a ghost presence haunting twentieth-century readings and stagings of the play. As readers in the so-called postmodern era we must be aware not only of the historical and cultural differences separating the *La estrella de Sevilla* from us and our era, but also of the acts of erasure that we perform in order to construct an Orientalist reading of slavery in the text. We tend to associate the practice of slavery with the East especially the Middle East—even today. But perhaps an Orientalist reading of the play is facilitated by erasing a presence from our own cultural heritage, by forgetting that the supposedly alien practice of slavery was the custom of this country not so long ago. This play's treatment of identity crises—subjective or national—reminds us that such pervasive questions are problems of not just Spanish history but our own as well. Perhaps by recognizing that fact, critics will continue to make *La estrella de Sevilla* a canonical play, not by ignoring its absences but by recognizing them and relating them to the absent presences of our own historical moment.[24]

Notes

1. See, for example, studies by Carrasco-Urgoiti (1976), Lida de Malkiel (1960), Márquez Villanueva (1975).

2. *Estrella* studies are indebted to research on the historical and political underpinnings of the play such as those by Aníbal (1934) and Kennedy (1975), although my point is that their focus has been Eurocentric.

3. Under a Renaissance architectural crown added in 1568, the Giralda remains the most impressive example of Almohad construction in Spain. It is the only remnant of the Great Mosque of Seville built in the last quarter of the twelfth century under the reign of Abu-Ya'qub Yusuf. Although the city was taken soon afterward (1248) by Fernando III of Castile, the Greco-Roman decoration was not added to the Giralda's Islamic-style base until the era of Spain's ascendancy as an imperial power. See Read (1974, 164–65).

4. All references to the play are from 1968 (1985) *Diez Comedias del Siglo de Oro* edited by José Martel, Hymen Alpern, and Leonard Mades. The translations are my own.

5. See the introduction by John M. Hill for the edition of *La estrella de Sevilla* by Frank Otis Reed and Esther M. Dixon, xxvii.

6. Western interpretations of encounters with Moslems produced images of Islamic rulers as powerful, cruel, and even despotic during a long and complicated history stretching from the rapid medieval expansion of Arabic and Moorish dominion to that of the Turks in the early modern period. See Said (1979, 59–62) and Daniel (1958, 109–33). A good example of the Spanish view is Bunés Ibarra's collection of sixteenth- and seventeenth-century chroniclers' comments on the sultans as unusually harsh, proud, daring, and powerful (1989, 314–15, 232, 90). Particularly interesting are their descriptions of luxurious Berber palaces as a demonstration of the vanity and tyranny of illegitimate and despotic rulers. Moreover, from the chroniclers' point of view the sumptuous palatial surroundings— gardens, seraglios, baths—were an indication that the rulers were excessive and "unnatural" in their sexual practices (59–60)! As Daniel demonstrates, such assumptions of sexual licentiousness have a history as long as the period of contact with the Islamic world (1958, 140–44, 242–43). And, as Said points out, more modern Orientalist suppositions about Moslem sexual practices have been generalized to include all "hot-blooded southerners'" (1979, 311).

7. Scholars have not yet produced evidence that the central dramatic conflict of the play has any basis in specific thirteenth-century historical events. Nevertheless, the sketch of Sancho IV depicted in the chronicles outlines the character of a Castilian king whose image might easily become the basis for a seventeenth-century questioning of monarchical power—either by rewriting medieval events or representing early modern ones in an older context. Interestingly, most studies on the imperialist ambitions or absolutist tendencies in Alfonso X and Sancho IV tend to refer to the rival codes of Roman and Gothic law without consideration of the possible subtle sociocultural influences of the Moorish encounter. See McDonald (1965 and 1990, xxxvii–lix), Craddock (1986), and González-Marcos (1982).

8. Harlan and Sara Sturm have written about the two Sanchos, although their discussion centers more on the dramatic roles of the pair than on their possible psychological relationship. Frederick A. de Armas has written extensively about the significance of twin-character relationships in the play (1994a and 1980). He sees an interplay of power and identity relations between the two Sanchos that is based on the justice/pleasure conflict, on Girardian notions about sacrificial victims, and on the interaction of astrological and mythological subtexts (1992, 16–17). I think that de Armas's conclusions and those of the Sturms can be extended to include an examination of the more psychoanalytic and sociological aspects of the paired Sanchos: 1) are the Castilian and Sevillian Sanchos cultural *and* sexual rivals for Estrella? 2) how extensive is their mutual admiration and how does it relate to thirteenth-or seventeenth-century indications of homosocial bonding opaquely grounded in concepts of honor and patriarchy? These are questions I plan to explore in more extensive research on the play.

9. I draw my description on the feminized exotic from Said's reconsideration of Orientalism, a more in-depth view "manifestly connected to the configurations of sexual, racial and political asymmetry underlying mainstream modern western culture, as illuminated respectively by feminists, by black studies critics and by anti–imperialist activists" (1985, 12).

10. See the "Canto de Orpheo" in Montemayor's *La Diana* (1970, 180–90).

11. It is important to remember how often supposedly "historical" *comedias* can be read as recreations in earlier contexts of seventeenth-century matters. In

La estrella de Sevilla I think it is significant that thirteenth-century issues of Castilian hegemony are a recreation of early modern struggles for Castilian and imperial Spanish power in the New World. The play's treatment of the Moor's otherness can be seen as displacement of Spain's newest encounter with the other in the Americas. (De Armas sees in such displacements the creation of a "homogenous" other [1991, 2]). Accounts of the struggle for Christian hegemony flow backward into the medieval past and forward into the early modern present and future. The momentum of the Reconquest seems to have poured into Seville and streamed out through the Guadalquivir on ships heading for the newly conquered lands.

12. See Gayle Rubin's landmark feminist reading of Lévi-Strauss's classic structuralist study on the exchange of women (1975), Karen Newman's comprehensive update (1990), and James Mandrell's cogent comments on the exchange factor in Don Juan studies, especially in *El burlador de Sevilla* (1992, 227–72).

13. The passage presents an interplay of concepts about women as coins of exchange, of northern "Germanic" blondness in women, of the possible Germanic (Visigoth) heritage of the Castilian Guzmán family, and of the power of German bankers. The juxtaposition of concepts is highly ironic when we consider the complex displacements of medieval, early modern European, and Spanish colonial conflicts in *La estrella de Sevilla*.

14. I thank Brian Dutton for having brought to my attention two particular examples from the fifteenth-century Spanish collection, the *Cancionero de Juan Alfonso de Baena:* "Este dezir . . . fizo e ordeno el dicho Alfonso Alvarez por porfya que tenian las monjas de seuilla E de toledo" (98. 11–12) and "Respuesta secunda de Suero de Ribera" (98. 326). Both are from the Bibliothèque Nationale, Paris, manuscript ESP 37, now printed in Dutton's vol. 3 (1991).

15. Estrella is also Orientalized in another way that resembles the treatment accorded the legendary Florinda, the daughter of Conde Julián violated by Rodrigo, the last Gothic king of Spain. Estrella is, in effect, blamed by Sancho IV for the death of her brother and the impossible predicament in which she and her beloved are placed. Estrella is told that "vos la culpa tenéis por ser tan bella" (2137; "It's your fault for being so beautiful"). Sancho IV rewrites the history of his encounter with this Orientalized woman. Her exotic brunette's beauty is to blame just as was Florinda's for the loss of Spain to the Moors. Curiously, however, the Christian Florinda became radically and ironically Orientalized by the process of blame when *Christian* legend adopted the *Arabic* "La Cava" (bad woman) to refer to her.

16. It is ironic, or course, that the Castilian, Christian king who behaves so despotically in the play should compare himself to one of the Magi, those representations—in the Christian mind—of Oriental wisdom, of concord between Orient and Occident, or of Oriental submission to Christian Occident.

17. Studies by Frederick A. de Armas (1994b, 1980), James F. Burke (1974), and Harlan and Sara Sturm (1969) have uncovered the extensive astrological subtexts of the play although they do not discuss the Islamic connections.

18. The majority of Arabic scientific texts translated and compiled under the reign of Alfonso X were astrological or astronomical. The *Picatrix*, translated under his direction in 1256, has been judged to be the most significant medieval text on astrological magic. See Deyermond (1984, 166). By the seventeenth century, the reputation of Arabic accomplishments in astrology may have been diminished in the popular mind and in some literary references by the image of the

Moor and his descendant the Morisco as necromancers and connivers. See, for example, Chejne (117), Brooks (238) and Márquez Villanueva (1975 and 1984).

19. The very setting for the flight of fancy has an Orientalist air. Sancho's "suffering" in this scene is exoticized and literary. His prison is really a sumptuous Sevillian palace equipped with musicians to amuse him and, in effect, to function as a chorus and a musical accompaniment to his histrionics. See also note 22 below.

20. Dante studies are indebted to the Spanish Arabist Asín Palacios for discovering the Islamic models and Moslem influences on the *Divine Comedy*. See Asín (1919) and an update by Southern on the general acceptance of his findings among Dante scholars (1962, 55–56, n.17).

21. I thank Charles Ganelin for this observation.

22. Nineteenth-century French recastings of *La estrella de Sevilla* clearly show the mark of growing European Orientalism. Alfredo Rodríguez López Vázquez tells me that the adaptations by Pierre Lebrun and Hyppolite Lucas made use of exotic Orientalist scenery to recreate an Orientalist image. See also the introduction to his edition of *La estrella de Sevilla* (1991, 23–30).

23. Natilde's name is illustrative of her status as the Christian subject's Islamic other. The letter "N" is the brief mark of difference and hierarchy separating her from varied Christian saints named *M*atilde, and, consequently, it is the sign that denies her the social and moral status to which a Christian is entitled. In addition, Natilde's speech—even when she banters amusingly with Clarindo (544–54)—does not betray signs of the conventional theatrical dialect used to portray blacks or mulatos in such settings. For these reasons it can be assumed that Natilde is a white Moslem. Interestingly, her identity—although typical of a slave in Christian homes during the thirteenth century—is a somewhat exotically historicized (re)-creation of slavery from the point of view of seventeenth-century Seville. By that time the typical slave in the city was black, frequently Christian, and served in an aristocratic household or that of a churchman, a wealthy artisan, or a merchant. In such homes, slaves were considered a prestigious sign of the luxurious lifestyle maintained by the proprietors. The most respected Christians of the early modern era, not unlike those of medieval times, fashioned their subjectivity in relation to their dominance over the other. On slavery in the era, see Bennassar (1979, 106–13), Domínguez Ortiz (1971, 162–64), Kamen (1980, 283–84), and Daniel (1975, 9 and 74).

24. I thank the following friends and colleagues whose suggestions helped shape the final version of this paper: Inés Azar, Emilie Bergmann, Dwayne Carpenter, Anne Cruz, Fred de Armas, Brian Dutton, Charles Ganelin, Mary Gaylord, Dan Heiple, Alfredo Rodríguez López-Vázquez, and Anita Stoll.

8

Star Gazing: Text, Performance, and the Female Gaze

Anne J. Cruz

In scene 8, act 2 of *La estrella de Sevilla*, King Sancho, his attempts at seducing Estrella in her own house stymied by her brother's arrival, is vengefully plotting Busto's murder with his *privado*, don Arias, when the latter sees a bulk hanging from the rafters of the Alcázar. Unwilling to focus on the sight, the monarch orders Arias to look at the object to determine what it is. The play's dialogue allows the spectators to understand the action: as Arias looks up at the bulk, he describes it as "una mujer colgada" ("a hanging woman") then as "ahorcada" ("hanged"). At the king's insistent questioning ("¿Mujer dices?" ["a woman, you say?"]), he repeats, affirming her gender, "una mujer" ("a woman"), but because of her condition, he corrects himself saying that she is no longer a woman: "Y está ahorcada, con que no lo viene a ser" (1241–42; "and she's hanged, so she's no longer one after all").[1]

The spectators know that the hanged woman is Natilde, Estrella's slave, since Busto had earlier admonished that she was to appear before the king for her part in the bungled seduction:

Busto.	Ven conmigo.
Natilde.	¿Dónde voy?
Busto.	Vas a que te vea el Rey:
	que así cumplo con la ley
	y obligación en que estoy.

(1157–60)

Busto.	Come with me.
Natilde.	Where am I going?
Busto.	You're going to see the King;
	That's how I obey the law
	and meet my obligation.

119

Nonetheless, despite his intention, Busto's threat is never carried out: the king never "sees" Natilde, whose body is viewed only by Arias. Neither is the body seen by the audience, as its ominous presence is noted solely through the *privado*'s description. What the spectators—and we as readers—must follow, then, is an interrupted gaze: the audience regards don Arias who, upon seeing the body, turns to look at the king, who intentionally looks away. And what is interrupted in the visual circuit as well is the recognition of the body as gendered, for, as punishment for her collusion with the king, Natilde loses not only her life, but her identity as a woman.

The slave's degendered corpse is a visual sign that points at once to the king's desire for Estrella and to its potential consequences. Yet Sancho's refusal to see both the body and the error of his ways cannot be conveyed verbally or textually, but must be apprehended in the very failure of its performance. Unlike predeterminately coded visual gestures such as a wink or a stare, the ocular movements of directing the gaze at something and of looking away ("saccades") have no inherent sign value other than what the audience may attribute to them at the specific time of their occurrence.[2]

While the king's gaze, interrupted by his misrecognition of the role he is playing, forms part of the production of meaning, it does not correspond easily to a totalizing conception of theater/ spectator relations in which all signs hold preestablished significance. In particular, such eye movements challenge what Keir Elam has classified as performance: the written meaning of a dramatic text expressed visually and aurally through the process of semiotization, the assigning of signification to actors and inanimate objects as sign-vehicles.[3] Moreover, Elam's reliance on spectator competence, as well as his faith in the interrelationship of both text and performance and their communicability, is manifest in his request that the spectator be "reasonably experienced" to understand the performance, since both encoding and decoding are based on codes (or ensembles of rules) that should be known to performer and spectator alike (1980, 34–35).[4] For Elam, the ideal spectator is "one endowed with a sufficiently detailed and judiciously employed, textual background to enable *him* to identify all relevant relations and use them as a grid for a correspondingly rich decodification" (1980, 93; my emphasis).

I underscore Elam's use of the masculine pronoun when referring to spectators, because he would seem to consider their gender irrelevant. In effect, his assumption that the "mastery" of theatergoing depends on the spectator's ability to infer its common rules necessitates that all spectators, regardless of gender, share and agree on the cultural values embedded in dramatic codes. For Elam, text and performance come together in his view of theater as a seamless communicative act. Despite his statement that theatrical communication begins and ends with the spectator, he stresses the spectator's role not as interpreter, but as participant in an "overall homogeneity of response." The spectator-spectator communication, he argues, moves the individual to "*integration* (the single audience member is encouraged in consequence to surrender his individual function in favour of the larger unit of which he is part" [1980, 97]). Other semioticians, while considerably more flexible, nevertheless fail to distinguish gender difference as a communicative rupture; for example, Marco de Marinis, who focuses on sociosemiotic variables, limits his studies to the dynamics of cognitive and emotional responses without, however, explicitly considering gender.[5]

In contrast to those critics who speak to an ideal spectator, feminist theater and film critics have insisted upon the fallacy of assuming an undifferentiated response from the audience and the need to point out the ways in which theater itself figures gender difference.[6] Jill Dolan (1988, 1) argues that

> [d]enaturalizing the position of the ideal spectator as a representative of the dominant culture enables the feminist critic to point out that every aspect of theatrical production, from the types of plays and performances produced to the texts that are ultimately canonized, is determined to reflect and perpetuate the ideal spectator's ideology.

Yet feminist critics would agree that theatrical production, like its reception, is never free from ideological tensions, conflicts, and contradictions. If Dolan's "resisting reader" can read against the grain, it is because s/he has learned to see beyond the naturalized theatrical representation and can point to its fissures, whether in text or performance.

In *La estrella de Sevilla,* one such fissure is the king's failure to look at Natilde's hanged body. Carrying no inherent code value but instead challenging the expected decodification from the audience, the uncompleted gesture itself suspends Elam's desired resolution of text and performance. Rather, it brings into play a third term that sheds light on theater's ideology of gender difference as well as on differences of reception according to gender. This third term, introjected in the space opened between performance and text, is what Jacques Lacan has called "the gaze." In defining his use of this term, Lacan (1981, 73–74) affirms "what determines me, at the most profound level, in the visible, is the gaze that is outside—I am looked at, that is to say, I am a picture." He explains further: "[I]n our relation to things, in so far as this relation is constituted by the way of vision, and ordered in the figures of representation, something slips, passes, is transmitted, from stage to stage, and is always to some degree eluded in it—that is what we call the gaze."

As Lacan's appropriation of the theatrical metaphor demonstrates, theater offers a field of vision where looks are displaced and reversed despite the mimetic constraints of representation. Yet, although masks may be exchanged, stage roles can never be completely dissolved or destroyed. Traditional theater thus both simulates and stands for presence since, like theatrical parts, social roles must be played out: they cannot escape being seen, caught in a scene, interpellated by the social order (Freedman 1991, 140). The play's audience cannot ignore the play of looks on stage, nor the gaze with which the play constitutes representation. In the *comedia,* the gaze that looks back upon the audience, staring it down, is that of the symbolic order which, regardless of its contradictions, plays upon the spectators' desire to see themselves as ego ideals, in turn as players pleasing to society.[7]

Lacan's theories of the gaze inform Barbara Freedman's recent studies of Shakespearean theater. She reminds us that traditional Western drama offers a dismal double bill, comic and tragic: either some version of *Oedipus* or its sister play, *The Taming of the Shrew.* For her, "[o]ne scenario identifies civilization with male payment for his own sexuality, the other identifies it with male control over disordered female sexuality. Both not only record but promulgate the values of a repressive patriarchal culture" (1988, 379). Freedman (1991, 63) points out besides that, as an Oedipal staging, theater literally represents our alienation from as well as our entry into society; its viewing thus assumes a gaze that looks back at us while it stares us down:

> The gaze comes into play when we realize that we are seen from a point within as well as from without with which we can never merge. . . . [T]he objectification of the self by an alien viewpoint enables, as it undermines, self-consciousness by calling into play an unconscious look.

My emphasis on Freedman's thesis is not to compare all of Spanish Golden Age theater to the two modes she considers Western dramatic Ur-texts, although, in the Golden Age *comedia*'s bipolar division of comedy and tragedy, both the *comedias de capa y espada*, with their requisite wedding finales, and the honor plays could at least partially carry forth the analogy. Instead, I wish to demonstrate the ways in which *La estrella de Sevilla* acts out, through the interplay of gazes, the characteristics of male domination as civilization, and the ordering of sexuality and gender to which Freedman calls attention. At the same time, I hope to show that the gaze itself creates a disturbance—however momentary—between performance and text that adds a separate, potentially subversive dimension to the theatrical performance and its reception, one to which female spectators might well have been particularly sensitive.

Indeed, if the king's interrupted gaze negates the "sign" of his unkingly behavior, the play's gaze reflects back on an audience that fully understands its consequences. These consequences, however, encode different meanings for different spectators. If, along with the king, male spectators interpret Natilde's hanged corpse as a phallic aggression against the state that demands the king's retribution, female spectators have reason to view it as a signal of female castration, a warning to them as women that Natilde's degendered state embodies masculine reaction against female power.

Thus, from Estrella's first unseeing rejection of the king to her final recognition of her brother's corpse, each visual (mis)apprehension creates a momentary opposition between performance and text, an undecided instance when Estrella may not subscribe to the letter of the law but instead act out an Imaginary and unwritten impulse. Ultimately, however, plot and narrative closure are achieved at the expense of her sexual difference, even as the male order is reinforced through its signifying dependency on the Other. As Freedman (1988, 381) explains, "[t]raditional drama therefore mimes socialization, juxtaposing the deconstruction of the gaze against the inevitability of a theatre of representation, the Imaginary as alterity against the Symbolic of Oedipally inscribed inevitability."

Insofar as it is enacted by the patriarchal/monarchical I/eye, "star gazing" in *La estrella de Sevilla* initiates the drama, propels it forward, and brings it to a close. Estrella's unmarried state compels her brother's surveillance; yet, although he is as unwed as she, and as prone to uncontrolled passion, his role as family patriarch ensures dominion over his sibling. The play's Oedipal narrative displaces the brother's incestuous desire onto the king. Estrella attracts the monarch's gaze from the first, as he asks

"¿Quién es la que en un balcón / yo con atención miré?" (131–32; "Who is the one on the balcony / that so caught my eye?"). Her darkness, set off against the insipidly pale ladies surrounding her, radiates an allure that extends beyond her attraction as a *sevillana* to the Moorish lands of Gibraltar that don Sancho wishes to conquer.

Fetishized by the king as an exotic Other, as a foreign land continually beyond his grasp, Estrella seems to him oblivious to her own visual powers:

Rey.   ¿Quién es la que rayos son
         sus dos ojos fulminantes,
         en abrasar semejantes
         a los de Júpiter fuerte,
         que están dándome la muerte,
         de su rigor ignorantes?

                                                    (136–140)

King.   Who is the one whose two fulminating eyes
         are lightning bolts,
         that burn and sear
         so like strong Jupiter's,
         that are killing me constantly
         without knowing their strength?

The young woman is not unaware of the power of her gaze, however; she has willfully fixed it on her betrothed, Sancho, with such intensity as to threaten the social order. The lovers are depicted as twins under the sign of Gemini, their differences fused and confused in their absorbing passion, their exalted courtship parodied in the hilarious amatory banter between the two servants. Estrella's desire for Sancho, codified in the Imaginary power of her gaze, thus bears comparison to the king's desire for her, his own desiring gaze posing a serious threat to the Symbolic order since it draws him away from his monarchical duties.

The thematic importance of the king's duality is underscored by his sharing identical names with his rival.[8] Yet the king and the lover share more than the same name—by also desiring the same woman, they are intended and represented as twins, their moral opposition merely apparent. In the same way, Sancho and Busto also appear as brothers, their homosocial relations strengthened through the bond of female exchange. The male gaze thus reopens the Oedipal wound, displaying and replaying male desire on several interlocking levels of displacement and deferral. The desire for Estrella manifested by the two Sanchos displaces the brother's incestuous desire for his sister, even while the monarch's passion supplants Busto's patriarchal role. Moreover, Sancho replays Estrella's role: unable to block the king's desire, he is feminized by the monarch's play of power.

While it would seem more logical for King Sancho to eliminate the lover rather than the brother, Sancho's alliance with the monarch entangles him in a web of complicity that will ultimately obviate the two men's desire. In offering Sancho to the king to carry out Busto's murder, the *privado* don Arias uses the same language as when he had earlier promised to obtain Estrella:

Don Arias. Pues yo darte un hombre quiero,
valeroso y gran soldado,
como insigne caballero.

(1205–07)

Don Arias. I therefore wish to give you a man,
courageous and a great soldier,
as your renowned knight.

The implied comparison reifies both Estrella and her lover, as Sancho's chivalric qualities are satirically inverted into those of a mere murderer. In the same way, the king's behavior toward his subjects shifts inexorably from one of protection to one of abuse. The king struggles to reinscribe Symbolic order through murderous means, checkmating Natilde's corpse by moving to assassinate Busto—at the cost, nonetheless, of the lovers' happiness and his own passion for Estrella.

The symmetrical pattern governing the two Sanchos becomes obvious by the manner in which the one perceives the other. Responding to the king's question "qué véis en mí (1440; "what do you see in me?"), Sancho reveals his own blindness, as he views the king solely as an image of righteousness and divine right:

Sancho. La majestad, y el valor,
al fin, una imagen veo,
de Dios, pues le imita el Rey:
y después dél, en vos creo.
y a vuestra cesárea ley,
gran señor, aquí me empleo.

(1441–46)

Sancho.   Your majesty, and your valor,
finally, an image I see
of God, since the King imitates Him:
and after Him, I believe in you.
and to your imperial law,
great lord, I dedicate myself.

Accepting the King's word as to what would constitute a crime of
lèse majesté, he vociferously proclaims his fealty, even to the point
of hypothetically killing his own brother: "Si es así, muerte daré, /
señor, a mi mismo hermano" (1522–23; "If such is the case, my
Lord / I'd even kill my brother"). When Sancho reads the king's
decree, he finds out that the hypothesis has indeed become reality:
the king has ordered Busto's death. He reads the decree again,
hoping that, as in the reshuffling of a deck of cards, another name
will appear. But as he reads twice more, confirming Busto's death
sentence, he can only posit his wish to please the king against his
desire for Estrella, which he now calls "loco amor." Incapable of
resolving the dilemma in which he finds himself, Sancho blames
Estrella, wishing he had never set eyes on her: "Nunca yo a Estrella mirara / causa de tanto disgusto" (1735–36; "would that I
never set eyes on Estrella / the cause of so much vexation"). By
ordering the lover to murder Busto, the monarch prompts him to
reject Estrella, as Sancho believes he must choose honor over love.

The king's initial momentary glance at Estrella sets the stage for
the rupture of the Symbolic order. It is, at the same time, a moment
in the play when performance and text are held in suspense—the
action begins to unfold only after don Arias ingratiates himself by
lecherously commenting on each woman attendant at court. The
monarch's desire is thus simultaneously incited and checked by
the *privado,* who identifies the king's choice as Estrella, but cautions that she is in her brother's charge, and will be wedded soon:

Don Arias.   Es doña Estrella Tavera
su nombre, y por maravilla
la llama Estrella Sevilla.

.   .   .   .

Casarla su hermano espera
en Sevilla, como es justo.

(161–166)

Don Arias.   Doña Estrella Tavera
is her name, and in admiration
Seville calls her Star.

. . . .
Her brother expects to marry her
in Seville, as is proper.

Anticipating the king's plans to seduce both brother and sister, don
Arias, in praising their worth, stresses their resemblance, since
Busto is not only unmarried, but is as valuable a catch as his sister:

Don Arias.   No es casado
que en la esfera sevillana
es Sol, si Estrella es su hermana;
que Estrella y Sol se han juntado.

(172–75)

Don Arias.   He's not married
since in the Sevillian heavens
he's the Sun, if his sister is Star;
so, Star and Sun have united.

Like Sancho, Busto takes on Estrella's role in that he denies the
king his desire while mediating her availability; the monarch will
attempt to seduce the sister by corrupting the brother.

Unlike Sancho, however, Busto sees through the king's ruse;
when the monarch tests his honor and sense of justice by offering
him an undeserved military position, Busto retorts that the king
should follow his example in telling the truth: "son mis verdades
espejos; / y así, en ellas os miráis" (399–400; "my truths serve as
mirrors / in which to see your self"). Sancho's blind willingness to
accept the king's mandate thus contrasts with Busto's understanding of the king's duties toward his subjects. Yet it is Sancho who
realizes that Busto has failed to inform the king of his engagement
to Estrella, and accuses him of hiding this fact from the king:

Sancho.   Mas no cumples con la ley
de amistad, porque debías
decirle al Rey que ya estaba
casada tu hermana.

(634–37)

Sancho.   Yet you do not obey
the laws of friendship, since you should
have told the King that your sister
was already married.

Busto's silence functions similarly to the king's interrupted gaze
in that it occurs in the absence of dialogue or action of any kind. As

such, it represents a lack that can only be given meaning belatedly. Again, performance and dramatic text are suspended until the moment is past; along with Sancho, who finds out too late, the audience is informed only afterward of Busto's unfortunate lapse, a lapse that discloses his own collusion with the patriarchy as he endeavors to impose his control of Estrella above Sancho and the king's.

Rather, Busto's failure to mention Estrella's engagement to Sancho is instead glossed over in his actual conversation with the king, where he reiterates his dominion over his sister by calling himself her husband: "Gran señor / soy de una hermana marido" (405–6; "Great lord / I am my sister's husband"). The displacement from fraternal to spousal control reflects upon the many occurrences in Golden Age plays, comedies as well as tragedies, where brothers are placed in charge of their sisters, their incestuous desires simultaneously maintained and forbidden by the patriarchal system. Elias Rivers (1980) has noted that we may perceive in this scene "the underlying sexual violence of two men fighting over a woman," as King Sancho challenges Busto's paternal role and symbolically claims his droit du seigneur not only by insisting upon his kingly right to marry off a female subject, but by ensuring the union through his superior economic power:

Rey.   Daréla, Busto, marido
        que a su igual no desmerezca.
        Y decidle que he de ser
        padrino y casamentero,
        y que yo dotarla quiero.

                                                              (419–23)

King.   Busto, I will give her a husband
        equal to her merits.
        and tell her that I will be
        her godfather and marriage broker,
        and that I wish to grant her a dowry.

Estrella has not remained passive, however. Fully involved in her love for Sancho, she wordlessly scorns the king's advances by literally turning her back on don Arias's offerings of riches and a wealthy husband. Unlike her earlier unseeing gaze, this gesture is especially meaningful to the play's contemporary audience. To turn one's back on the king or, as in this case, the king's ambassador and representative, is tantamount to treason. It is, therefore, as much her disdain as Busto's rejection that unleashes the king's vengeance on the family.

Yet the sign by which Busto retaliates against monarchical abuse ultimately turns against him and his sister. Natilde's body, hanged in the violent aftermath of the king's intrusion into Busto's house, stands as much for Estrella's increasing repression as it does for Busto's impending murder. Unknowingly, Estrella writes her lover to seek Busto out, since the brother plans to give Sancho her hand in marriage. Preparing for her wedding, she breaks a hand mirror; yet, instead of interpreting this as an evil omen, she innocently awaits Sancho's loving gaze as the mirror's replacement:

> *Estrella:*   y pues tal espejo aguardo,
> quiébrese el espejo, amiga;
> que no quiero que con él,
> éste de espejo me sirva.
>
> (1913–16)

> *Estrella.*   And while I await such a mirror,
> may my own mirror break, friend;
> since once he's arrived,
> I won't need this one any longer.

Immediately following this incident, the servant Clarindo returns from having delivered Estrella's letter with Sancho's hyacinth ring as his prize. Estrella, wishing to possess her beloved's ring, eagerly exchanges it for her diamond. Noting that the ring's stone is split in two, Clarindo reminds Estrella of the hyacinth's melancholic nature, yet she again refuses to take the accident as an evil portent:

> *Estrella.*   No importa que esté partida;
> que es bien que las piedras sientan
> mis contentos y alegrías.
> Ay, venturoso día!
>
> (1936–39)

> *Estrella.*   No matter that the stone's broken;
> it's good for stones to feel
> my happiness and joys.
> Oh, happy day!

Both the broken mirror and the split hyacinth ring foreshadow the degendered condition in which she will find herself. Yet she can see neither her bleak future forewarned in the mirror's shards, nor does she recognize in the ring's split stone the echoes of the mythical Hyacinth's accidental death by his lover, Apollo—a premonition of the break in Sancho and Busto's homoerotic alliance. Instead, Estrella mistakenly takes both omens as positive signs of her good fortune and forthcoming marital bliss ("Esta, amigos, ha sido estrella mía . . . ¿Qué valor hay que resista / al placer? (1940, 1944–45; "what valor can resist / so much pleasure?"). Nonetheless, pleasure will not only be resisted, but proscribed. The mirror's breaking signifies Estrella's plight—she had earlier challenged her gendered role in the Symbolic order through her agency as a willing lover. Now, she cannot "see" the threat her sexuality poses to the play's patriarchal figures: her brother, her lover, and her king.

Yet if, earlier, Estrella's gaze had dismissed one Sancho to fixate instead upon another, the spectacle of her brother's corpse forces her to confront her untenable situation. The sight of her murdered brother metamorphoses her into an inverted Medusa, unfeeling precisely because she remains alive despite her brother's death:

Estrella.   ¡Mi hermano es muerto, y le ha muerto
            Sancho Ortiz! ¿Hay quien lo diga?
            ¿Hay quien lo escuche y no muera?
            Piedra soy, pues estoy viva.

                                                        (1961–64)

Estrella.   My brother's dead, murdered by
            Sancho Ortiz! Can anyone say such a thing?
            Who can hear this and not die?
            I must be stone, since I'm alive still.

Once again, performance divides from text at Estrella's recognizance of Busto's body, a despairing moment in which she cries out for her own death, invoking the suicides of other abandoned lovers:

            ¿No hay cuchillos, no hay espadas,
            no hay cordel, no hay encendidas
            brasas, no hay áspides fieros,
            muertes de reinas egipcias?
            Pero si hay piedad humana,
            matadme.

                                                        (1967–71)

            Are there not knives, swords,
            Is there no rope, no burning coal,
            no wild asp that caused the death of Egyptian queens?

> If, however, there is any human pity,
> kill me.

The moment of desperation disappears all too soon, however, and the distraught figure seeking to end her life transforms instead into a veiled guide who frees Sancho from jail and piously forgives her brother's death. Protecting her from the lover's gaze, Estrella's veil uncovers for us—and I would add, for the women in the audience—the role Estrella has accepted in the patriarchy. Mary Ann Doane (1989, 107) discusses how, in film, the sight of a veiled woman isolates and contains female representation:

> [T]he veil functions to visualize (and hence stabilize) the instability, the precariousness of sexuality. At some level of the cultural ordering of the psychical, the horror or threat of that precariousness (of both sexuality and the visible) is attenuated by attributing it to the woman, over and against the purported stability and identity of the male. The veil is the mark of that precariousness.

Only after Sancho insists that she reveal her identity, and only after she admits her love for him, does Estrella unveil her own lack of self. The veil, like her admission of love, serves to conceal an absence, temporarily repressing Estrella's final acceptance of her own castration. No longer struggling to burn brightly, Estrella's light finally flickers out. Closing the breach between performance and text, she returns, unmoved and immovable, to the confines of the patriarchy.

The illusion signified by the veil underscores the play's deceptively seductive ending, the disparity between what Estrella appears to be and what she has become. For despite Estrella's seeming independence in rejecting Sancho's marriage proposal, she acts not for her own sake, but on the king's behalf. Planned by the monarch, Busto's murder by Sancho ensures that she will spurn the lover for having killed her brother. The king anticipates her reaction and, indeed, states that he has already married her to a Castillian prince. Estrella's forgiveness of Sancho at this point precipitates the kings' public confession, which, as Frank Casa (1987, 54) has ascertained, represents "not only his re-integration into the divine order of things, but also a ritual cleansing through which social order is re-established."

But what, then, of Estrella? Her integration into the Symbolic order is accomplished at the price of her very subjectivity, since in the end, deprived of desire, she is married to a man she has not met and whom she cannot love. Like Natilde, whose degendered corpse she has come to resemble, Estrella signifies the proscription of desire by law, by the Lacanian nom/non du père (Sullivan 1990, 48). As such, she exemplifies to the spectators not only what a woman cannot do (performance), but what a woman cannot be (text). I do not think it too extreme to suggest that seventeenth-century female spectators would recognize the proposal by both text and performance of an ideology inscribed by the concerns of the male dominant culture (Dolan 1988, 1).

The play's last scene offers the final confrontation of king, lover, and beloved. Estrella's assent when mandated by the king to marry Sancho ("Que se haga / vuestro gusto. Suya soy" [2998–99; "May your will be done. I am his"]) is rightly interpreted by the lover as an act of passive resistance; Sancho realizes that her acceptance lacks volition, and retracts his promise. Although Estrella's final words temporarily challenge the king's orders, she is still caught in the trap initially set by the king. No matter how she responds, she is sacrificed to the Symbolic order:

> *Estrella.*   Señor, no ha de ser mi esposo
> hombre que a mi hermano mata,
> aunque le quiero y le adoro.
>
> (3014–16)

> *Estrella.*   My lord, he who has murdered my brother
> will not be my husband,
> even though I love and adore him.

Yet despite the play's final interpellation of the female subject into the Symbolic order, the momentary ambiguities of the players' gaze allow us to perceive as well the play's ideological fissures. Because the moments of dramatic visual movement remain uncodified by semiological systems, they differentiate the performance from its dominant text by signalling where any potential subversive shifts in meaning may take place. In questioning cultural constructions, even for an instance, the female gaze in particular disrupts textual narrative coherence. While Estrella's anxiety to become an ego ideal—to be seen as pleasing to the Symbolic order—is manifest in her final rejection of Sancho and in her objectification as a pawn in the monarch's social reintegration (his own denial of desire), the female gaze in *La estrella de Sevilla* exposes the means through which dominant ideology is naturalized and circulated. As Freedman (1991, 142) well puts it,

[s]ince theater is always placing the living body's energies in tension with a constraining form, it is always recording the cost of entry into the symbolic. But by staging that form we displace it; we view from another angle the looks that inscribe us, and so look back.

Accordingly, as a critical act, star gazing asks for more than the passive acceptance of what Henry Sullivan (1990, 50) deems all too categorically "the [play's] submission to the primacy of the signifier." By refocusing our critical perspective on Estrella, rather than on the king—that is to say, by shifting from the male I/eye to the female eye/I, and from the play's stare at the audience to the players' visual exchanges—we become aware that the signifying gaze slips, as Lacan notes, from stage to stage. Once our own gaze readjusts, it calls into question the seamless relation of text to performance that supposedly engenders the ideal (male) spectator response. Finally, and most important, in replicating the play's disruptive female gaze, our critical eye reproduces its resistance to the tyranny of symbolic form.[9]

Notes

1. *Don Arias.* En el alcázar está / un bulto pendiente al viento. *Rey.* ¿Bulto dices? ¿Qué será? *Don Arias.* No será sin fundamento. *Rey.* Llega, llega, Arias, a ver / lo que es. *Don Arias.* Es mujer colgada. *Rey.* ¿Mujer dices? *Don Arias.* Es mujer. *Rey.* ¿Mujer? *Don Arias.* Y está ahorcada, / con que no lo viene a ser. (1229–38; *Don Arias.* There, at the palace is / a bulk hanging in the wind. *King.* Bulk, you say? What can it be? *Don Arias.* It must be there for a reason. *King.* Go, go, Arias, see / what it is. *Don Arias.* It's a hanged woman. *King.* A woman, you say? *Don Arias.* It's a woman. *King.* A woman? *Don Arias.* And she's hanged / so she's no longer one after all.) All translations are my own.

2. Tim Fitzpatrick (1990, 13) describes recent studies sponsored by the U.S. Army Human Engineering Laboratory that divide eye movements into fixation, the focus on a specific element of the visual scene; and saccade, the movement of the point of regard to select a visual target upon which the eye will then focus. Fitzpatrick's interest lies mainly in the spectator's visual scanpath and how plays are structured audiovisually to attract, hold, and direct the audience's visual attention. His remarks on potentially expressive features, however, confirm that spectators are likely to assign interpretation even if none inheres: "Faces, hands, objects (particularly moving ones) all attract attention both for obvious perceptual reasons but also due to cognitive expectancies that they will be rich in information. Scanning is thus seen to be largely interpretation- and hypothesis-driven."

3. See Elam (1980, 19 ff.). Although indicated by dialogue or in the stage directions, a look or gaze toward or away from an object does not carry sign value. Elam (1980, 187) relegates it to a "channel function," through which "characters operate (acoustic or visual), together with physical, psychological, emotional and ideational states expressed by the speaker, references entailing movements, etc."

4. While Elam (1980, 38) does not suggest that there is only one message to each performance, its univocality is ensured in that, following Abraham Moles, he believes that the performance's multiple messages are synthesized and interpreted as an integrated text by the spectator.

5. De Marinis's (1984; 1986) relativist approach to spectacle/spectator relations allows for difference in what he calls spectator psychophysiological disposition, which, while it includes attention and interest controlled in part by the play's performance, does not directly address gender difference.

6. Feminist theater and film criticism has increased considerably over recent years; early studies of English Renaissance theater include Carolyn Ruth Swift Lenz et al. (1980) and Lisa Jardine (1983). Feminist studies of Spanish Golden Age plays begin with Melveena McKendrick (1974). Film studies include Laura Mulvey (1975; 1989), Teresa de Lauretis (1983), and Kaja Silverman (1983).

7. In assigning the *comedia* to the Symbolic order, I do not advocate a deterministic reading, but mean that its social force is ultimately conservative. Traditional criticism has thus overlooked the *comedia*'s contradictions to focus on its ideological function. See especially José Antonio Maravall (1981) and José María Díez Borque (1978).

8. Frank P. Casa (1987) has addressed the issue from the perspective of the king's "two bodies."

9. I am most grateful to the UC-Irvine Organized Research Initiative on Woman and the Image for research funding.

9

Madness as Philosophical Insight

Daniel L. Heiple

THE short mad scene in act 3 of *La estrella de Sevilla* was severely criticized by early critics. Menéndez y Pelayo (1949, 174) claimed it was further evidence the play had been ruined by Claramonte: "la [escena] del delirio de Sancho Ortiz, tan insulsa, tan fría, tan desatinadamente escrita, tiene . . . que ser de aquel adocenado plagiario" ("the scene of the delirium of Sancho Ortiz, so insipidly, so coldly, so crazily written, has . . . to be by that inept plagiarist.") In evaluating this criticism, one must remember that he had only the much butchered *suelta* version on which to base his impressions of the play. Even though the much fuller version had been published by Foulché-Delbosc, other early critics, searching for the identity of the author of *La estrella,* tended to agree with Menéndez y Pelayo's conclusion. Leavitt called the scene "confused, jumbled and aimless" (1931, 15). In a long article, Spitzer (1934) came to a defense of the mad scene, arguing for its structural coherence. He cited the other passages in which characters nearly lose their minds and showed the relevance of this scene to the action of the play.

Later critics have viewed the mad scene more favorably. William McCrary (1971, 511) saw the split personality of Sancho as a perfect example of the inner struggle the character faces:

Perhaps nowhere in the play is the *sparagmos* more vividly imitated than in the much debated mad scene. The spectator witnesses a splitting apart of the *entendimiento* [understanding] from the *fantasía* [fantasy]. For a while the two faculties discourse with one another . . . about the origins of the *sparagmos* itself—*ambición* [ambition] and *soberbia* [pride]. Cause . . . and effect . . . meet in a schizoid dialogue that recapitulates the entire course of the action. No more brilliant and shattering representation of the paroxysm of alienation can be imag-

ined. The mad scene . . . is a virtual lens which dramatically magnifies
the central essence of the action allegorically.

In a very innovative study, James Burke (1974) relates Sancho's
madness to the medical ideas concerning melancholy in the period,
regarding his madness as the result of adust melancholy, which
results from the burning of the choleric humor. This form of madness was considered the gravest and most dangerous. He argues
that melancholic purification resulted from the influence of Saturn,
the melancholic planet that dominates the action of the play and
is the planet represented by Estrella. He concludes that the mad
scene is thematically related to the planetary influences and humors whose imagery dominates the play.

Sara and Harlan Sturm (1970, 290) find the scene to be thematically relevant to the action of the play:

> This "mad scene" . . . represents the low point in the fortunes of both
> Sancho's. The presentation of the delirium, far from being a defect in
> the play as some critics have suggested, is, as Brooks notes, "symbolic
> interpretation of what has gone before", pointing up the differences
> between Sancho's concept of honor and that represented by the King.
> It is also the key to the dramatic identity-relationship of the two
> characters.

These quotations, along with others that could be cited, show that
this scene has been treated more sympathetically since it was restored to full integrity.

Several recent studies of madness in Golden Age literature have
the objective of identifying the signs that represent the discourse
of the mad in literature (Valesio 1971; García-Varela). This is an
important element in the study of madness in literature, especially
in the theater where brevity requires that the madness be immediately apparent to the audience. Various signs of alienation and
melancholy and various associations based on humoral sciences
provide clues to this semiotic of the discourse of madness. In her
recent book *Melancholy and the Secular Mind in Spanish Golden
Age Literature,* Teresa Soufas has gone beyond the study of the
signs indicating madness to study how melancholy was not only a
mental alienation, but also a sign of intellectual alienation from
society, providing the perfect vehicle in a closed society, like that
of Golden Age Spain, for the veiled criticism of society's values
and norms.

A further development occurs with the study *Folly and Insanity
in Renaissance Literature* by Ernesto Grassi and Maristella Lorch.

In this monograph, the authors look to writings on folly, such as Ficino's praise of divine furor and Erasmus's *Praise of Folly,* as the profoundest contributions of the Renaissance to philosophical discourse. The authors argue from the beginning that folly, not reason, is the element that is unique to human intelligence, even maintaining that folly, not reason, distinguishes human mentality from that of animals. They argue that we can observe that animals use elementary reason to solve various problems, a type of mental activity that goes beyond the simple instincts attributed to them by ancient and medieval scholastic philosophers. Folly, the ability to assume an ironic or contradictory stance when faced with a problem, is available only to human intelligence. Folly implies a consciousness of existence (which, it would seem, animals do not have, or at least cannot express). It is the ability to express consciousness of existence and to understand existence in contradictory and paradoxical terms that are elements unique to human intelligence. The Golden Age expression, "el mundo al revés" ("the world topsy-turvy"), conveys the sense of irony that only human intelligence can understand through consciousness of existence (Grant 1972; Lafond 1979). From the study of the signs of mad discourse we have been led to the study of madness as a sign of one of the most characteristic forms of human expression, the sense of irony and paradox, the reversal of our understanding of events and existence.

Madness flourished as a motif in Renaissance literature. Its expression usually served one of two seemingly contradictory ends: either the criticism of society, the idea first expressed in Sebastian Brant's *Ship of Fools,* that all of society suffers from some form of madness, or conversely the idea that the mad have a gifted understanding and are the only ones with access to truth and prophetic vision. The first idea, that the world is insane, supported by the saying attributed to King Solomon that the number of fools is infinite, produced satires of the foibles and defects of society and social conventions. The tone of the criticism could range from that of religious tracts railing against sinners to the reflective or satirical essay on the eccentricities of human activity. The second idea, that the mad are wise and gifted seers, is supported by the Platonic ideas of divine furor and the Pauline claim that the blessed are fools in the eyes of the world. Both ideas flourished in Renaissance literature.

Erasmus's *Praise of Folly* attempts to combine both traditions. Folly is praised as a necessary ingredient to the insanity of the world. Folly provides the masks with which people hide the truths that cannot be faced. Erasmus asks, "Who would be so foolish as to unmask the actors and expose that everything was a farce? . . . would he not ruin the play? And would everyone not think he deserved to be chased out of the theater with brickbats as a madman?" (1964, 118–19). We all contribute to the play and pretenses with which social convention is maintained. Erasmus also praises Folly itself as a superior form of understanding, both religiously and philosophically.

It is, of course, the mad who provide the ability to reverse our understanding of society's pretenses. The type of humor practiced by court jesters in the houses of powerful nobles provides a type of unmasking of the courtiers and their pretenses. Madness is a privilege, not a formal *hidalguía* (title of nobility), but a position carved out and maintained by undercutting the social pretensions of courtiers—a satirical or ironical humor that can be maintained only at the expense of continually pleasing the prince and undoing and angering the people who surround him. Much of the humor concerning madness is precisely this type of social commentary, in which the mad person speaks the truth that the rest of society must conceal in order to maintain the pretenses of order and civility (Márquez Villanueva 1985).

As the Renaissance collections of jokes and the humor of *graciosos* (comics) in the *comedia* and the wit of the madman in Cervantes's *El licenciado Vidriera* (*The Glass Magistrate*) clearly demonstrate, this irony could verge on cruelty. A number of proverbs from the period warned against the mad: "Allegándose el loco, finge negocio" ("If the madman approaches, pretend to be busy"; Martínez Kleiser 1978, 37.153), and "Al loco y al toro, déjales el coso" ("Leave the madman and the bull the whole street"; 1978, 37.159). Even though the dangers of the mad, who could of course be violent, were compared to those of the bull, one suspects that the dangers were more than physical. One element that seems common to the representation of madness is the case in which a questioner tries to provoke a mad person. In some of the popular jokes of the period the questioner puts him or herself in the position of being criticized, such as the *hidalgo* (squire) from Segovia who visited an insane asylum, only to be recognized by one of the inmates who reported to him and his friends that the *hidalgo*'s family was of *converso* (Jewish) origin, but he need not worry since he was probably illegitimate anyway (Arguijo 4v, 27). Or the sinner who, making fun of a madman, asked who were the most insane people in the world and was told: "Los que creen que hai premio de pena i gloria en la otra vida, i de contino andan embueltos en el pecado, como vos" ("Those who believe there is a reward of suffering and glory in the afterlife, and are continually involved in sin, like you"; Mondragón 1953, 165–66). In a number of examples in Cervantes's *El licenciado Vidriera* the questioner tries to establish a pact with the madman, which always provokes the mad Vidriera to insult his questioner. In these jokes the desire for entertainment backfires and the inquisitive audience becomes the uncomfortable butt of the joke, a situation that takes its justification from the fact the spectator seemed to invite and provoke a response.

The mad Vidriera not only criticizes falseness, but he also rebukes those who are pretentious enough to feel themselves above criticism. The least hint of this in a questioner brings a sharp retort. The acquaintance who dressed as a *licenciado* (magistrate) without having the degree is a good example because he tries to get Vidriera to go along with his pretense, but the madman does not compromise his ideals of truth and doubly wounds, first for the pretentiousness itself and second for the attempt to gain approval for his deception:

A lo cual dijo el amigo: —Tratémonos bien, señor Vidriera, pues ya sabéis vos que soy hombre de altas y de profundas letras. Respondióle Vidriera: —Ya yo sé que sois un Tántalo en ellas, porque se os van, por altas, y no las alcanzáis, de profundas. (1962, 2. 59–60)

To which his friend said: "Let's treat each other nicely, Mr. Glass, since you know I am a man of high and profound learning." Glass answered: "I know you are a real Tantalus in it, since it passes you over because of its height, and you don't get it because of its depth."

Others who try to curry favor receive similar putdowns. A mule boy, assuming himself above criticism, took the liberty of insulting the madman in asking his question:

De nosotros, señor Redoma, poco o nada hay que decir, porque somos gente de bien, y necesaria en la república. (1962, 2. 53)

There's very little or nothing to say about us, Mr. Flask, because we are good people and necessary for the republic.

This provokes a long discourse on the evils of the boy's profession, which serves to rebuke his pretensions. Vidriera attacks pretentiousness by direct insult, saving the strongest insults for those who claim to be above criticism. This situation of course plays on the old question of whether the mad person is more sane than the sane one. The pretentious who feel they have nothing to lose are humbled and proved wrong, and it is the madman who delivers this truth. For a moment they change roles, the sane having proved themselves to be mad in their pursuits and the fool stating the truth with a cutting sharpness that is well deserved. This reversal of roles is precisely what Cervantes was trying to achieve in order to censure the world and praise folly. When Vidriera comments on the learning, "las letras" ("the learning"), of the false licentiate: "sois un Tántalo en ellas, porque se os van, por altas, y no las alcanzáis, de profundas" ("you are a real Tantalus in it, because it passes you by, because of its height, and you don't get it, because of its depth"; 1962, 2. 59–60), there, crystallized in one situation is a double paradox: the worldly fool presuming to be what he is not and the real fool speaking with the keenness of a seventeenth-century wit.

The mad scene in *La estrella* is short and almost mechanical, and it consists mainly of social criticism. Rather than apologize for the humor of the scene, I would argue that it is necessary as an element of comic relief. Coming after Estrellas's attempt to liberate Sancho from prison and preceding King Sancho's psychological defeat, the intrusion of humor is necessary to keep the audience from laughing at the serious pathos presented in the play. During the mad scene, Sancho Ortiz has a brief flight of fancy, a journey to hell that consists mainly of satirical commentaries on various social stations in Golden Age life, the very same commentaries, as Leavitt pointed out, that one can find in Quevedo's and other writers' satires. The idea of Hell as the antithesis of reason, the real world in reverse, lies at the basis of these satirical sketches. The difference is that in *La estrella,* as in Cervantes's *El licenciado Vidriera,* the roles of the sane and the mad are reversed. Sancho, who has followed a path of loyalty and service to his monarch, is imprisoned and condemned to death. The king, the real culprit, who has been ruled by his passions and ordered the unjust death of a subject, is free and above punishment. This situation represents the reversal of reason in its system of rewards and punishments.

Cases of real madness in Golden Age *comedia* often arise from an insoluble dilemma. A character is faced with an impossible situation and is driven to madness. Such is the case of the protagonist in Lope's *La locura por la honra (Madness because of Honor)*, who loses his sanity because he cannot avenge himself by killing the royal personage who seduced his wife. In other words, madness often arises from a personal crisis motivated by social situations, the failure of established society to incorporate the individual. In *La estrella de Sevilla* the madness results from the collision of two powerful social codes that dominated seventeenth-century thought: the divine right of kings and the idea of individual rights encapsulated in personal honor. The divine right of kings, represented by Sancho's transgressions of his subjects' rights to virtue, is maintained by the power vested in the monarchy, the same power that renders Sancho Ortiz helpless and produces the dilemma that results in his madness. As in other plays, madness is an individual response to social codes that place the individual in insoluble situations.

During the first two decades of the seventeenth century, the period of the corrupt and powerful ministers of Philip III, the playwrights had idealized an alliance between the monarchy and the lower classes to curb the excesses and abuses of the nearly unlimited powers of the nobility. Such plays as Lope's *El mejor alcalde el rey, Peribañez,* and *Fuenteovejuna* seem to propose a new and curious alliance of a monarchy that was not interested in power with the disenfranchised lower classes who had very few rights and nearly no power. But the idea of a revitalized monarchy and a newly empowered lower class held great attraction during reign of Philip III.

In the 1620s and 1630's this message disappears as the problems of a philandering monarch come to dominate political plays such as Lope's *El castigo sin venganza (Punishment without Revenge)* and the anonymous *La estrella de Sevilla.* The dramatization of the problematics of royal licentiousness seems to arise from the character of Philip IV, especially in his early years. Apparently encouraged by the Conde-Duque de Olivares as a strategy to divert the king's interests from governmental affairs, the young Philip devoted a great deal of time to amorous pursuits. The Convent of the Royal Conception was founded on the sight of the house of the first noble mistress to bear him a child (which gives a new twist to name Real Concepción). All of the French travelers present anecdotes with details very similar to the situation in *La estrella de Sevilla.* All three may in fact be versions of the same anecdote, which may be false or may be adapted from the play itself. In all three stories, the king has bestowed many honors on the woman's guardian as means to corrupt him with appointments that keep him away from home. The king is accompanied on his nocturnal visit by his minister, and he is surprised by the return of the guardian who lectures him and allows him to escape because the presence of the king is revealed and the guardian had suspected the king in the first place. In all three accounts, the king was injured in the scuffle. While it is impossible to determine whether these anecdotes are elaborated from the plot of *La estrella,* or the plot is molded from events such as these, the fact remains that the new king pursued respectable women illicitly at night, and both the anecdotes and the play are logical extensions of possible confrontations. A number of political plays of the early part of the reign of Philip IV criticize the monarch and, in the case of *La estrella de Sevilla,* place restrictions and responsibilities on the king in view of the rights of the nobility.

Sancho's mad scene incorporates elements from both traditions of Renaissance madness. It begins by satirizing the professionals, referring to "más de mil sastres mintiendo" (2405; "more than a thousand tailors lying" and "una legión de cocheros" (2413; "and a legion of coachmen"), to which Sancho replies: "Si andan coches por acá, / destruirán el infierno" (2414–15; "If there are coaches here, they will ruin Hell"). They pass to the satire of lawyers. Sancho asks: "Pero si el infierno es, / ¿cómo escribanos no vemos?". ("but if this is Hell, why don't we see notaries") and Clarindo answers: "No los quieren recebir / por que acá no inventen pleitos" (2416–19; "They do not want to admit them to prevent them from bringing law suits"), and they pass to visionary scenes of gamblers, *malcasados* (unhappy spouses), fops, writers, and other elements common to seventeenth-century satires, as Leavitt pointed out. The difference in this play concerns the characters who announce the satire: one is said to be mad and the other is playing along with him. As in many jokes on madness and in *El licenciado Vidriera,* satire becomes the truth spoken by the mad person. Like the court jester, the mad person is free to unmask the pretensions of those whose commitments to society and pretense prevent them from admitting their flaws. The idea of falsehood and deceit dominate the images: such as the "mil sastres mintiendo" ("a thousand tailors lying") and the vision of Virgil whose tongue has been cut out by Dido "en premio / del testimonio y mentira / que le levantó" (2453–45; "in payment for the testimony and lies he brought against her"). The idea of madness as revelation of truth, either through satire or through the penetrating visions of the mad, is integrated into one scene in which a madman and his servant present satirical observations as the penetrating insights of the mad.

Various aspects of the imaginary hell visited by Sancho and Clarindo deserve commentary. The first concerns its manner of presentation, which is completely portrayed through description in the dialogue. Typically, one of the characters asks what an object is (incidentally describing it in the process) and the other answers. This was most probably performed on a stage without props, especially since it is a purely imaginary setting whose existence in the minds of the characters is transferred to the imaginations of the audience. It is important to note, however, that the staging of this scene differs in no substantial way from other scenes in the play that are either narrative, such as the descriptions early in the play of the ladies on the balconies, or the scenes in Busto Tavera's house in which the audience would need to imagine various parts of the stage as entranceway, hallways leading to various rooms, and so on. The descriptions of the ladies on the balconies provide a very direct comparison, the main difference being that the king and Arias state they saw the figures on the balconies, while in the mad scene only Sancho Ortiz is supposed to see the apparitions and Clarindo pretends to see them. Both scenes, however, correspond in structure in that one character describes and questions and the other identifies, whether it is the king asking Arias to name the women he saw standing on the balconies or Sancho and Clarindo exchanging visions of hell. Both scenes are dramatized as poetic descriptions of figures and actions that are not visually represented to the audience.

One element of the hell visited by Sancho and Clarindo that has barely been commented on are the allegorical figures that populate it. In addition to the satirical figures, the tailors, writers, and lawyers that appear in this hell, Sancho reports seeing "la Soberbia . . . ardiendo" (2407; "Pride . . . burning"), "la Ambición / tragando abismos de fuego" (2411; "Ambition swallowing chasms of fire"), and Clarindo describes "la necesidad, haciendo cara de hereje" (2441–42; "necessity looking like a heretic"). Finally Clarindo reports seeing "el tirano Honor, / cargado de muchos necios / que por la honra padecen" (2474–76; "the tyrant Honor, carrying many fools who suffer for honor"). These figures clearly belong to the characters in the play. Soberbia and Ambición characterize Sancho el Bravo, whose ambition will, as is stated so many times in the play, make him ruler in Castile and Seville; through pride, he must add Estrella to his conquests. Necesidad and Honor belong to Sancho Ortiz, who is constrained in prison waiting to die because he honorably held to his word to kill his best friend. He himself, as McCrary and the Sturms point out, recognizes his place with the "muchos necios / que por la honra padecen" (2476–77; "the many fools who suffer because of honor") and his personality splits as he dialogues with himself, assuming the roles of both Honor and his own chastised self. These allegorical characters carry the presentation of madness beyond the simple satirical vignettes that often are associated with this scene. The allegories allow for a direct moral commentary on the action of the play without resolving any of the problems. In addition to the satirical figures associated with hell in the seventeenth century and the funny lines about how coaches and lawyers would just ruin the place, the allegorical figures return the discourse to the central themes of the play.

One final aspect of the mad scene that needs commentary is the way in which the scene is unraveled by the beginning and ending comments. Sancho says he will suffer the punishment ordered by law and the confusion ordered by heaven:

> Consiento
> que me castiguen los hombres
> y que me confunda el cielo.
> Y ya, Clarindo, comienza.
> ¿No oyes un confuso estruendo?
>
>   (2363–67)

> I will allow
> men to punish me
> and heaven to confound me.
> And now, Clarindo, it is beginning.
> Don't you hear a confused roar?

The fact that the character is conscious of the altered state that is about to overtake him seems to make it less a real mad scene than a tour de force of the imagination. At the end of the scene, Clarindo adds another touch of unreality when he says, rather illogically, that he must stop Sancho or his master will lose his mind:

> ¡Válgame Dios!
> Si más proseguir le dejo,
> ha de perder el juicio.
> Inventar un enredo quiero.
>
>   (2503–5)

> God help me!
> If I let him go on,
> he will lose his mind.
> I need to invent a trap.

Sancho's consciousness of the approaching confusion of his mind and Clarindo's admission that he must stop the madness or Sancho will lose his mind seem to indicate that the scene before us is somehow less than a real mad scene.

Madness and the infernal vision it presents serve as an sign for the very disturbed world portrayed in *La estrella de Sevilla*. The satirical traditions of madness in which the world is mad and the mad are the only vessels capable of speaking the truth come to represent the topsy-turvy situations in the play. Sancho's situation really is an example of the world-values reversed. As the central allegory of the mad scene makes clear, he has been forced, by doing the right thing, to destroy his best friend, as well as his and Estrella's chances of happiness and integration into society; the loyal and virtuous are punished and the guilty go free. The paradox could not be greater, and the mad scene, with its comic relief and deeply inscribed traditions of the world gone mad and of the mad-person as someone with privileged access to an ironic and para-doxical, but perhaps more logically correct, interpretation of the world, represents more fully the paradoxes of the human under-standing of existence.

10

Of Material Girls and Celestial Women, or, Honor and Exchange

JAMES MANDRELL

At the end of Leandro Fernández de Moratín's *El sí de las niñas* (*The Girls' Consent*), which premiered in Madrid in 1806, Don Diego remarks as to the confusion resulting from the attempt to marry a young woman to an old man without taking into account the question of love. This confusion, Don Diego claims, "resulta del abuso de autoridad, de la opresión que la juventud padece; éstas son las seguridades que dan los padres y los tutores, y esto lo que se debe fiar en el sí de las niñas" (283; "results from the abuse of authority, from the oppression from which the young suffer; these are the measures taken by parents and guardians, and the trust that ought to be placed in the girls' consent [literally: in the girls' right to say yes]"). With the aging Don Diego's realization of the folly of his plans to wed the nubile Doña Francisca, Moratín makes a not so subtle point relating to the rights of individuals in society, particularly women. At the same time, he advocates an equilibrium between the interests of parents and families in a child's betrothal and the desires of the parties directly involved in making the marriage vows. In so doing, Moratín's play both reflects the world to which it refers and seeks to shape that world, to advance a specific idea with respect to social progress, of which a woman's right to negotiate matrimony, to say yes—or no—is an integral part. Yet, as the play makes clear, there is a way to go before the concept of love is so universally accepted as to be self-evident and unquestioned, and this is the case well into the twentieth century. We could say that *El sí de las niñas* mirrors social concerns pertinent to the late-eighteenth and the early-nineteenth centuries and that, in ideological terms, it advances a cautious polemic regarding love and marriage.[1]

My purpose in beginning with reference to *El sí de las niñas* is to suggest the ongoing significance of matrimony to the social questions confronting Spain and then to make a leap by claiming that the Spanish *comedia* of the Golden Age is no different from other literary texts. It is both reflective *and* implicated in the shaping of what we might loosely refer to as reality or the real world, which is to say that, in Aristotelian terms, the *comedia* is not merely an imitation of the actions of men, but also a powerful determinant of those very actions. In this light, most texts can be read as a confrontation between old and new, can be seen to mark a boundary between the present and one version of the future.

Anthony Cascardi makes this argument quite cogently in terms of Tirso de Molina's *El burlador de Sevilla* and its relationship to the modern or the modern world. According to Cascardi, *El burlador de Sevilla* evidences a somewhat contradictory ideological aesthetic in its generic confrontation between the old and the new, which has to do with

> on the one hand, a culture in which interpersonal relationships are determined by kinship ties and by bloodlines, in which actions are evaluated according to an archaic heroic ethos, and in which social functions and roles are sedimented into near static hierarchies; on the other hand, a culture in which the categories that determine personal worth are based largely on standards of possessive individualism . . . in which the central cultural myths are those of personal and social progress (the latter to be achieved largely through the technological domination of nature and through the medium of free economic exchange) . . . (1988, 152–53)

For Cascardi, the result of the tension between the traditional and the modern is a drama in which there is a simultaneous acceptance and repudiation of the new. Thus, concludes Cascardi, "the psychological mobility of Don Juan, which is perceived as a threat to the ethical foundations of society, is overcome once it is discovered that within it lies an extreme concern for honor, the very basis of self-consciousness in a 'traditional' world" (1988, 155–56). In this light, *El burlador de Sevilla* articulates a moment at which traditional notions of value, in relation to individual worth as it translates into honor, are being replaced by what Cascardi refers to as "free circulation" (1988, 162). The value of women remains constant even as the nature of the *meaning* of that value alters in conjunction with the shift from the kinship structures characteristic of feudalism to the (bourgeois) family associated with capitalism. In other words and as seen in this culture, women are of value even as the understanding of their worth and use changes to adapt to a new sense of the economy of exchange; the value of women is paramount even as there occurs a shift in the meaning that is attached to that value and in its expression.

So what has all of this to do with *La estrella de Sevilla,* or even more acutely with material girls and celestial women? In what follows, I will propose a reading of *La estrella de Sevilla* that is at once less and more radical than it appears to be, *less* radical in that it presumes that the *comedia* is about its eponymous heroine, that the protagonist of the play is indeed the Estrella of the title and not King Sancho, and *more* radical in that it considers the question of women in terms of the economies of honor and exchange, which might be one and the same thing. Ultimately, I believe it is possible to read this drama as a confrontation between old and new such that we find two types of women portrayed—to wit, the material girl and the celestial woman of my title—and that these are necessarily related to the topics of honor and exchange as they are characteristic of the Golden Age and are adumbrated in *La estrella de Sevilla.*

> *Boys may come and boys may go*
> *And that's all right you see*
> *Experience has made me rich*
> *And now they're after me*

Before beginning with the more radical aspects of my argument, I should like to suggest why the less radical notion of Estrella's role as protagonist is so crucial. Even a cursory examination of the secondary literature relating to *La estrella de Sevilla* will prove that "Sancho," either in his guise as King Sancho IV or as the two Sanchos, has displaced Estrella as the putative subject of the *comedia.* Harlan H. Sturm and Sara G. Sturm speak first of Estrella's "symbolic role" as the light leading to recognition of a higher order, and they conclude that, in terms of astronomy, "the play's title, *La estrella de Sevilla,* has double significance, for Seville itself is a star which will guide the King. The play is in this sense about a king who must learn the true nature of monarchy from his subjects themselves" (1969, 194, 196). The ancillary nature of Estrella is next taken up by William C. McCrary, and it then becomes almost an article of faith. McCrary remarks:

> What is peculiar is that neither Busto, nor Sancho, nor Estrella can be regarded as the protagonist although one comes away from the play with the impression that their collective misfortune is central and that one of them should be designated the hero. . . . Estrella intervenes

periodically in all three acts but primarily as the object of masculine attention in one form or another. Compared to the male characters, she is more a contemplator and victim of the action than an agent of it. . . . If the play can be said to have a protagonist, then, it is the King. . . . He, and he alone, undergoes a vital and central dramatic change from one *stasis* to another. Busto, Sancho, and Estrella are subordinate to this evolution of the Monarch's role. (1971, 505–6)

Once Estrella becomes a celestial woman, the metaphorical light that leads to truth, she ceases to bear any meaning as one of the female characters in the drama. I would go so far as to suggest that *La estrella de Sevilla* becomes, in this type of reading, an enactment of male fantasies of empowerment as one critic after another becomes "kingly" in his attempt to marry Estrella to one figure or another in the *comedia* itself (by seeing her as part of a sociobiological or semiotic dyad) or one interpretation or another.[2] In this way, Estrella becomes almost incidental as a character, permitting James F. Burke to conclude that "*La estrella de Sevilla,* then, shows us a moral awakening on the part of the King and Sancho Ortiz and perhaps for Estrella also if she is inspired to seek a religious vocation" (1974, 156)—if, in other words, she links her star and her future to God the father.[3]

These critics are, to be sure, merely following the lead of the text itself. Throughout the drama women are described in terms of astronomy and celestial metaphors, forcing them to become, in essence, longed for but unobtainable objects. For example, Estrella is, as McCrary notes, "the object of masculine attention in one form or another," and, as an object of desire, she is placed beyond the reach of the men who covet her, becoming like the stars. As a celestial woman, she becomes the quintessential floating signifier who is endowed (*dotar*) with—but does not bear her own—meaning. Typically, Estrella is paired with various male characters (or, in Burke's thinking, with God) who do or would like to confer upon her a particular role or symbolic value as, say, a sister, a lover, a wife; and it is through the substitution of the male characters in a pattern of "twinning" that Estrella serves to unify *La estrella de Sevilla,* the play to which she lends her name as its title even if she cannot claim to be its protagonist. In fact, Estrella is the only female character in the drama to be paired with a masculine other (indeed, she is the only character in the drama who figures in all of the mixed pairs), which should distinguish her as an individual. But, as Frederick de Armas points out in his most recent study of *La estrella de Sevilla,* and apropos of yet another set of twins in the drama, "Busto and Sancho Ortiz can also be seen as twins since the latter will soon substitute for the former through marriage with Busto's sister" (1994a, 21) all of which means that, as boys come and go, as she is "twinned" with one male character or another, Estrella exists as the necessary yet secondary element in an equation involving three terms: herself and two men, two families, a critic and one of the male characters in the text. Estrella is, then, always the projection of masculine desire and is always in service to that desire as she is continually joined with something else.

And yet, given that boys may come and boys may go and that Estrella has a brother, an admirer, and a future husband, what would happen if we were to restore to the celestial Estrella her materiality and individuality and if we were to take into consideration the equally material—and materialistic—Natilde? What does *La estrella de Sevilla* have to say about the ideation of woman in the Golden Age and questions of honor and exchange?

> *Some boys kiss me, some boys hug me*
> *I think they're o.k.*
> *If they don't give me proper credit*
> *I just walk away*

We begin to restore proper credit to Estrella—and to Natilde— by first leaving her practically to one side to consider *La estrella de Sevilla* as a drama about honor and exchange, since it is obvious that the question of "credit," in the sense of an exchange, is of paramount importance from the first scene on. As the king enters Seville, he acknowledges the city's significance to the consolidation of his power in the realm and he repays his subjects' investment in pomp and circumstance by reimbursing them for the reception as well as by deciding to situate his court there. Seville becomes, then, Madonna's material girl in the sense that she embraces the King in exchange for the credit she is due as an imperial city.

In fact, the plot of the *comedia* could be expressed simply in the language of honor as it relates to and is upheld by exchange. King Sancho enters Sevilla and essentially purchases its support. While entering the city he spies the beautiful Estrella whom he desires. In conversations with don Arias, the King decides that he can best obtain Estrella by entering into an exchange with her brother that appears to have to do with honor. As don Arias explains: "a su hermano honrar podrás. . . . Favorécele; que el dar, / deshacer y conquistar / puede imposibles mayores. / Si tú le das y él recibe, / se obliga; y si es obligado, / pagará lo que le has dado" (193–203; "You could honor her brother. . . . Favor him; for giving, undoing, and conquering can accomplish greater impossibilities. If you give [something] to him and he accepts [it], he will be obligated; and if he is obligated, he will pay for what you have given him").

King Sancho sets out on precisely this course of action and calls Busto to his side as he creates a virtually untenable situation for Estrella's brother when he claims that he, Sancho, will marry Estrella in his name "con el hombre que la merezca" (417, "with the man who merits her"), which contravenes the arrangements already made by Busto to give Estrella to Sancho Ortiz. If Busto assures Sancho Ortiz that the matter will be dealt with in his favor—since "están hechos los conciertos / y escrituras, serán ciertos / los contratos" (644–46; "the agreements and documents are completed, the contracts will be fulfilled")—there is nonetheless a serious problem, which is aggravated when the king attempts to enter the Taveras' home and to lie with Estrella. For King Sancho to enjoy Estrella's favors, he must somehow treat the Taveras' honor lightly. Yet, once he is caught making his way to Estrella's boudoir by Busto, he has been shamed by a subject and must restore his own honor, and he is shamed once again when Busto hangs the traitorous Natilde outside the king's palace. As Elias L. Rivers puts it:

> Coming into this community from the outside, King Sancho IV of Castile attempts to seduce Estrella but is repeatedly thwarted, and thus secretly shamed, by her brother, Busto. To shame a man is to accuse him of being without honor, to impugn his manhood. The skirmishes of honor between King Sancho and Busto are fascinating dramatic scenes in which formal courtesy cannot fully disguise the underlying sexual violence of two men fighting over a woman. (1983, 79).

This implicit shaming means that the king must seek retribution in Busto's death, which he finds by entering into another contract, this time with Sancho Ortiz.

La estrella de Sevilla reads, then, like a treatise on the nature of contractual obligation as it relates to personal honor. One who fulfills an obligation will be treated fairly. One who enters into a contractual relationship without possessing the means to do so will be dealt a harsh blow. As the *comedia* draws to a close, we witness the extent to which exchange is involved in what has transpired. Sancho's killing of Busto is presented as a gift of death (*dar muerte a uno*) in which the idea of exchange is embodied in the anaphoric use of *por* by don Arias in the probing questions he directs to the imprisoned murderer (2299–2307). Sancho Ortiz "gives" Busto the "gift of death" in exchange for everything mentioned by don Arias, for the supposedly friendly protection of the king and on his behalf, for the right to marry the woman of his choice with the king's blessing, and out of his sense of obligation as Sancho's subject. In return, the king gives Estrella her brother's killer and then admits his own culpability in Busto's death. In the latter instance, the admission is couched in the language of exchange. Don Arias urges the king: "Pague Sancho Ortiz: así / vuelves, gran señor, por él, / y ceñido de laurel, / premiado queda de ti" (2706–9; "Let Sancho Ortiz pay: you'll then return for him and, crowned with laurel, he'll be rewarded by you"). The drama ends when the king fulfills his remaining promises by marrying Estrella to a nobleman of the court only to submit to his obligation to Sancho Ortiz and to agree that Estrella should marry her brother's killer. In this way, King Sancho regains his honor as a ruler and Estrella and Sancho Ortiz maintain their personal honor.

> *Some boys try and some boys lie but*
> *I don't let them play (No way!)*
> *Only boys that save their pennies*
> *Make my rainy day*

It would probably be a good idea at this point to specify what is involved in my attempt to play the games of "exchange" and "honor."[4] By exchange, I refer to all forms of giving, be it the giving of a gift, where an exchange of one thing for another is presumably not to be found, be it an exchange in its more literal sense of a barter, trade, or purchase. This follows on Marcel Mauss' study of prestation, where he claims that something given entails an obligation, something to be given in return. The acceptance of a gift is a challenge to one's honor, a challenge to repay a debt; Mauss comments, "Food, women, children, possessions, charms, land, labour, services, religious offices, rank—everything is stuff to be given away and repaid. In perpetual interchange of what we may call spiritual matter, comprising men and things, these elements pass and repass between clans and individuals, ranks, sexes and generations" (1967, 11–12). In the economies of exchange in *La estrella de Sevilla,* things are indeed given in the expectation that something will be given in return, agreements are made—and broken—and all of these relate to the ways in which an individual's honor is enhanced or devalued.

King Sancho is more than aware of the implications of giving as a form of obligation and of the significance of honor. When don Gonzalo de Ulloa and Fernán Pérez de Medina each approaches Sancho to ask to be appointed the general of Archidona, the king wants to use this position not in the interests of the state or as an honor for a faithful subject, but first as a means of drawing Busto into his confidence and second to distance the brother from Estrella. In using the perquisites of his royal office in this way, Sancho demonstrates the economy of giving in which the granting of a privilege or favor inevitably occurs at the expense of another and, oftentimes, of another's honor, as Busto himself realizes: "Tanto favor. . . . / No puedo entender por qué. / Sospechoso voy: quererme, / y sin conocerme honrarme . . . / El rey quiere sobornarme / de algún mal que piensa hacerme" (439–44; "Such favor. . . . I can't understand why. I must be suspicious: to favor me, and without knowing me, to honor me . . . The king wants to buy me for some evil he's thinking of committing on me").

That king Sancho would seemingly honor Busto while plotting his dishonor indicates the extent to which honor is not an unambiguous notion in *La estrella de Sevilla*. Although honor indeed serves as a touchstone for much of the action and dialogue, Sancho Ortiz voices a highly cynical view of honor that not coincidentally has to do with money. As Sancho Ortiz crosses through the Inferno in his delirium, he spots "el tirano Honor, / cargado de muchos necios / que por la honra padecen" (2474–76; "That tyrant Honor, the burden of many fools, who suffer for honor"). He continues by observing that "el verdadero honor / consiste ya en no tenerlo" (2482–83; "true honor consists in not having it") and that "Dinero, amigo, buscad; que el honor es el dinero" (2486–87; "Seek out money, my friend; money is honor"). The equation of honor with money and of "true honor" with what is, in this formulation, the essence of poverty echoes one of the most succinct expressions of honor, which is to be found in Lope de Vega's *Los comendadores de Córdoba*(*The Commanders from Córdoba*).[5] Here Lope repeats the idea that honor "es una cosa / que no la tiene el hombre" ("is something that man doesn't possess"). Moreover,

> honra es aquella que consiste en otro;
> *ningún hombre es honrado por sí mismo,*
> *que del otro recibe la honra un hombre;*
> ser virtuoso hombre y tener méritos,
> no es ser honrado; pero *dar las causas*
> *para que* los que tratan *les den honra.*
> El que quita la gorra cuando pasa
> el amigo ó mayor, *le da la honra;*
> el que le da su lado, el que le asienta

el lugar mayor; de donde es cierto
que la honra está en otro y no en el mismo.
(290b-291a; emphases mine)

(Honor is that which inheres in others. *No man is honorable in and of himself; rather he receives it from others.* To be virtuous and meritorious is not to be honorable, but *to give others* with whom one deals *reason to give one honor.* He who removes his hat when passing a friend or an elder, *gives him honor,* as does he who seats him at his side or in the place of honor. From this it is plain that honor rests with others and not with oneself.)

Honor is otherness, something apart and distinct from the individual involved. Yet it is also subject to exchange: in Julian Pitt-Rivers's words, it is "entitlement to a certain treatment *in return*" (1966, 22).

It is also important to understand that there is always the sense if not the reality that contractual obligations and thus the reciprocal nature of honor are predicated on the illusion of a basis of egalitarian and free exchange, much as Marx ironically describes his "Eden of the innate rights of man" (1967, 1: 176). According to Marx, this illusory realm of free exchange is based on

Freedom, Equality, Property and Bentham. Freedom, because both buyer and seller of a commodity, say of labour-power, are constrained only by their own free will. They contract as free agents, and the agreement they come to, is but the form in which they give legal expression to their common will. Equality, because each enters into relation with the other, as with a simple owner of commodities, and they exchange equivalent for equivalent. Property, because each disposes only of what is his own. And Bentham, because each looks only to himself. The only force that brings each of them together and puts them in relation with each other, is the selfishness, the gain and the private interests of each. Each looks to himself only, and no one troubles himself about the rest, and just because they do so, do they all, in accordance with the pre-established harmony of things, or under the auspices of an all-shrewd providence, work together to their mutual advantage, for the common weal and in the interest of all. (1967, 1: 176)

The irony is to be found, of course, in the fact that exchange is not based on "free will." Rather individuals are constrained by their own resources and by the class restrictions that bring them together in a way that contradicts the very notion of an exchange of "equivalent for equivalent." Marx thus suggests what others have termed the notion of the "rational economic man" who lives in a world of "pre-established harmony." In conjunction with their critique of such so-called neoclassic economic theories, Martin J. Hollis and Edward J. Nell assert that, according to the neoclassicist, "the market place is not a battlefield but an orderly shopping centre where, even if the odd customer is short changed or the odd item shop-lifted, people in the long run get what they pay for and pay for what they get" (1975, 216). Nancy C. M. Hartsock explains, "Exchange is voluntarily engaged in, and therefore must be mutually profitable and nonexploitative. The argument about the mutual profit of interaction is closely linked to the assumption that all exchanges are voluntary and therefore must be engaged in for gain" (1983, 23).

Clearly, the notion of free exchange, what Cascardi calls "free circulation," is an illusion in *La estrella de Sevilla,* but it is operative as an illusion as various characters set out to make deals and to enter into obligations as if they were free to do so, as if they had saved their pennies. In the end, some boys try and some boys lie, but all subjects owe fealty to the king, who is in turn obligated to his subjects to uphold the law and to respond to the authority embodied in a ruler. Yet King Sancho, Busto (if mistrustfully), Natilde, Sancho Ortiz, and even Estrella embark on exchanges destined to bring about nothing but unhappiness and the frustration of those desires they sought to fulfill (with the possible exception, that is, of Estrella, who does obtain Sancho Ortiz's freedom).

So how do Estrella and Natilde fit into a reading of *La estrella de Sevilla* as a play about honor and exchange? Their role in this drama is twofold. On the one hand, each woman is viewed as an object of exchange. On the other, both women set out to enter into exchanges on their own, and this is where we find the confrontation between old and new to which I alluded earlier and to which I now turn.

> *They can beg and they can plead*
> *But they can't see the light (That's right!)*
> *'Cause the boy with the cold hard cash*
> *Is always Mister Right*

That women are objects of exchange in *La estrella de Sevilla* is so evident as almost to constitute a critical banality. Almost all of the male characters—to say nothing of critics of the drama—want to "see the light" but are constrained by their ability to negotiate successfully or to pay for the honor with cold hard cash. Moreover, the nature of women in general and of Estrella in particular as commodities is not merely a given, but is considered in terms of coinage. Exchange implies credit as well as a full economy driven by desire and acquisition and backed up by the guarantee of honor, an economy in which women are the coin of the realm. In the second scene of the first act, don Arias and King Sancho discuss the sights of the city, which include the "divinas bellezas" ("divine beauties") or women, in the language of money, where women are like currency and are liable to be exchanged among men (83–90). This is quite literally the case, as the king attempts to establish an implicit exchange with Busto for Estrella and then to marry Estrella to a man of his choosing, as the plans and agreements ("conciertos y escrituras") and contracts ("contratos") between Busto and Sancho Tavera and as Sancho Ortiz's agreement with the king all indicate. Even Sancho Ortiz asks the woman in question, Estrella, in a conflation of the celestial woman with the material girl who is owned, "Divino ángel mío, / ¿cuándo seré tu dueño?" (477–78; "My divine angel, when will I be your master [owner]").

Sancho Ortiz's is not an idle question. As a drama dealing with honor and exchange, *La estrella de Sevilla* is about the ways in which Estrella's exchange and exchange value will either augment or diminish the honor of the men involved in circulating her. For the King to acquire Estrella, he must impugn Busto's honor, as Busto naturally comprehends. When Sancho first attempts to enter the Taveras' home, he is rebuffed by Estrella's brother; and when Busto catches Sancho as he is about to enter Estrella's bedroom, he understands the situation in terms of the possible cost to Estrella's and to his reputation. With the two men at a standoff, Sancho attempts to wriggle free, and Busto to find a way to let the man he realizes is the king leave without revealing his identity. The King admits, "no es mi intención ofenderte, / sino aumentar más su honor" ("it is not my intention to offend you, but to increase your honor even more"). This strikes Busto as highly ironic; he remarks, "¡El honor así se aumenta!" ("Honor is increased thus!"), which prompts the King to threaten, "Corra tu honor por mi cuenta" (998–1007; "I shall bear the cost of your honor").

If women are a currency to be exchanged by men, then the gold standard, that which backs the value of women in an exchange, is honor itself. When the king goes to Busto's home under the cover of night to lie with Estrella, he presents the situation as if he were making a deposit in the account of Busto's honor. It is in the exchange of women, then, that men find and represent their own worth, since in controlling the circulation of women, in controlling their value, men can establish themselves in relation to one another.

Estrella is not, however, the only woman involved in this economy, the only woman to have a "dueño" ("master" or "owner"),
as the surprising case of Natilde makes plain. When don Arias
approaches Natilde to bribe her into allowing King Sancho to enter
Busto's home, we learn of yet another way in which women are
possessed by men (827–49). As a slave, Natilde belongs to a particular class of women who are quite literally owned by men. The
agreement into which she enters with don Arias grants Natilde her
freedom along with a generous amount of money in return for
which she will show the king to Estrella's bed. The terms of the
obligation of each party are clear, and, as the subsequent action
demonstrates, Natilde holds up her end of the bargain, as does the
king. When don Arias comments to the king with respect to what
has transpired, "Todos con el interés / son, señor, de un mismo
modo" (926–28; "When it comes to interest, sir, they're all just
alike"), he could, of course, be speaking of King Sancho himself.
As the King admits, "Recelo / que me vende el sol del cielo / en
la Estrella de Sevilla" (914–16; "I suspect that they're selling me
the sun in the sky in the Star of Seville"). As a consumer, then,
the king has purchased Estrella at the price of releasing Natilde
from slavery. Or, in another sense, Natilde has sold herself and her
assistance to the king in return for her freedom.

The problem with this exchange is that Natilde is technically
unable to dispose of herself or her labor. As a slave she is owned
by Busto, and, because she is his property, he and he alone controls
her exchange. This means that she is not free to enter into a barter
with others in which she is the object being bought or sold without
reflecting negatively on the honor of her master. In Marx's words,
Natilde and the king cannot "work together to their mutual advantage, for the common weal and in the interest of all" because neither is free as private individuals to initiate the type of agreement
they finally attempt to complete. In this regard, the king's intention
to compensate Busto by giving him another slave ("yo le daré
otra esclava / a Busto" [924–25]) is merely pathetic; it doubles the
exchange and opens yet another breach in the relationship between
the two men, since, as Busto notes, all of this takes place at the
expense of his honor ("¡A costa de mi honor!" [1155]), which, as
he admits, has also been sold by the slave girl: "Esta me vende,
que está / avergonzada y humilde" (1119–20; "She's selling me,
since she's ashamed and humble").

Natilde is, of course, in a much more lamentable predicament
than Estrella, at least for us as modern readers. But the respective
situations of the two women are really not so different, since it is

possible to understand them both as being caught up in a society and culture in which the exchange of women is central to the honor of men, which means that Mauss is only partially correct in his formulation of "prestation" and commodities. Claude Lévi-Strauss modifies Mauss's stance somewhat and claims that women are a special kind of commodity in culture, which can be identified as *patriarchal* culture: a "fundamental difference exists between the women who are exchanged and the goods and services which are also exchanged. Women are biological individuals, that is, natural products naturally procreated by other biological individuals. Goods and services on the other hand are manufactured objects" (1969, 23). But women are not of particular significance because they are "biological individuals . . . naturally procreated by other biological individuals," but, rather, because their primary function is that of procreation itself. Men, by controlling women, can control the functioning and ongoing stability of society. Moreover, the exchange of women is, for Lévi-Strauss, constitutive of the fundamental difference between nature and culture, since it operates in opposition to incest, in concert with the central tenet of civilization, the incest taboo (1969, 481).

La estrella de Sevilla can thus be read as a drama about the construction of social stability and the elaboration of individual honor by means of the licit exchange of women. Yet, in the case of Natilde, exchange violates the principle of ownership that is exemplified in the circulation of women; and in the king's nefarious attempt to possess Estrella we witness yet another exchange gone awry. This would suggest that *La estrella de Sevilla* is about the ways in which an economy of honor and exchange based on the control of women is liable to create social and political chaos, and not the stability theorized by Lévi-Strauss and others, when it is misunderstood and misused.

> *Some boys romance, some boys slow dance*
> *That's all right with me*
> *If they can't raise my interest then I*
> *Have to let them be*

Although Natilde's attempt at exchange is doomed to failure and death, Estrella herself appears to be much more adept at initiating and controlling those exchanges in which she is directly involved. In contrast to Natilde's eager demonstration of a misplaced self-interest, Estrella presents herself as the modest maiden subject to the will of the men who dispose of her being. When, for example, don Arias approaches her in her home on behalf of the King, telling her that Sancho "daráte villas, ciudades, / de quien serás rica hembra, / y te dará a un rico hombre / por esposo, con quien seas / corona de tus pasados / y aumento de tus Taveras" (805–10; "will give you towns, cities, in which you will be a wealthy woman, and he will give you a wealthy man as a husband, with whom you will be the crown of your ancestors and will increase the glory of the Taveras"), she turns her back to him, rejecting the offer, as she must if she is to be considered an honorable woman. Later, don Arias will seek to arrange the same type of exchange with Natilde, to whom he offers not a husband and riches beyond compare, but the much more humble—yet coveted—freedom. The result is much the same: at the drama's end, Estrella has not been physically possessed by King Sancho, but she nevertheless admits, "Que se haga / vuestro gusto. Suya soy" (2997–98; "Let your will be done. I'm yours") when he first says he has planned for her marriage to a grandee and then offers her to Sancho Ortiz. Although the King's sorry efforts at romance fail to raise Estrella's interest, she remains an object and an object of exchange who has passed from the hands of her brother to those of the man who brought about his death. Ultimately she succeeds only in saving Sancho Ortiz's life—no small feat—and in then denying him as a husband.

In fact, and in conclusion, the difference between Natilde and Estrella is to be found in their respective answers to the offer of some type of contractual obligation. Natilde answers in the affirmative, Estrella in the negative. What we find when we consider Estrella as a woman and not some transcendental signifier, as a material girl and not a celestial woman, is a character who is constrained by her social role as a woman to circulate in accordance with the needs of the men around her. When a woman like Natilde tries to liberate herself and to purchase her freedom, when she says yes to an offer made directly to her by a man, she finds the finality of death instead of the fulfillment of individuality. This would be the new woman, who struggles toward the opportunities of a world in which "free circulation" is the predominant manner of economic organization and in which women as well as men can enter into contractual relationships. But the world portrayed in *La estrella de Sevilla* is obviously not ready for a woman who acts as an agent of self-interest, since this would destabilize the code of honor and the social hierarchies on which male identity rest. Thus, Estrella can refuse those offers made directly to her, but she cannot escape from a culture in which she is such an important medium of exchange. If Moratín suggests the power that might be found in "el sí de las niñas" ("the girls' consent"), the author of *La estrella de Sevilla* convincingly asserts that, at this moment in Spanish society and culture at least, a "no" is as good as it gets.

Notes

1. The polemic might not have been so cautious. See Moratín's *advertencia,* added to the 1825 Paris publication of the drama, in which he speaks of the reception of *El sí de las niñas,* the première, and social progress (1982, 162). As regards the question of love in the eighteenth century, particularly as it pertains to women, see Carmen Martín Gaite (1987).

2. Recall that King Sancho tells Busto, "Daréla [a Estrella], Busto, marido / que a su igual no desmerezca. / Y decidle que he de ser / padrino y casamentero, / y *que dotarla quiero*" (419–23; "I will give Estrella, Busto, a husband of whose equal she would not be unworthy. And tell her that I will be her sponsor and matchmaker [literally: that I wish to endow her]").

3. In this regard see, too, Sara H. Sturm and Harlan G. Sturm (1970), the three studies of Frederick A. de Armas (1979, 1980, 1994a), and Jack Weiner (1981).

4. My argument at this point derives from that of Nancy C. M. Hartsock (1983), and it in fact parallels that in my study of Don Juan, in particular the discussions of honor in the second chapter (1992, 77–78) and of women in commodity exchange in the fourth chapter (1992, 252–59).

5. Donald R. Larson has an extended discussion of this *comedia* and the topic of honor (1977, 38–54). Melveena McKendrick, however, views the presentation of honor in *Los comendadores de Córdoba* with some skepticism (1984).

Part IV
Text, Authority, and Performance

11

The Authority of the Text

SUSAN L. FISCHER

ONE of the legacies of poststructuralist thought is that we can no longer view literature as reflecting life, but rather as operating on it; however much literature may seem to reflect life directly, it is perforce portraying it through the cultural system in which it functions, whether that means the historical period of production or the contemporary moment of recreation, reception, and contemplation.[1] With specific reference to "Shakespeare for the 1990s," Jean E. Howard questions the notion that a literary text "does or can have a determinate and unchanging meaning" (1986, 138), arguing instead that "contemporary response theory . . . can help us see that as a work is read in different times, its meaning *must* change, perhaps profoundly, since meaning is not *in* the text, but is created by the dynamic interaction between text and reader. Consequently, as readers change, so, inevitably, does textual meaning" (139). The reading process enables the individual reader to engage actively in the creation of meaning vis à vis his or her own historicity; texts and readers mutually exert pressure on one another:

> Acts of reading and interpretation are never simply unmediated discoveries of what is *in* the text. They are always, in part, creative acts in which specific readers, located firmly in history and possessed of particular reading conventions, confront the alien matter of a text and try to have it "make sense." In this confrontation the text is not passive. Texts are rhetorical objects shaped to guide our responses and to put pressure on our expectations . . . . Both empirical and theoretical studies of response suggest that readers and audiences are not simply black sheets upon which texts inscribe their meanings. As we read, we both discover *and* create. (Howard 143–44)

Theories of reading and interpretation which suggest that meaning arises from the interaction between the strategies of the text and

the strategies of the reader are thought to offer the most explana-
tory power, for neither functions as a negligible force. Wolfgang
Iser has proved to be one of the more moderate, less subjective of
the reader-response critics, insofar as his model takes into account
most fully the written—objective—text that imposes certain limits
on the reader's creative participation. Iser's phenomenological approach to the act of reading "lays full stress on the idea that, in
considering a literary work, one must take into account not only
the actual text but also, and in equal measure, the actions involved
in responding to that text" (1974, 274).

If we are willing to posit the "death of the author" of *La estrella
de Sevilla*—despite recent scholarly efforts to resurrect him in the
name of Claramonte[2]—we are left only with the playtext and its
multiple readers, both intratextual and extratextual. In this vein, I
should like to propose a series of intratextual readings—legitimate
interpretations and aberrant misunderstandings—performed by
three characters in the play (the two Sanchos and Busto Tavera),
thereby examining the way in which the reading process itself
might function as a textual strategy through which *La estrella*'s
subversive nature is perhaps made manifest. Reader response,
then, is intended to provide more than just a theoretical framework
for deciphering the operations governing the production of new
readings. *La estrella de Sevilla* becomes a forum for the simultaneous exposition and application of Iser's model of the text-reader
interaction.[3]

The problem at the play's outset involves King Sancho el Bravo's
lust for Estrella and his willingness to subscribe to the wrong-
headed advice of court favorite Arias to heap royal favor on Busto,
brother and protector of the desired woman, in the hope of obliging
him to assent to the monarch's desires. Busto's initial response to
the sudden offer of unexpected favor is one of confusion and tur-
moil, which he attempts to diffuse by contrasting his status with
that of a grandee who, unlike himself, is privileged to keep a hat
on in the presence of royalty (309–12). The king grasps Busto's
intention here: "¡Notable filosofía / de honor!" (313; "Remarkable
philosophy of honor"). But if initially his response is that of a
"competent" reader, Sancho el Bravo immediately loses sight of
the textual signals he has just deciphered, proclaiming Busto general of Archidora in any case (322). The contrast between "correct"
and "incorrect" decodings of information is heightened when
Busto, upon reading aloud the petitions of more deserving con-
tenders for the post, discovers the injustice of the king's action
and urges the application of reason and justice. The monarch's

retort reveals his growing uneasiness as he tries to suppress the voice of conscience—"Basta; que me avergonzáis / con vuestros buenos consejos" (397–98; "That's enough; you shame me with your good counsel")—to which Busto replies, "Son mis verdades espejos; / y así en ellas os miráis" (399–400; "My truths are mirror reflections in which you should see yourself").

If we view this first exchange between Busto and King Sancho in the light of Iser's model of reader response, we are presented with two disparate readings of the content of the petitions and, by extension, of political and social convention, expressed poetically by the juxtaposition "consejos / espejos." Iser maps out three domains for study: first, there is the text which, with its skeleton of "schematized views" that must be actualized or concretized by the reader, constitutes a potential for the production of meaning; secondly, there is the reader's processing of the text through the formation of mental images in order to construct a consistent and cohesive aesthetic object; and finally, there are the conditions that give rise to and govern the text-reader interaction, that is, the communicatory structure of the (literary) work.[4] The process of *Konkretisation,* according to Iser (1978), is steered by two main structural components in the text: first, a repertoire of familiar literary patterns and themes as well as allusions to familiar social, historical, and cultural norms; and secondly, strategies used to foreground the familiar elements against an unfamiliar backdrop or horizon. Through such techniques of defamiliarization or "negation," the function of the conventional aspects of the repertoire can be reassessed extratextually, in real life (61).[5] Literary texts in general, Iser argues, constitute a reaction to contemporary situations, targeting problems that are conditioned but not resolved by contemporary norms. Put another way, they are acts of communication whose function is to reformulate existing thought-systems in order to effect "the imaginary correction of deficient realities" (85).

Busto then, by challenging the king to examine his unorthodox behavior against the backdrop, or mirror reflection, of a subject's counsel, effectively calls into question many of the established social and political norms that dominated the first quarter of the seventeenth century. Of particular interest here is the system of *privanza* that became an accepted feature of national life following the death of Philip II, partly because, as J. H. Elliott (1963, 298) explains, his descendants were "men who lacked both the ability and the diligence to govern by themselves." This was especially the case during Philip III's reign (1598–1621), ruled as he was by the Duke of Lerma, whose "choice of confidants was uniformly disastrous" (299). That the defamiliarization of the social convention of the *privado* in *La estrella* was probably meant to be subversive becomes all the more apparent when Busto, having engaged in what Iser calls "incessant acts of ideation" (or formation of images in the mind), organizes the discrete segments of his audience with the king so as to construe a possible connection between them:

> (*Aparte.*)   Tanto favor. . . .
> No puedo entender por qué.
> Sospecho voy: quererme,
> y sin conocerme honrarme. . . .
> El rey quiere sobornarme
> de algún mal que piensa hacerme.
>
> (439–44)

[(*Aside.*) Such favor. . . . I can't understand why. I am suspicious: to desire me and without knowing me to honor me. . . . The king wants to bribe me for the evil he intends to do me.]

If Busto's synthesis enables him to see the king's behavior for what it is—an act of bribery—Sancho himself accurately discerns his subject's personal worth and integrity: "El hombre es bien entendido, / y tan cuerdo como honrado" (445–46; "The man is clued in and as wise as he is honorable"). It is again the *privado* Arias who sends the king off in the wrong direction, asking how many men actually remain honorable when the scale of royal privilege is tipped in their favor (447–64). Interestingly, Elliott (297) says the following about the failure of leadership during the time of Philip III: "Where the sixteenth century had produced innumerable 'mirrors' for princes, the seventeenth century devoted its attention to 'mirrors' for favourites, on the assumption that, since they could not be abolished, they might at least be improved." Busto, however, provides a negative, rather than a positive, mirror image of the *privado* for the king to see, which will be reduplicated in the figure of Sancho Ortiz, namesake and rival for the heart of Estrella.

It should be apparent by now that, as Elizabeth Freund (1987, 145) aptly puts it, there is no "immaculate perception"; rather, the meeting place of the objective, self-sufficient text (the artistic pole) and the subjective experience of an individual reader (the aesthetic pole) is based on an incomplete set of instructions—full of "gaps" or "blanks" or "indeterminacies"—that must be filled by the reader, according both to his or her disposition and to the perspectives offered by the text. Meaning is not directly accessible or even present either in the reader or in the textual object, but is something that arises in the process of interaction between the two. The reader is therefore free to fill in the gaps, but at the same time is constrained by the patterns supplied by the text; in short, "the text proposes or instructs, and the reader disposes, or constructs" (142). Since the gaps in a text can be filled in varying ways, every text is potentially capable of many different realizations. For no two readers, then, will the reading experience be the same; Iser's (1974, 282) analogy in this regard is stellar, particularly in the light of *La estrella de Sevilla:* "Two people gazing at the night sky may both be looking at the same collection of stars, but one will see the image of a plough, and the other will make out a dipper. The 'stars' in a literary text are fixed; the lines that join them are variable."

Sancho el Bravo's error is that, upon gazing on Estrella, he erroneously forms in his mind an image of the "sun" that he deems within reach:

> Encubierto pienso ver
> esta mujer en su casa,
> que es Sol, pues tanto me abrasa,
> aunque Estrella al parecer.
>
> (465–68)

[Clandestinely I intend to see this woman in her house; she is the Sun, for she sets me ablaze, although she is to all appearances only a Star.]

The king is bound to fail in this case because, in Iser's (1978, 167) terms, he will not cease "joining the lines" or "filling the blank exclusively with [his] own projections," rather than modifying his perceptions with data provided by objective reality. At this juncture, however, he knows that Estrella is already betrothed, but only because Arias (and not Busto) has told him so (165–66). Sancho Ortiz, when he hears Busto's reasons for feeling both sadness and happiness after his interview with the king, foregrounds the segment pertaining to sadness and anger ("el triste" and "enojo," 626, 629) and allows the happiness over his friend's appointment as general of Archidona to recede into the background. Ortiz, however, suspects that this "tyrant" of a king (665) will not sacrifice what he wants for what is right—"gusto" for "lo justo" (650, 647)—but will forever twist the law to suit his whims despite Estrella's pending marriage. Therefore, for Ortiz, the "laws of friendship"

(634–35) should prevail over one's obligations to the king, which is not what Busto implies when he says "el Rey es Rey; / callar y tener paciencia" (661–62; "The King is the King; be silent and have patience"). In creating a virtual text about the future behavior of the king, brother and lover have different views on how to join the unconnected segments; unfortunately, Ortiz's way of filling in the gaps turns out to be the more accurate.

Nevertheless, the moment Busto encounters the king about to enter his house, he makes Estrella's imminent marriage known to the royal visitor, saying what any man concerned about his honor "should":

> Dirán,
> puesto que al contrario sea,
> que venistes a mi casa
> por ver a mi hermana; y puesta
> en buena opinión su fama,
> está a pique de perderla;
> que el honor es cristal puro,
> que con un soplo se quiebra.
>
> (737–44)

[Even if the opposite is true, they will say that you have come to my house to see my sister; her untarnished reputation is on the verge of becoming damaged, for honor is like pure crystal in that it will shatter with only a single puff of air.]

If at first Busto has correctly deciphered the subtext of Sancho el Bravo's unexpected visit, he is soon made to lose sight of the overall textual scheme, for he is whisked away by the king while Arias bribes the slave Natilde with the promise of liberty in exchange for free access to Estrella that night. Natilde's frankness about the power of gold to engender vice and immorality mirrors Arias's candor about the corruptibility of men of honor when tempted by the system of *privanza*:

> Natilde.   ¿Por oro,
> qué monte tendrá firmeza?
> El oro ha sido en el mundo
> el que los males engendra,
> porque, si él faltara, es claro
> no hubiera infamias ni afrentas.
>
> (862–68)

[*Natilde*. What mountain will not be moved by gold? Gold has been that which engenders evil the world over, because, if it were lacking, iniquity and insults would clearly not exist.]

Arias.   Si honra en una balanza
              pone; en otra poner puedes
              tus favores y mercedes,
              tu lisonja y tu privanza;
              y verás, gran señor, cómo
              la que agora está baja
              viene a pesar una paja,
              y ella mil marcos de plomo.

                                        (457–64)

[*Arias*. If (Busto) places his honor on one scale, on the other you can place favors and rewards, flattery and privilege; and you will see, my Lord, how the one which is tipped from the weight comes to be as light as straw, and the other as heavy as a thousand marks of lead.]

Slave and royal favorite alike have a clear understanding of the false values underlying their social system; that they openly subscribe to those degenerate norms ultimately causes their validity to be called into question. By accepting the king's "aumento," Busto also has bought into the system of the privileged, even if against his better judgment. The difference is that initially Busto had been better able to scrutinize the determinate elements of the king's proposal and so make more judicious links among the units of "suspended connectability" (Iser, 1978, 198) in the political text before him. Now those good perceptions have receded temporarily into the background as he simultaneously moves toward the court with the status of gentleman-in-waiting—"Goce vuestra señoría / la llave y cámara" (869–70; "May your lordship enjoy your access to the royal chambers")—and away from his home to carouse with his companions.

Act 2 of *La estrella* shows the workings of Iser's (1978) concept of "wandering viewpoint," which he adopts from Husserl's discussion of temporality to refer to the "modified expectations" and "transformed memories" that inform the reading process. The wandering viewpoint "permits the reader to travel through the text . . . unfolding the multiplicity of interconnecting perspectives which are offset whenever there is a switch from one to another" (118). Every text is bound by a temporal sequence that involves an active interweaving of anticipation and retrospection; we are constantly evaluating and perceiving events with regard to our expectations for the future and against the background of the past. The process of recreation is one where "we look forward, we look back, we decide, we change our decisions, we formulate expectations, we are shocked by their non-fulfillment, we question, we muse, we accept, we reject" (1974, 288). An unexpected occurrence can therefore cause us to reformulate our expectations and to reinterpret the significance we have given to what has already occurred. This is precisely what happens to Busto when he returns unexpectedly at night and wanders into a face-to-face encounter with the king, who has entered his house "solo, embozado y sin gente" (1024; "alone and covered up") to deflower his sister.

Busto, first in pretending not to believe Sancho el Bravo's pretending to be the king (1022–40), and then in treating Sancho as through he were a man passing himself off as the king (1049–84), has radically modified his previous impressions of his sovereign, expressed earlier to Sancho Ortiz as follows: "el Rey es Rey; / callar y tener paciencia" (661–62; "The King is the King; be silent and have patience"). Contrary to all expectations, this king clearly has dared to offend a subject in so base a fashion (1029–30) and, moreover, by his behavior he has shown himself to be the opposite of "el Rey, mi señor, / del Africa horror y espanto, / . . . cristianísimo y santo" (1061–63; "the King, My Lord, horror and terror of Africa, a sainted Christian"). Such observations made to the king's muffled face are a step toward directing attention to flaws in the current thought system in the hope of bringing about its reformulation or, as Iser (1978, 85) puts it, "the imaginary correction of deficient realities." Busto expresses his righteous indignation thus:

> Y sin más atropellallos
> contra Dios y contra ley,
> así aprenderá a ser rey,
> del honor de sus vasallos.

> (1081–84)

[And without further trampling on your subjects, a crime against God and against the law, you will learn to comport yourself as a king ought from the honor of your subjects.]

That La estrella was meant to be a subversive work in its time seems clear when we consider Elliott's (1963, 304) description of the status quo during the reign of Philip III:

Here was a régime which, at a time when Castile stood most in need of government was content merely to follow where others led; a government which preferred panaceas to policies, and which had nothing but high-sounding phrases and empty gestures to offer a society that desperately needed a cure for its many ills.

If Busto's viewpoint has wandered among the various segments of his political world, his focus on a particular perspective—King Sancho's contemptible conduct—has caused a "theme" to be formed, the reaction to which will be conditioned by the "horizon" established from past attitudes toward honor and revenge.[6] The tension between theme and horizon, foreground and background, Iser says, creates a "mechanism that regulates perception," although the "ultimate meaning of the text" perforce transcends any individual perspective (1978, 98). Busto's perspective on the king's lust leads him to corroborate his worst fears by tricking Natilde into revealing what she thinks he already knows about the royal scam (1121–26). The slave's method, however, of bridging the gaps between the unconnected segments in Busto's contrived text turns out to be dead wrong:

> (*Aparte.*)   (Si él no guardó
> el secreto ¿cómo yo,
> con tan infelice estado,
> lo puedo guardar?) Señor,
> todo lo que el Rey te dijo
> es verdad.
>
>   (1126–1131)

[(*Aside.*) (If [the king] did not keep the secret, who am I, in my wretched condition, to keep it?) Sir, everything the king said is true.]

But if Busto ends up putting Natilde to death for her disloyalty, he will himself die a victim of imperial wrath for having affronted his majesty on two counts: first, by humiliating him albeit *en flagrant délit* (1185–89), and then by flouting a royal decree in having the slave killed (1231–44). For now Busto, in looking back over recent events as he recounts them to Estrella, anticipates further dishonor to his family; thus, he alters prior decisions so as to hasten Estrella's marriage to Sancho Ortiz and prepare his own departure from Seville (1380–85). The key point here is that, although Busto's individual perspective on the king's transgression is correct and although he was justified, if foolhardy, in defending his house against the royal intruder and in exacting vengeance against the enslaved enabler, the "ultimate meaning of the text"—that is, the effect of probing the thought systems underlying Seville's political organization—will emerge from the intermingling of other textual perspectives, principally those of Sancho Ortiz. Ortiz, like Tavera before him, will serve not simply as a reflector, but rather as a refractor, of the king's person; this parallel becomes all the more apparent if we recall Busto's earlier words to Sancho el Bravo: "Son mis verdades espejos; / y así en ellas os miráis" (399–400; "My truths are mirror reflections in which you should see yourself").

In one sense, Sancho Ortiz exists as Iser's sort of ideal, "implied reader" who is simultaneously attuned to the social and political norms of the day[7] and free from "ideological" biases; commitment to an ideological position, Iser states, hampers proper understanding and so precludes a correct reading.[8] From the first moments of his audience with Sancho el Bravo, Ortiz challenges the mandate that a certain man be killed in secret, thereby questioning the validity of a political norm that appeared to contradict what had been operant in society before the Castilian monarch's arrival in Seville:

> Pues, ¿cómo muerte en secreto
> a un culpable se le da?
> Poner su muerte en efeto
> públicamente podrá
> vuestra justicia, sin dalle
> muerte en secreto, que así
> vos os culpáis en culpalle,
> pues dais a entender que aquí
> sin culpa mandáis matalle.
>
> (1477–86)

[Well then, how is it that a guilty man is to be killed in secret? You can have him publicly executed; to conceal such a death throws the guilt back onto you, for you imply that you ordered him killed without just cause.]

Ortiz, from the very start, places the king on the defensive, as his retort shows: "Sancho Ortiz, no habéis venido, / sino para dalle muerte" (1506–7; "Sancho Ortiz, you have been summoned solely to effect his death"). Ortiz is again horrified when the king demands that he kill the transgressor unawares: "¡Señor! . . . / ¿me quieres hacer traidor? (1529–30; "My Lord! Do you wish to turn me into a traitor?"). Next, Ortiz is shocked by the king's act of proffering two letters—one to exonerate him from any potential blame (1545–46) and another to identify the guilty party (1597–98). Ortiz's response to Sancho el Bravo's written offer of surety is one of indignation, for a gentleman's word of honor need not be substantiated in writing:

> A la palabra remito
> la cédula que me dais,
> con que a vengaros me incito,
> porque donde vos estáis
> es excusado lo escrito.
>
> (1567–71)

[Substituting the spoken word for the document you gave me, I spur myself on toward avenging you, because your royal presence makes written proof unnecessary.]

Consequently, he tears up the first letter and asks only that he be allowed to marry the woman of his choice as a reward for carrying out the King's wishes (1585–87).

Ortiz's act of destroying one letter and of setting aside the other brings to mind the overall process of constituting the (literary) work, which, in Iser's (1978) model, has two poles: the "artistic" or the "author's text" and the "aesthetic" or "the realization accomplished by the reader." In light of this polarity, "the work itself cannot be identical with the text or with the concretization, but must be situated somewhere between the two. It must inevitably be virtual in character, as it cannot be reduced to the reality of the text or to the subjectivity of the reader" (21). Meaning, therefore, is seen as the result of an interaction between text and reader, as "an effect to be experienced," not an "object to be defined" (10). When Ortiz finally reads the letter containing the death warrant for friend and brother Busto Tavera—which comprises only one segment of the complex playtext the king has authored—he finally "sets the work in motion, and so sets himself in motion too" by trying to relate "the different views and patterns to one another" (21):

> ¡Perdido soy! ¿Qué he de hacer?
> Que al Rey la palabra he dado . . .
> de matar a mi cuñado,
> y a su hermana he de perder . . .
> Sancho Ortiz, no puede ser.
> Viva Busto.—Mas no es justo
> que al honor contraste el gusto:
> muera Busto, Busto muera.
>
> (1711–18)

[I am lost. What am I to do? Because I have given my word to the King that I will kill my brother-in-law, and I will lose his sister. Sancho Ortiz, this cannot be. Long live Busto. But it is not right that a man's pleasure oppose his word of honor: die Busto, let Busto die.]

Ortiz's thoughts on life and death, love and honor, "gusto" and "justo," Busto and Bravo, continue to shift back and forth between "foreground-and-background" (Iser, 1978, 95), until the various segments are organized, a connection is construed between them, the theme of "Busto muera, Busto muera" (1758) emerges, and the synthesis thought of as comprehension or meaning is produced. Henceforth, meaning for Ortiz will consist only of the *fait accompli* the reasons behind the action are deemed the responsibility of someone else to acknowledge:

> Yo lo maté, no hay que negallo;
> mas el porque no diré:
> otro confiese el porqué,
> pues yo confieso el matallo.
>
> (1877–80)

[I killed him, there is no denying it; but I shall not divulge the motive: let another confess the motive, for I confess the deed.]

In the process of creating meaning, then, Ortiz has virtually authored a playtext full of gaps or unspoken dialogue or unwritten text (variously termed "blanks" and "vacancies" by Iser),[9] which are what induce communication. The "open silences"[10] in Sancho Ortiz's text will ultimately constrain Sancho el Bravo to complete the textual structure and "speak the speech" of his complicity (*Hamlet* 3.2).

The king's shift in role from "author" to "reader" forces him into the untenable position of having to process someone else's invention rather than impose his own, and he continually seeks to put Ortiz's *author(ity)* to the test. It is no surprise, therefore, that the king embodies the sort of reader Iser (1978, 167) cautions against, one who attempts to complete the blanks in the text exclusively with his own projections. First, he tries to wrest from Ortiz a public confession of the reasons behind his killing of Busto, presumably to test whether the Sevillian subject would dare to implicate the real perpetrator (2032–44). Then, smitten once more by Estrella, Sancho el Bravo accedes to her request to take vengeance into her own hands, but not before blaming Ortiz's death on her irresistible beauty rather than on his own lewd behavior (2134–41). Her reply—

> ¿Qué ocasión dió, gran señor, mi hermosura
> en la inocente muerte de mi hermano?
> ¿He dado yo la causa, por ventura,
> o con deseo, a propósito liviano?
> ¿Ha visto alguno en mi desenvoltura
> algún inútil pensamiento vano?
>
> (2142–47)

[My Lord, what role did my beauty play, in the innocent death of my brother? Have I by chance given you cause, either by desire or lewd suggestion? Have you ever seen any vain thought in my comportment?]

—makes the king suspect that the perspective embodied in the words, "Es ser hermosa, en la mujer, tan fuerte, / que, sin dar ocasión, da al mundo muerte" (2148–49; "Is beauty in a woman so powerful that, without provocation, it destroys the world?"), is only partial and might need modifying. That he has begun to take responsibility for the tragic onslaught of events suggests that he has finally initiated the process of letting go of a few projections:

> Yo incité a Sancho Ortiz: voy a libralle;
> que amor que pisa púrpura de reyes,
> a su gusto no más promulga leyes.
>
> (2271–73)

[I incited Sancho Ortiz: I am going to free him; for the line of kings that treads on love no longer enacts laws at his whim.]

Iser's concept of "negation," or the act of probing the validity of received norms and systems (1973, 213), is useful for understanding Sancho Ortiz's scrutiny of Sancho el Bravo's Sevillian rule, which, based as it is on the codes of individual desire ("gusto"), reflects a sociopolitical organization desperately in need of reform ("justo"). Although Ortiz refuses to speak in name of the king and so make him accountable, he has virtually usurped the man and the office, for not only does he deserve the title of "Sancho el Bravo" for his dauntless fulfillment of a promise, but also he has displayed kingly qualities in his commitment to duty. His behavior is intended to make the king face himself: "que conozca que en Sevilla / también ser reyes sabemos" (2336–37; "Let it be known that in Seville we also know to act as kings should"). He will continue to hold his ground in the hope that the royal figure will out:

Haga quien se obliga hablando,
pues yo me he obligado haciendo,
que si al callar llaman Sancho,
yo soy Sancho, y callar quiero.

(2330–33)

[Let the one who has so obligated himself act by speaking out, for I have obligated myself by acting, and I, Sancho, wish to remain silent even if they call for Sancho.]

In effect, he is asking no more of the sovereign whose baptismal name he shares than he is of himself:

Quien es quien es, haga obrando
como quien es; y con esto,
de aquesta suerte los dos
como quien somos haremos.

(2344–47)

[Let the one who has knowledge of who he is act upon that knowledge; therefore we will both comport ourselves according to who we are.]

Ortiz's subsequent bout with madness, and particularly his imaginary dialogue with honor turned tyrant, reveal the extent to which conventions have gone awry and a reversal is needed if society is to prosper; Honor's words are telling:

el verdadero honor
consiste ya en no tenerlo. . . .
Dinero, amigo, buscad;
que el honor es el dinero. . . .
Riendo
me estoy: ¿palabras cumplís?
Parecéisme majadero;
que es ya el no cumplir palabras
bizarría en este tiempo.
(2482–83; 2486–87; 2489–93)

[true honor consists of no longer possessing it. . . . My friend, seek money, for honor is money. . . . Are you being true to your word? You seem like a fool to me, for the failure to keep one's word is gallantry in these times.]

When we recall Iser's notion that the (literary) text calls conventions into question, making them "become subjects of scrutiny in themselves" (1978, 61), it is not surprising that the playtext Ortiz has obliged the king to decode has brought him face to face with both his failure as a leader and his abuse of the system. This time, when King Sancho hears Arias's version of Sancho Ortiz's challenge—

> Dijo al fin que él ha cumplido
> su obligación, y que es bien
> que cumpla la suya quien
> le obligó comprometido
>
> (2650–53)

(At last he confessed that he has fulfilled his obligations, and that it is appropriate for the person who implicated him to do the same)

—his response is conditioned by the horizon of perspectives established from past readings of Ortiz's indomitable silence: "Callando quiere vencerme" (2654; "He wants to vanquish me with his silence"). Arias, whose current viewpoint has been informed by conversations with Ortiz (cf. 2299–2348), makes some attempt to modify the king's perceptions, saying that, if a subject is expected to fulfill his obligations to a monarch, then a monarch is equally responsible to a subject (2660–65). (Interestingly, Arias did not display such high moral standards initially when he encouraged the king to pursue his lust for Estrella by conferring special honors and privileges on Busto Tavera!)

Finally Sancho el Bravo, finding himself in a no-win situation, begins producing an accurate reading of the political (con)text. In response to an almost desperate—"¿Qué he de hacer?" (2699; "What am I to do?")—Arias remains true to form by suggesting that his majesty flatter the Sevillian council into prescribing exile for Ortiz rather than death, so as to demand punishment and yet save face. Consequently, the king convinces himself that, through his decision to marry off Estrella to some grandee of the court, through his confession of repentance, albeit insincere—"¡Cómo estoy arrepentido, . . . / de mi flaqueza (2728–29; "How I repent of my weakness")—and through his determination to "cumplir la palabra, / sin que [su] rigor se entienda" (2803–4; "keep his word without his cruelty becoming known"), he has, in Iser's terms, created meaning from the totality of interacting perspectives. Nevertheless, since no two readers are identical, no two readings, or concretizations, of a text will be the same, even when they are the work of the same reader. That all parties do not come up with the same "reading" of current events in Seville is therefore no shock: on the one hand, the prison warden reveals that Sancho Ortiz has elected death over liberty despite Estrella's generous act of forgiveness (2767–69), and on the other, the magistrate proclaims death by beheading to be the council's verdict for the prisoner's supposed crime (2900–2902).

It is here that Iser's concepts of foreground and background, theme and horizon, become most explicit, as well as the notion that the text itself can never be grasped as a whole, but "only as a series of changing viewpoints, each one restricted in itself and so necessitating further perspectives" (1978, 68). Sancho el Bravo's acts of comprehension, or his process of "realizing an overall situation" (68), have been structured by a series of futile attempts to build up a consistent view of varying textual segments from among the shifting perspectives of his social and political worlds. That he is finally willing to engage in open dialogue with the other, rival Sancho—albeit prompted by Arias's emphatic "Hablad" (2968; "Speak")—*suggests* that he has filled in all the textual gaps and so produced the synthesis we call comprehension or meaning. Admitting publicly to having coerced Sancho Ortiz into killing Busto Tavera—"Digo que es verdad" (2073; "I admit that it is true")—he adds, however insincerely, that the overall process of "reading" to which he has been subjected has affected him deeply or, in Iser's terms, caused a "heightening of self-awareness" (1978, 157): "Admirado me ha dejado / la nobleza sevillana" (2834–35; "The nobility of Seville has left me amazed"). That done, the king thinks that by endorsing the marriage of his namesake to the once coveted Estrella, he has at long last effected a meaningful denouement of a complicated plot, and he expects the book to be closed. Nevertheless, there remains one final twist, one last gap to be filled in before the king's journey through the Sevillian (con)text can reach closure: the proposed union depends for its realization on the mutual consent of both parties ("la conformidad," 2999), which the couple can no longer grant:

> *Estrella.* Señor, no ha de ser mi esposo
> hombre que a mi hermano mata,
> aunque le quiero y le adoro.
> *Sancho.* Y yo, señor, por amarla,
> no es justicia que lo sea.

(3014–18)

[—My Lord, the man who has killed my brother will not be my husband, even though I may love and idolize him. —And as for me, Lord, because I love her, I agree that justice will not permit me to be her husband.]

Sancho el Bravo's response to this unexpected coda is one of total disbelief, a blank and a void: "Toda esta gente me espanta" (3021; "They all terrify me"). The logical solution of course is to marry off Estrella to some grandee as she "deserves." Perhaps then, should the king ever be asked with respect to "la estrella de Sevilla"—"And what's her history?" (as was Viola/Cesario in musing to the Duke Orsino about Viola)—he might be able to respond, as did Viola, "A blank, my lord. She never told her love" (*Twelfth Night* 2.4.108–9).[11] Iser's view of blanks, however, is not that they forestall the production of meaning but rather that they chart a course for its creation (1973, 198). In fact, the *gracioso's* final boding implies that "esta tragedia"—the text of *his-story* and *her-story*—will live on and derive "eterna fama" (3025–27) because, as both intratextual and extratextual respondents to *La estrella de Sevilla* surely know from experience, "readers and audiences are not simply blank sheets upon which texts inscribe their meanings. As we read, we both discover *and* create" (Howard 1986, 144). The authority of the text, then, lies as much with the reader as with the author.

Notes

1. This essay owes its existence to a series of lectures delivered by Wolfgang Iser at The School of Criticism and Theory in 1978. I am further indebted to my training in Gestalt methods at the Gestalt Institute of Cleveland (1981–82), and to Sonia March Nevis for helping to keep that Gestalt ground figural for me.

2. See the recent edition of *La estrella de Sevilla* by López-Vázquez (1991) that attributes the play to Andrés de Claramonte. All references to *La estrella*, however, are to the edition by Alpern and Martel (1968). Translations from the Spanish are mine; a word of thanks goes to Grace M. Burton for a suggestion or two in that regard.

3. See Fischer (1979) for the application of Iser's theory of response to Calderón's *La cisma de Ingalaterra*.

4. Iser (1978, 21) provides a succinct description of the shape of his model, which will be referred to again below: "The literary work has two poles, which we might call the artistic and the aesthetic: the artistic pole is the author's text and the aesthetic is the realization accomplished by the reader. In view of this polarity, it is clear that the work itself cannot be identical with the text or with the concretization, but must be situated somewhere between the two. It must inevitably be virtual in character, as it cannot be reduced to the reality of the text or to the subjectivity of the reader. . . . As the reader passes through the various perspectives offered by the text and relates the different views and patterns to one another he sets the work in motion, and so sets himself in motion too."

5. In Iser's (1978) own words, a text represents "a reaction to the thought system which it has chosen and incorporated in its own repertoire" (72); and the repertoire in turn assumes a dual function: "It reshapes familiar schemata to form a background for the process of communication and it provides a general framework within which the message or meaning of the text can be organized" (81).

6. The terms "theme" and "horizon," which Iser (1978, 98) borrows from Alfred Schütz's phenomenological theory, involve the selection from multiple perspectives in a text. Freund (1987, 145) captures the essence of Iser's thinking here: "The journey through perspectives and shifting themes and horizons is accomplished by virtue of the reader's incessant acts of ideation, as she/he organizes segments and construes connections between them, always preoccupied by gap-filling activities that ultimately produce the synthesis we think of as comprehension or meaning."

7. For Iser (1978), the concept of the implied reader "embodies all those predispositions necessary for a literary work to exercise its effect—predispositions laid down, not by an empirical outside reality, but by the text itself"; in other words, he "has his roots firmly planted in the structure of the text; he is a construct and in no way to be identified with any real reader" (34). This so-called "transcendental model" (38), however, has been deemed problematic; Holub (1984, 97), for example, argues that "although Iser postulates a 'transcendental construct,' in reality his reader approximates the ideal of an educated European. Throughout *The Act of Reading* we encounter a competent and cultured reader who, contrary to Iser's wishes, *is* predetermined in both character and historical situation. This reader must be attuned to the social and literary norms of the day." Theoretical debate notwithstanding, the construct works to facilitate an understanding of the role and function of Sancho Ortiz in *La estrella de Sevilla*.

8. "The more committed the reader is to an ideological position, the less inclined he will be to accept the basic theme-and-horizon structure of comprehension which regulates the text-reader interaction. He will not allow his norms to become a theme, because as such they are automatically open to the critical view inherent in the virtualized positions that form the background. And if he *is* induced to participate in the events of the text, only to find that he is then supposed to adopt a negative attitude toward values he does not wish to question, the result will be open rejection of the book and its author" (Iser, 1978, 202).

9. According to Holub (1984), "a satisfactory definition" for the term *blank* is impossible to find, even in *The Act of Reading*. For our purposes, however, the distinction between blanks and vacancies is not crucial; in general, a *blank* refers to "suspended connectability in the text," while vacancies specify "non-thematic segments within the referential field of the wandering viewpoint" (Iser, 1978, 198). As Holub puts it, "The blanks and vacancies thus chart a course for reading a text by organizing the reader's participation with their structure of shifting positions. At the same time they compel the reader to complete the structure and thereby produce the aesthetic object" (94).

10. The term is Philip McGuire's (1985) and is defined as follows with regard to Shakespeare in performance: "An open silence is one whose precise meanings and effects, because they cannot be determined by analysis of the words of the playtext, must be established by nonverbal, extratextual features of the play that emerge only in performance. Such silences are usually required by Shakespeare's words, and they occur most often during the final scene of a play" (xv).

11. Freund (1987, 134) appropriately associates these verses with Iser's theory of reader response.

12

Intertextuality in the Theater of Lope de Vega

CARMEN HERNÁNDEZ VALCÁRCEL

Translated from the Spanish by Carolyn Nadeau

La estrella de Sevilla is an especially conflictive *comedia* with respect to the problems of attribution that have arisen over the years. It is not my intention to return to this debate nor to decisively demonstrate who was its author because, most importantly, I believe that many hands and alterations have intervened in the current state of the text. Moreover, the method I use to determine the authorship of this work is not so scientifically rigorous as other methods.

I am going to do an intertextual study of the themes, motifs, and characters of this and other plays whose attribution to Lope is indisputable. Naturally, only those more objective systems such as the study of metric combinations or of certain semantic or lexical aspects can approach a scientific proof of the authorship of a disputed play. However, the thematic characteristics I am dealing with will help either to reinforce or to discard these hypotheses. Meter is an especially strong argument against Lope's authorship of *La estrella de Sevilla*. But the thematic similarities with other Lope plays, the distribution and selection of motifs, and Lope's way of exploring a variety of solutions to similar situations complicate the question a great deal.

Lope de Vega, extraordinarily prolific in his dramatic production, had to utilize certain methods that would facilitate creating the enormous number of themes and characters found in his plays. One of the most useful is a limited use of intertextuality, that is, the creation within his many works of a network of repetitions within a polyphonic structure. One theme or character may appear numerous times, and by this repetition Lope introduces motifs and even themes that establish variations in the plays' development (Hernández Valcárcel).

The central theme of *La estrella de Sevilla* can be defined by the term *the gallant king* because the action of the *comedia* is set off by the desires of Sancho the Brave for Estrella Tabera. This term establishes a series of motifs or isotopes that are related to the functions the characters act out (Forastieri 1976):

1. The king falls in love with the lady upon seeing her.
2. The king confronted with the difficulties at hand:
   a. tries to bribe her brother
   b. bribes the slave
3. The lady resists the king.
4. The king breaks into the lady's dwelling.
5. Nighttime encounter between the king and the lady's brother, the latter confronts the king.
6. The suitor has to kill his lady's brother.
7. Imprisoned, the suitor becomes love crazy.
8. Dénouement.

This distribution of motifs is almost identically repeated in two authentic *comedias* by Lope, *La niña de Plata* (*The Silver Damsel*) and *La paloma de Toledo* (*The Dove of Toledo*). The similarities even extend to their titles, which all allude to the nickname a girl receives from her fellow citizens in recognition of her beauty and charm. These plays have the same syntactic construction:

1. *La niña de Plata*
2. *La paloma de Toledo*
3. *La estrella de Sevilla*

The thematic expositions with respect to the selection and distribution of motifs in the three plays are as follows:

1. A king or future king (Henry of Trastamara/Sancho the Brave) falls in love with a lady as he enters Seville (1 and 3) or Toledo (2).
2. The brother of the lady is favored by the king.
3. One of the leading men close to the lady sees the king in her home and confronts/does not confront the king (Don Juan, Paloma's suitor and Busto, Estrella's brother, knife the king in the dark. Don Juan, the Stunning Beauty's suitor, is hidden and sees Henry but does not confront him.

4. The three ladies resist the royal pursuits.
5. The three suitors debate over jealously and love.
6. The three kings' duty prevails over their passion.
7. Three weddings by the kings' hand.

La estrella de Sevilla contains one exception to the usual motifs, a common technique Lope employs as he very consciously breaks from commonplaces to create distinct solutions. When the king confirms Sancho and Estrella's wedding, she refuses to marry her brother's murderer. This surprises the spectator, who expects marriage as the usual dénouement.[1] This is an uncommon ending that approaches solutions similar to those in *El príncipe perfecto I* (*The Perfect Prince I*) and *Querer la propia desdicha* (*Desiring Your Own Misfortune*), whose authorship is undeniable.

There is still more. The theme of *the gallant king* in Lope's work is not limited to two or three texts but is central to a considerable number of his plays. Solely among historic plays, sixteen, not including *La estrella de Sevilla*, incorporate this theme:

1. *El postrer godo de España,* 1599–1608 (*The Last Goth in Spain*)
2. *El primero Benavides,* 1600 (*The First Benavides*)
3. *El príncipe despeñado,* 1602 (*The Assassinated Prince*)
4. *La corona merecida,* 1603 (*The Deserved Crown*)
5. *La reina doña María,* 1604–8 (D) (*The Queen Doña María*)
6. *La ventura en la desgracia,* h. 1610 (D) (*Fortune in Misfortune*)
7. *La niña de Plata,* 1610–12
8. *La paloma de Toledo,* 1610–15
9. *El príncipe perfecto I,* 1614?
10. *El príncipe perfecto II,* 1616 (*The Perfect Prince II*)
11. *Lo cierto por lo dudoso,* 1612–24 (*The Finding of Truth Through Doubting*)
12. *La primera información,* 1620–25 (*The First Piece of Information*)
13. *La lealtad en el agravio,* 1623–25 (D) (*Loyalty in Vengeance*)
14. *La carbonera,* 1620–26 (*The Charcoal-Burner*)
15. *El piadoso aragonés,* 1626 (*The Pious Aragonese*)
16. *El guante de doña Blanca,* 1627–35 (*Doña Blanca's Glove*)

(D) = Doubtful Authorship
(h) = holograph

To this overwhelming list, I add three more plays that I consider to present, in essence, the same theme, but with significant thematic changes that I will develop later:

1. *Peribáñez y el Comendador de Ocaña,* h. 1610
2. *Fuenteovejuna,* 1612–14
3. *El mejor alcalde, el rey,* 1620–23 (*The King Is the Best Judge*)

The theme reappears again in the frontier ballad plays. However, here it is not the central theme but rather a secondary one:

1. *Los hechos de Garcilaso de la Vega y moro Tarfe,* 1579–83 (*The Exploits of Garcilaso de la Vega and the Moor Tarfe*)
2. *El hijo de Reduán,* 1588–95 (*The Son of Reduan*)
3. *El sol parado,* 1596–1603 (*The Stopped Sun*)
4. *El hidalgo Bencerraje,* 1599–1608 (*The Moorish Nobleman*)
5. *El primer Fajardo,* 1610–12 (*The First Fajardo*)
6. *La envidia de la nobleza,* 1613–18 (*The Envy of the Nobility*)

As one realizes by examining the chronology, the motif is very prevalent in Lope's *comedias* (twenty-five texts without counting *La Estrella*) and spans thirty-five years of Lope's dramatic production. It constitutes more than twenty-eight percent of all of Lope's extant historic plays, the type of *comedia* to which I have limited my investigation. Moreover, it appears as a secondary motif in some other works such as, *El aldegüela* (*The Little Village*) and *El sol parado.* Both pertain to the subgroup, *the commander vs. the village woman,* along the line of works such as *Fuenteovejuna* or *El mejor alcalde el rey.*[2]

I have labeled the group of plays under discussion *the gallant king* because in a very high percentage the king is the protagonist. *El piadoso aragonés* is the only play (apart from the commander's cycle) where the tragic protagonist is not the king. But this *comedia* is anomalous in the motifs it includes. In many other cases the protagonists are princes at the time the play takes place, even though they will be kings in the near future. Again, the conflict they are presented with is identical to the other plays in which the character has already been crowned king.

The historical plays with which I am dealing include many motifs that coincide with those in *La estrella.* One can distinguish between those motifs common to all—the pertinent ones—and those that appear in more than one play but not in all—the nonpertinent ones.

Other motifs can be added (the lady's attitude toward and solution of the conflict, the father's or husband's solution, the suitor's attitude toward his rivalry with the king) but they seem more relevant for character studies than for thematic and motif studies, and so I shall leave them for the present.

Three subgroups can be established within this group of plays. They are classified according to the social nature of the protagonists and the scenes and environments in which they move.

1. Court (king or prince-lady)
2. Country (commander-villager)
3. *Morisco* environment (king or governor-lady)

La estrella de Sevilla is appropriately incorporated into the first group, considerably the largest and rightly named *the gallant king*. In this group the amorous dialogue is generally established in courtly environments and the protagonists are a king or prince who sexually pursues a lady. All the previously listed plays are included here, except three that belong to the second subgroup.

As is natural in a subgroup of such far reaching dimensions as the first above, one can and should establish various lesser subgroups whose thematic motifs more intensely agree while maintaining the basic characteristics of the main category to which they belong. Generally, the theme of *the gallant king* arises during the period of the king's pursuit of the lady and is the nucleus of the play. When a conflict is resolved in one way or another, the play ends. So, then, the motifs that make the groups of plays different are either temporal or related to the dénouement. For this last aspect, one can establish three possibilities:

1. Happy ending A: the king's duty prevails over his desire. The lady marries her suitor.
2. Happy ending B: the king's desire prevails over his duty. The lady accepts the king and has bastard children.
3. Tragic ending: desire prevails over duty. The king is punished.

Type one is the most common. The theme of the play consists in developing the conflict provoked by the king's whims and its effect on a pair of lovers. In the end royal good sense prevails and the suitor's role cedes to the inherently just king's role as the king himself takes charge of marrying the couple. In spite of being the most commonly repeated situation, it appears relatively late in

Lope's dramaturgy; not until 1603, in *La corona merecida,* does it surface for the first time.

Type two chronologically appears somewhat earlier, with *El primero Benavides,* dating to 1600. Although I have classified it as a happy-ending work, one must keep in mind that I am referring to the ending of the king-lady love story, which in this case is not the central theme of the play. These *comedias* begin at a point in time which is later than those of group one. The process of seduction has ended and the lady, instead of resisting the king, has consented to his desires and their love has given fruit to one or several children, who on occasion are presented as the play's central theme: the bastard. This grouping is very small:

1. *El primero Benavides*
2. *El piadoso aragonés*

Type three only has two examples, both fairly early. Here, the king, overwhelmed by his passion, conquers the lady and achieves his desires. The unjust royal action requires punishment that implies the loss of the kingdom and the king's life. The two plays that deal with this theme are:

1. *El postrer godo de España*
2. *El príncipe despeñado*

The first play that explores this solution is also chronologically first within the group of *the gallant king* plays. It derives from the old legend of *Rodrigo el último godo,* the last Visigothic king of Spain and how he lost rulership over the peninsula. Thus, in Lope's theater the theme of the king in love with a lady initially comes from the epic legends. As of 1602, with the appearance of *El príncipe despeñado* it extends to plays where the legend functions as a historic framework. In this first example the type of tragic ending that prevails is divine punishment for the king—no longer expressed in military and political terms but rather through a private solution where the outraged husband opts for a secret vengeance. But Lope perceives that the plays with an historic framework require a happy ending, one that rewards the integrity and merit of the lady. These works rapidly develop happy endings of type one.

In these types of plays one can fairly see the tendency toward thematic systematization. This facilitates both rapidly writing the plays and experimenting with solutions that include different developments of some given standards. But, in this sense, still more parameters can be established. This is the case with two consecutive plays, *El príncipe perfecto* I and II (one a continuation of the other), in which Lope's experimentation is evident and undeniable. These two works are not only a cycle in which a continuation of the first theme is found in the second, but they also show two sides of *the gallant king*. The circumstances are such that the second part perfectly fits within the commonplace norms and includes all the characteristic motifs. The crown prince falls in love with the lady of his closest friend and vassal, and experiences the standard conflict between love and duty. This dichotomy is mirrored in the love and jealousy the suitor then feels. The denouement is still the same: the prince renounces his feelings and the couple gets married.

The exception is found in *El príncipe perfecto I*. The initial conflict is the same: the suitor drives the prince to his own lady's door. But the prince's attitude is different here. As the perfect prince that he is, he puts friendship before love along the lines of another familiar Lope commonplace, although not so common in the historic plays: the theme of two friends. The prince's attitude is anomalous and so is the lady's. She experiences an uncontrollable passion for the prince. This feminine character type appears from time to time in Lope. So it is, then, that, when Lope de Vega decides to write the first play, he opts for revolutionary solutions within the commonplaces. He inverts the typical situations: the lady loves the prince and he rejects her. In the second part, Lope reworks the commonplace as he had contrived it sixteen years earlier.

In this different treatment of the commonplace, one also notes a second experiment with another theme. The two plays are essentially a dramatization of the theory and practice of the makings of a perfect prince, along the lines of a great many works found in the didactic treatises that deal with the education of a prince. In revising the possible situations that a prince may confront, there arises, in the first work, the idea of fidelity to a legitimate wife, which impels don Juan to leave his old lover and reject his friend's lady. The second demonstrates the king's attitude toward the unrestrained love of his own son, the crown prince, whom he should educate and guide. He advises his son not to allow passion to lead him to unjust action. He tells his son a parable:

> Y pues me pedís consejo
> para vos, y como padre,

desta manera os advierto.
A cazar el blanco armiño
van los cazadores diestros,
y alrededor de la cueva
le ponen de lodo un cerco.
El sale para buscar
por la campaña el sustento,
y en viendo el lodo se para,
tan turbado solo en verlo,
que allí se deja coger;
porque más quiere ser muerto
que ensuciar tanta blancura.
Harto os he dicho; entendedlo.

(B.A.E. 52, 129)

And since you are asking me for advice, as a father, in this way I will inform you. To hunt the white ermine the smart hunters go around the cave laying a circle of mud. The ermine leaves to look for food on the plain and when he sees the mud he stops and is so upset just by seeing it, that he allows himself to be caught because it is better for him to die than to dirty such whiteness. Enough I have told you; understand it.

Let me now turn to the classification of characters. The protagonist has specific traits. First, one must keep in mind that the protagonists in this type of play can be classified according to the social class to which they belong. The majority are young kings, or princes who will soon be crowned. Inherent in such a person are the responsibilities that go with the position. But one group of characters, preserving the general functions I am about to specify, has a lower social status. This subcategory of plays, although very well known, contains very few *comedias* (three compared to twenty-two). It has as protagonists a country nobleman, normally a commander, whose characteristics are similar to those of *the gallant prince*. On the other hand, the third subcategory that I established in the thematic study, the *morisco*, is not pertinent now to the character study, because the functions and motivations of plays with a moorish environment are identical to the Christian courtly plays I am going to analyze.

The king is present in both subcategories but with a very different function. Typically, the king rules with inherent sociopolitical functions. When he affects the love story, it is to restore order. This role is still played out in the group of country plays. Here, the king cedes his role as protagonist to the nobleman and continues to exercise his role as arbitrator, punishing, in this case, the nobleman who violates the norms.

But, in the majority of plays, the historical king (Peter the Cruel, Sancho the Brave, Alfonso VIII) plays a very different role from the one normally assigned to him in the Baroque theater as he takes the role of the noble protagonist in love. Within the subcategory of plays that deal with *the gallant king,* only one, as I have already mentioned, includes a character who, although he is crown prince, will die before reigning: *El piadoso aragonés.* The rest fluctuate between their unleashed passion for a lady and their obligations, which demand that they respect morals and laws. From this perspective, one could consider this type of play as a very peculiar educational theory for princes, not often expressed in the works but always implicit: one that exclusively focuses on the love I have just explained.

This type of royal figure, when in love, is characterized by two attitudes. One can be labeled Machiavellian; it imposes royal pleasure above and beyond laws and social conventions. In these cases the king, arguing that he can die from love and that his life is more valuable than the lady's honor, tries to disregard her honor. With very few exceptions, all these plays begin with this Machiavellian attitude and develop toward a providential ending, imposing good sense on the king who, in turn, dominates his passion and definitively restores order. *El príncipe perfecto I* constitutes the only notable exception. Here, the future Juan II adopts a providential attitude from the beginning of the love conflict.

The plays in which a providential denouement is imposed end with the restoration of social norms, while those in which the king persists in his determination and forces the lady to break moral and divine laws bring about death as a punishment from heaven, the only authority that can prevail over royal power. In the plays with country noblemen, when they transgress these norms, they are punished by a higher authority, the king, who is the supreme judge representing divine power on earth. The only difference between the king and the nobleman is that, while the king is not punished unless he consummates the affront (even if he is caught in the lady's antechamber), the village nobleman does pay even his unfulfilled desires with death (*Peribáñez*).

The king's attitude toward the remaining characters in the play focuses on achieving his desires. At the first opportunity, in one way or another he tries to bribe the man responsible for the lady, offering him positions of importance and sometimes managing to send him off on some mission. Secondly, he usually takes advantage of one of the servants, either his own or someone else's, to facilitate his entrance into the lady's house. These devices are identical for both the kings and the country nobleman. King Sancho sends don Martin, the lady's husband, away in *El príncipe despeñado*. In the same way, the commander of Ocaña tries to distance Peribáñez. In *Peribáñez*, Luján and Leonardo have the same role as don Arias in *La estrella de Sevilla* or as Ruy and Alvaro in *La lealtad en el agravio*. The only difference is that the king's servants who act as go-betweens are knights and the commander's servants are villagers. In *Peribáñez*, this difference in the servant's circumstances is pointed out to Luján by the commander.

Luján.	pero caúsame risa en ver que hagas tu secretario en cosas de tu gusto un hombre de mis prendas.
Comendador.	No te espantes; que sirviendo mujer de humildes prendas, es fuerza que lo trate com las tuyas. Si sirviera a una dama, hubiera dado parte a mi secretario o mayordomo, o a algunos gentilhombres de mi casa. . . . pero la calidad de lo que quiero me obliga a darte parte de mis cosas, Luján; que aunque eres mi lacayo, miro que para comprar mulas eres propio: de suerte que yo trato el amor mío de la manera misma que él me trata. (B.A.E. 41, 286)

Luján.	But it makes me laugh to think that for achieving your own pleasure you make a man of my talents your secretary.
Commander.	Don't be afraid. When serving a lady of humble dress, it is better that someone of your category does it. If I wanted to serve a courtly lady, I might have asked my secretary or steward or some gentleman in waiting to act the part. . . . But the quality that I want obliges me to involve you in my affairs, Luján. Even though you are my footman, I realize you are also your own man when it comes to buying mules. So, I will treat my love in the same way my love treats me.

The kings have four attitudes regarding the lady. Some are less frequent but still meaningful. In a couple of examples, the king reaches the point of rape and thus brings about divine punishment (*El postrer godo, El príncipe despeñado*). In *El piadoso aragonés*, Carlos, the prince of Viana, adopts a mixed attitude of gallant seduction and breaking-and-entering into the lady's room via servant bribery as in *La estrella de Sevilla*. The difference is that Busto returns home in time as if sent by providence.

The most common solution is that the king ultimately respects the lady. This does not mean that he does not adopt drastic attitudes that usually lead to breaking into her dwelling, but rather that his attempts fail because of coincidental situations. The intentions and attitude of the king, in this scheme, are always the same. The only difference is that normally fate prohibits him from realizing his intentions, much to his chagrin.

Now I will look at the other characters' attitudes toward the king. They can be classified into three types: the lady, her father or brother, and the suitor. The lady resists the king, with greater or lesser success, and only in the case of *Los Benavides* willingly accepts the king because of his divine image. In general, she hides the situation from her friends and relatives and tries to resolve the problem alone. However, she can also decide to tell what happened. Normally, the lady's solution to the royal pursuit is fairly paradigmatic. The most drastic is suicide (*El postrer godo*). But, commonly, in accordance with the happy ending that both Lope and his public enjoyed, the conflict ends in marriage or a happy life for the lady and the husband with whom she was previously married.

This brings me to another interesting point about this group of plays. The men who have custody of the lady's honor, whether father or brother, upon sensing the king's pursuit, decide to marry her as fast as possible so that another guardian will be responsible for her honor. This is precisely what the brothers in *La corona merecida* and *La estrella de Sevilla* do. Lope's love of playful experimentation with a given situation allows him to redevelop the idea of marrying the pursued lady in *La primera información*. Instead of giving the initiative to her relative, he gives it to the king himself, who tries to ease the queen's jealousy and maintain a front for fulfilling his desire without scandal.

Lastly, the third type of character who should be pointed out are the suitors. In general, they are the men who first court the lady, although the role of the brother, too, follows a similar typology. In various cases, the man, whether he is her suitor or her brother, confronts the king in the lady's darkened house. This happens in *La niña de Plata, La estrella de Sevilla, Lo cierto por lo dudoso,* and *Peribáñez*. It also occurs in a much more confusing scene in *La ventura en la desgracia*.

The attitudes that the men adopt when faced with this circumstance are very interesting and clearly explain a solution that may otherwise be surprising if the events were not taken into account. Generally, the man, once he recognizes the king, refuses to confront him out of respect and may even become imprisoned and insulted on the king's behalf (*La ventura en la desgracia, Lo cierto por lo dudoso*). Naturally, the other possibility is the opposite. Peribáñez doubts if he should kill the commander because he is a villager. Later, he decides to, precisely because the commander had named him captain. In this way, the commander's cleverness, having contrived the plan of distancing the husband, turns against him. Nonetheless, Peribáñez's unlawful act of confronting the commander can be pardoned by the king because, after all, he belongs to an inferior noble class.

Likewise, Busto Tabera, Estrella's brother, confronts the king and pretends not to recognize him, but, in this case, Busto lets him go. This is a more serious crime, a lèse majesté, as Lope himself says, and deserves inevitable death. *La estrella de Sevilla* comprises this solution, which, whether Lope's or not, enters into the inalterable logic of reward and punishment that structures all of his plays. If the king had ordered Busto's death to facilitate access to Estrella, it would have been an illegal and immoral action. But that is not the way it happens. The king becomes furious because of the disrespect that Busto's act of aggression supposed, and his anger even extends to Estrella, whom he threatens with death. In this way, the king's supposed cruelty is no more than an act of justice in the context of total respect and submission to the monarchical figure.

The painful circumstance that Busto's best friend must be in as he is forced to kill Busto is the same conflict as that of another Lope character. In *La primera información* the king orders the killing of Enrique by his best friend, Lucidoro. But, as in many plays, this character's conflict moves from the primary to the secondary level and he makes the opposite decision; he is incapable of killing his friend.

All things considered, in this category of plays, one finds a surprising regularity in both the king's attitude toward the lady and the lady's toward such a delicate situation. Clara, in *Los Benavides,* is the exception that confirms the rule for nineteen plays. In contrast, Lope habitually experiments with and diversifies secondary characters through, of course, relatively different situations.

The direction of the characters' functions is extraordinarily regular and becomes clear with these outlines of some of the more significant plays:

LA CORONA MERECIDA

Queen <----> *Alfonso VIII* -->Lady Sol<-->Don Alvaro
Elvira   Iñigo/Pedro

LA VENTURA EN LA DESGRACIA

Queen<-->Sancho the Brave-->Sancha<---->García

LA NIÑA DE PLATA

Enrique------->*Dorotea*<-->Don Juan
Master   Teodora

LA PALOMA DE TOLEDO

King   ------>   *Violante*<--->*Don Juan*
Fernán Pérez   Elvira   Galván

LA ESTRELLA DE SEVILLA

Sancho the Brave--> *Estrella*<--->Sancho
Don Arias   Natilde

This same outline also functions for *Lo cierto por lo dudoso*, *La primera información*, *La lealtad en el agravio*, *La carbonera*, and *El guante de doña Blanca*. Changes are made at the level of secondary characters, who, however, fulfill identical functions. For example, in *La niña de Plata* Teodora is not the protagonist's servant but her aunt, yet she carries out the same function as Natilde, the slave in *La estrella de Sevilla*. Also, the suitor can be a husband (*El príncipe despeñado*, *La lealtad en el agravio*), but his essential functions do not change (See the entire outline).

I have analyzed the state of character functions in the plays with a Christian king as protagonist, and so there is little to add about the Moslem king and the commander plays. In the first case not even the slightest difference of functions occurs; the variations are thematic in nature. While the gallant Christian king occupies the main action of the play, the function of the Moslem gallant king is relegated to a secondary position.

Regarding the commander type, a sociological change occurs in the women whose passions they awaken. But this does not affect at all the functions or the final outcome, as I have already pointed out. The most important difference in these plays in relation to the rest lies in the direction of character relationships. Here, there is vertical interaction among the different social classes, while the former presents horizontal direction within the same social class.

After reviewing a considerable number of Lope plays whose themes and character classification very significantly coincide with *La estrella de Sevilla,* I am not bold enough to affirm that the play is Lope's. It is always easier to imitate themes, structure, and characterization than meter and semantic traits. Nevertheless, so as not to avoid formulating my opinion on the question, I think that, as we know the play today, it has many elements not common to Lope but also many that have his unmistakable seal. I believe that a first draft of the play reveals Lope's brilliant expertise in re-creating themes from his other plays. At least eleven plays with the same theme had been written before *La niña de Plata* and *La paloma de Toledo,* and many others were written after. Nevertheless, the interventions of Clarindo, certain metric forms that Lope did not use, and questions of detail suggest a later adaptation by Andrés de Claramonte.

Notes

1. Alfredo Rodríguez López-Vázquez has related the conflict of Estrella to Doña Jimena's in the epic legend of the Cid. In fact, both women debate over the blood of their brother or father and the murderer whom they are in love with. But in the epic legend Jimena opts for the solution that is in perfect harmony with the usual denouements of this type of play: matrimony. Lope, Claramonte, or whoever may have conceived the dénouement of *La estrella de Sevilla* once again breaks with the commonplace. No one better than Lope breaks with his/her own and others' commonplaces in search of diversity within a certain systematization.

2. Within this same sector one might incorporate another play that the critics consider not by Lope, *Los novios de Hornachuelos* (*The Reluctant Bride and Groom from Hornachuelos*). Another work whose attribution to Lope has been rejected, *El milagro por los celos y don Alvaro de Luna* (*Jealousy's Miracle and don Alvaro de Luna*), belongs to the first subcategory of plays that I am establishing.

3. The numbering refers to the first list of sixteen plays. Number 17 refers to *La estrella de Sevilla,* while numbers 18–20 refer to the three commander plays: (18) *Peribañez,* (19) *Fuenteovejuna* and (20) *El mejor alcalde, el rey.*

13

The Analysis of Authorship:
A Methodology

ALFREDO RODRÍGUEZ LÓPEZ-VÁZQUEZ

Translated from the Spanish by Christopher B. Weimer

SINCE S. E. Leavitt first proposed Andrés de Claramonte as author of *La estrella de Sevilla* (1931b) until my recent edition in which author and work have been reunited (1991), critics have offered various and disparate solutions to the question of the work's authorship. Generally speaking, an attribution is nothing more than a hypothetical proposal in order to fill a documentary lacuna. Its verisimilitude compared with all other proposals must be based on critical postulates that, as in any activity aspiring to scientific status, must rely upon clear, exhaustive, and verifiable methodological principles. It is worthless to insist on concepts that are already stale (although effective in critical practice based on scholastic models) and that are neither debatable nor try to be so, precisely because they are based on modern forms of the old argument of authority. This substitutes for solid proofs and avoids approaching the problem from the direction from which it has been necessary to approach any problem since Descartes called attention to the importance of *method* in critical discourse.

Returning to Leavitt (1931b), who omitted any clear exposition of the methodology on which he based his reasoning, it must be lamented that the critical debate that followed his proposal was founded on the famous principle of authorship. Not even one of Leavitt's proposals has lost any force; not even one of the counterarguments used to confront them can resist empirical verification. In their day they were useful in spreading uncertainty, beginning with a very well-founded and coherent critical exposition. Those who opposed the Leavitt theory used as counterhypotheses arguments that permitted empirical verification but did

195

not include such verification. Since reviews of Leavitt's book did not offer any proofs to verify their conclusions the reader could be led into error through believing that the counterhypotheses were supported by prior proofs, which was not the case. Methodological coherence would have demanded that the alternative hypotheses to that of Claramonte (Ruiz de Alarcón, Tirso and Vélez de Guevara) be submitted to the same proofs, sketched but not carried out, in order to screen the hypothesis of Claramonte's authorship.

The edition that I have prepared for Cátedra is based on a system of proof that amplifies data already put forward in previously published articles (1983, 1984). I have not seen any clear evidence against what was advanced in these articles, and beginning there I have developed the hypothesis that *La estrella de Sevilla* must have been written around 1618 in Seville, which agrees with biographical and stylistic observations concerning Andrés de Claramonte. I will not repeat here what I have already stated in the prologue of this edition. I will expound upon the methodological bases of what would be a discussion or debate centered on the authorship and on the proposition of said edition, contributing a model beginning with an index, which I have not utilized for the edition. This index proceeds in reality from the scrutiny and analysis of one of the methodological errors incurred by doña Blanca de los Ríos in her attribution of *El burlador de Sevilla* (*The Trickster of Seville*) to Tirso,[1] an error recently repeated and amplified by Fray Luis Vázquez (1989).

Blanca de los Ríos carried out a commentary on citations from *El burlador de Sevilla* that she also encountered in works by Tirso de Molina, and concluded that these coincidences demonstrated "with mathematical certainty" Tirso's authorship. The first counterargument turned out to be very simple. It suffices to prove that these citations are also to be found in other authors of the period and, therefore, are general, foreseeable references. The proposal also involves verifying this in the alternate candidate for authorship, Andrés de Claramonte. It follows that in the verification process some features of interest appear: there is at least one reference in *El burlador,* that to Tifis, pilot of the ship *Argos,* which does not appear anywhere in the vast work of Tirso, and in contrast does appear, and repeatedly, in various works of Claramonte, in spite of the fact that Claramonte's corpus is considerably less than that of Tirso. We have here, therefore, a qualitative selection (the filter of a rare reference) and a quantitative selection (with a lesser corpus, the searched-for condition is fulfilled in greater measure). We have subsequently broadened this analysis in order to present as evidence the fact that the statistical difference between Tirso's and Claramonte's works from a similar period proves to be quite marked and that it statistically presents a deviation very favorable to Claramonte with regard to this group of classical references.

The present study develops the same type of methodological approximation: selection of classical references from *La estrella* and verification in the works of Claramonte and in the works of Tirso, Vélez de Guevara and Ruiz de Alarcón. I consider the statistical results to be conclusive.

The group of classical/Biblical/hagiographic references for the "texto breve" (short version) of *La estrella* is the following: Anáxagoras, Augusto, Júpiter, Porcia, Lucrecia, Dionisio, Bruto, Tarquino, Cain, Abel, Fálaris, Majencio, Saul, David, Atlante. The question is: how many of an author's plays do we need in order to locate these fifteen references? The complementary question is: on what date is the greatest similarity of references to this group from *La estrella de Sevilla* produced?

Obviously it is unthinkable that we can locate with exactitude all these references in a single *comedia* by one author. We can construct an index based on the use of such references in at least two *comedias,* finding approximate percentages. The filter of the period permits us to sustain a coherent hypothesis with the probable date of the text's editing. Then, moving to a subtheory of the general analytic model, we would be able to reinforce this hypothesis with comparisons of meter, of which we have at our disposal samples that have been quite well analyzed, thanks to the work of Morley and Bruerton, Williamsen and other scholars. In the case of Claramonte there is an immediate and spectacular response. Using only two perfectly datable *comedias, Deste agua no beberé (From This Water I Will Not Drink)* and *La infelice Dorotea (Unhappy Dorotea),* which are encompassed by the years 1617–20, we encounter twelve of those fifteen references, some of them repeated in both plays. The repetition could be a subindex of interest, but I will limit myself to the global references—in *Deste agua no beberé:* Caín, Abel, Tarquino, Lucrecia, David, Saul, Júpiter, Atlante, Porcia, Lucrecia; in *La infelice Dorotea:* Júpiter, Fálaris, Majencio, Dionisio.

As is seen, the text of *Deste agua* contains a very high approximation to the group of references from *Estrella,* coinciding with other similarities that we have already pointed out upon comparing these two works. That from a group of 15 references, one work alone repeats nine is something exceptional. It is a question of sixty percent correspondence. With *Dorotea* we reach an eighty percent correspondence, upon adding Fálaris, Majencio, and Dionisio, which were not in *Deste agua*. The suspicion we have formulated that the writing of *La estrella de Sevilla* dates from 1618 fits very well with these data. Fálaris, Majencio, and Dionisio are the novelty in references with regard to *Deste agua* and they return to use in 1620 with the writing of *Dorotea*.

Once this index is adjusted, we can then compare it with indices of works by Tirso, Vélez, or Ruiz de Alarcón. For Tirso we will choose a work in which there has been detected a link with a scene from *La estrella de Sevilla*. This work is *Cómo han de ser los amigos* (*How Friends Must Be*), staged by Pinedo and sold to Juan Acacio in 1612. We have already suggested in our edition that Claramonte could very well have borrowed a scene from this work for his composition of *La estrella*.

The grouping of classical references in *Cómo han de ser los amigos* is this: Sinón, Marte, Dédalo, Teseo, Endimión, Liguria, Noé, Nestor, San Onofre, Jonás, Ovidio, Eneas, Acates, Fénix, Darío, Zopiro, Campos Elíseos, Pilades, Orestes, Teseo, Peristeo, Eurialo, Niso, Pitias, Damón.

It would seem difficult to encounter greater diversity. Of the twenty-five references in *Cómo han de ser los amigos,* not even one coincides with the fifteen references in *La estrella de Sevilla*. It can be argued that the work was already written around 1612 and that, if we designate the date 1618 for the writing of *La estrella de Sevilla,* we should search for a work by Tirso closer to that year—for example, *Don Gil de las calzas verdes* (*Don Gil of the Green Breeches*), performed in 1615. The classical references are: Venus, Marte, Troya, Escitia, Argos, Hipócrates, Avicena, Galeno, Salomon, Baco, Narciso, Babel, San Antonio, Lucrecia, Abel. In this case, from a total of sixteen references we have two coincidences with *La estrella de Sevilla*. Taking into account that these two references, Lucretia and Abel, are also in Claramonte, and even repeated there, it seems that we find ourselves on the margin of statistically foreseeable coincidences. In *Palabras y plumas* (*Words and Feathers*), also dating from around 1615, we find the following references: Cupido, Adonis, César, Parténope, San Onofre, Eneas, Troya, Marte, Europa, Venus, Hércules. There are only eleven references but not even one coincidence with the fifteen of *La estrella*. In contrast, we see various correspondences among the three texts by Tirso, which repeat references. This confirms the probability of repetition as a trustworthy investigative index. Concerning *La estrella de Sevilla,* the comparison between Tirso and Claramonte proves Claramonte's similarity to the microsystem of references in *La estrella*. With two *comedias* by Claramonte, we encounter eighty percent of the references; with three by Tirso, only a meager, perfectly predictable 13.3 percent.

As an alternative to Claramonte, the most solid candidate for authorship is without a doubt Vélez de Guevara. Like the Murcian writer, Vélez never published his work during his lifetime, making it feasible to consider attributions of *comedias* of dubious authorship, without the existence of the difficulty that affects Tirso and Ruiz de Alarcón, who *did* publish, but not these *comedias* whose authorship is under discussion. On the other hand, Vélez's style is technically very similar to Claramonte's, although Vélez is the better versifier. In fact this tells against an attribution to Vélez, since *La estrella* does not stand out for the quality of its verse, but rather for the vigorous construction of the plot and the potent sense of tragedy and of political denunciation in the work. In this, Vélez is an author very close to Claramonte.

Toward this end, we have searched for a wider corpus by Vélez. It consists of: *La serrana de la Vera* (*The Mountain Woman of La Vera,* 1613), *El conde don Sancho Niño* (*Count Sancho Niño,* ca. 1620), *La luna de la sierra* (*The Moon Maiden of the Mountains,* ca. 1620), *Reinar después de morir* (*Ruling after Death,* 1620–30), *El verdugo de Málaga* (*The Hangman of Málaga,* ca. 1620–30?), *Más pesa el rey que la sangre* (*The King Matters More Than Blood,* ca. 1635?). Obviously we run into the difficulty caused by the lack of precise dating. I personally believe that *El verdugo de Málaga* is of a date earlier than that proposed by María Grazia Profeti; this belief is based precisely on the metrics, which use *redondilla* more than *romance*. Be that as it may, the result of the search is this—in *La serrana de la Vera:* Jordán, Semíramis, Evadnes, Palas, Troya, Galeno, Esculapio, Acaya, Efesia, Fénix, Venus. Of the eleven references in this work, not one coincides with those of *La estrella de Sevilla*.

In *El conde don Sancho Niño:* Cleopatra, Marco Antonio, Tisbe, Píramo, Hero, Leandro, Paris, Elena, Marte, Narciso, Nerón, Vulcano, Trajano, Augusto, Dédalo, Argos, Troya, Faetón, Helicona. Of nineteen references, one (Augusto) coincides with *Estrella*.

In *La luna de la sierra:*
Diana, Adonis, Palas, Venus, Marte, César, Adán, Poncio Pilato, Campos Eliseos, Endimión, Fénix. Of eleven references, not one coincides with *Estrella*.

In *Reinar después de morir:*
Narciso, Fenix, Parca, Cupido, Peneo, Parténope, Palas, Venus, Amaltea, Abel. Of the ten references, one (Abel) coincides.

In *El verdugo de Málaga:* Venus, Marte, Troya, Héctor, Judas, Faetón, Milón, Alcides, Golias, Narciso, Barrabas. Out of eleven references, not one coincides with *La estrella.*

In *Más pesa el rey que la sangre:*

Babilonia, Cleopatra, Hércules, Sansón, Marte, Adonis, Jerjes, Orontes, Adán, Alcides, Pitón, Olimpo, Palinuro, Acates, César, Amiclas. None of the sixteen references coincides.

On the whole, I believe that we have at our disposal an acceptable corpus and striking results with regard to the hypothesis of Vélez as author of *La estrella.* Making use of six *comedias* yields only *two* classical references matching those of *La estrella.* Perhaps another sampling, using a *comedia* with a date very close to the 1617–18 that we have postulated, might be able to offer a surprise. In any case, however, the sampling of Vélez corresponds to his most representative works and to those whose verification is most accessible.

The sole candidate remaining to us is Ruiz de Alarcón, who, as a resident of Seville during various years and as author of *Ganar amigos (Winning Friends),* a work inspired by Lope's *La niña de Plata (The Silver Damsel)* and therefore close in spirit to *La estrella de Sevilla,* represents an interesting hypothesis. It is necessary to make the same case for him as for Vélez. Alarcón is also a splendid, occasionally exceptional, versifier. It is difficult to connect him technically with a work whose weak point is precisely its versification. It must be pointed out that Alarcón is likewise very painstaking in depicting secondary characters, which are another of the weaknesses of *La estrella.*

For Alarcón we have also chosen an ample corpus. Together with *Ganar amigos,* which seems to us obligatory, we have at our disposal *La prueba de las promesas (The Test of Promises), Las paredes oyen (The Walls Have Ears), Los pechos privilegiados (The Privileged Hearts), La verdad sospechosa (Suspect Truth)* and *Mudarse por mejorarse (Changing for the Better).* These works are all thematically related to motifs in *La estrella de Sevilla.*

In *La verdad sospechosa:* Atlante, Apolo, Alejandro, Midas, Narciso, Faetón, Eridano, Cupido, Alcides, Marte, Ovidio, Tarquino, Marcial, Dido, Virgilio, Troya. Out of sixteen, two references coincide, Tarquino and Atlante.

In *Mudarse por mejorarse:* Diana, Marte, Júpiter, Venus, Adán, Sinón, Nerón, Troya, Tántalo, Cipariso. Of ten references, one (Júpiter) coincides with *Estrella.*

In *Las paredes oyen:* Diana, Narciso, Faustina, Hippia, Egira, Febo, Dafne, Júpiter, Gorgona, Cupido, Marte, Venus, Flora, Europa, Apolo, Acates, Sinón, Momo, Dictis, Marcial, Fanio, Adán, Jordán, Faetón, Vulcano. Out of twenty-five references, one of them (Júpiter) coincides.

In *Los pechos privilegiados:*
Atlante, Faetón, Júpiter, Alcides, Neso, Deyanira, Vulcano, Dafne. Of these eight references, two (Júpiter and Atlante) coincide, and they had already appeared in the previously seen corpus.

In *La prueba de las promesas:*
Marte, Cupido, Minerva, Numa, Quinto Fabio, Neptuno, Boreas, Venus, Leteo, Momo, Plutón, Himeneo. None of the twelve references coincide with *Estrella*.

Until this point we have indices very similar to those of Vélez and Tirso. A *comedia* normally repeats one or two references (or there is no correspondence) with respect to *La estrella*. In fact, for these three authors, the repeated terms—Júpiter, Atlante, Tarquino, Lucrecia and Abel—form a unit that appears in its entirety in the two Claramonte works that we have seen. We are within normal bounds. On the other hand, in *Ganar amigos,* whose connection to *La niña de plata* and *Deste agua no beberé* I have made manifest in my edition of *La estrella de Sevilla,* the index of coincidences is significantly greater and similar to that which Claramonte introduces in *La infelice Dorotea.*

In *Ganar amigos:* Barrabas, Atlante, Morfeo, Leteo, Tarquino, Júpiter. The coinciding references (Júpiter, Tarquino, and Atlante) are not a novelty, inasmuch as they already appeared in the other *comedias.* However, it is curious to observe that, with fewer global references, there is a greater resemblance to *La estrella.* In any case, we again encounter a statistical fact: with more (between three and six) works analyzed, the maximum index of coincidence of classical references in any of the authors considered alternatives to Claramonte does not exceed twenty percent; with only two *comedias* from the period 1617–20, Claramonte presents an eighty percent correspondence. I believe this to be conclusive.

Even now we have not concluded the analysis; some points of interest remain to be analyzed. We have already alluded to the relationship between *La estrella de Sevilla, La niña de plata, Deste agua no beberé* and *Ganar amigos. La niña de Plata* is without a doubt the work that serves as a matrix for the other three. Its 1613 staging is established and its 1617 edition coincides with the performance year of *Deste agua no beberé.* It is probable that *Ganar amigos* belongs to the same period. Both Claramonte and Ruiz de Alarcón took advantage of the subject developed by Lope, exploiting the Sevillian theme, the rivalry between Pedro *el Cruel* and his brother Enrique, and the motif we will label *Lucrecia-Tarquino*. It is interesting to note that, if Lope does not explicitly mention the names of Lucrecia and Tarquino, he indeed clearly alludes to their history. During the attempted violation of Dorotea by the *infante* Enrique, the *Niña de Plata* says the following:

> mas como Roma ha tenido
> la matrona venerable
> que ha honrado con su laurel
> a la castidad triunfante,
> haz tu gusto, pues no puedo
> defenderme ni librarme
> (*arrójase al acero de Enrique y él la detiene*)
> pero deja que tu acero
> mi infeliz sangre derrame
> para que tenga Sevilla
> una mujer que se mate.

> but just as Rome has had
> the venerable matron
> who has honored with her laurel
> triumphant chastity,
> take your pleasure, since I cannot
> defend nor free myself
> (*she rushes toward Enrique's sword and he stops her*)
> but let your sword
> spill my unhappy blood
> in order that Sevilla may have
> a woman who kills herself.

This is the culminating moment in the dramatic tension of the work. Lope does not allude by name to Lucrecia and to King Tarquino, but he places on Dorotea's lips their history and its dénouement. This motivates Enrique's change of heart and he abandons his purpose. Both Claramonte and Ruiz de Alarcón use the same structural device and both allude expressly to Lucrecia and Tarquino. Claramonte deviates in terms of character but not of epoch when he projects the Tarquino motif in *Deste agua no beberé* onto King Pedro. And in *La estrella de Sevilla* the motif deviates again toward yet another character, also a king and also in Seville: Sancho IV, *el Bravo*.

In addition, we will now examine a very interesting question concerning the classical references of *La niña de Plata*: Cleopatra, Venus, Ulises, Homero, Horacio, Cupido, Ifis, Anajarte, Jupiter, Dario, Alejandro. Ifis and Anajarte are relatively unfamiliar characters. It has already been seen that they do not belong to the global unit that we have formulated. On the other hand, they do reappear in another work by Claramonte, *Púsoseme el sol, salióme la luna* (*My Sun Set, My Moon Rose*), definitely composed by 1618, and the name Ifis also reappears (although he is not the lover of Anajarte, but a pilot instead) in a passage from *El nuevo rey Gallinato* (*The New King Gallinato*), a work staged in 1604.

Finally, here we will be able to complete the investigation of references shedding some light on an important aspect of the text. Until now we have analyzed the textual references of *La estrella* that both the longer and shorter versions have in common, references unmistakably attributable to the author and not to the adaptation. But the longer version incorporates other references of extraordinary interest:

v. 498: "otro Cástor y Pólux en el suelo" ("another Castor and Pollux on the earth");

v. 509: "caminan con las plantas de Saturno" ("they walk with Saturn's feet");

v. 935: :"por manzanas paso a Colcos" ("for apples I go to Colcos").

The mention of Saturn as a planet enters fully not only into the astrological theme, but also into one of the internal motifs of *La estrella*, that of melancholy. This idea also appears in *La infelice Dorotea:* "Marte y Saturno se encuentran, / Venus y Mercurio oponen / al malévolo planeta" (222–24; "Mars and Saturn meet, / Venus and Mercury oppose / the malevolent planet"). This reference, simultaneously classical and astrological, is part of the deeper idea in *La estrella* that conceives Saturn's influence as a pernicious one. A slowly orbiting planet is dealt with here, one related to the concept of melancholy. There exists another reference in *El inobediente* (*The Disobedient One*) that confirms this: "las perezosas plantas de Saturno" ("Saturn's lazy feet"). The allusion to Colcos, related to Jason, is a reference typical of Claramonte, as commentators since Leavitt (1930, 1931a) have seen. In fact, it is even a very concrete reference because it links the rhyme *Colcos-Remolcos* to *Jasón-Colcos*. And at this point we will introduce a most interesting detail. As is known, Ruth Lee Kennedy had assigned *La estrella de Sevilla*'s date of composition to 1623, based upon the allusion to "cuellos escarolados" and to the decree of that year. María del Carmen Hernández Valcárcel observed the same allusion while editing *Gallinato* and proposed the same time period. In this last case the documentation confirms that *Gallinato* was already performed in 1604; in *La estrella* the analytic indices point to 1617. But there also exists, according to what we have seen, the possibility of a longer version prepared after the original date of composition. It follows that the reference to *cuellos escarolados*, like the reference to Colcos, is not in the short versions. This lends weight to a general hypothesis that is confirmed by specific documentation: around 1623, the date at which Claramonte was in Madrid participating in the famous attack on Ruiz de Alarcón, and at which time it does not appear that he had his own company at his disposal, Claramonte was selling his *comedias* to other companies—*La estrella de Sevilla* in the longer version. He himself had updated the text, introducing the contemporary references.

The last lexical detail that fixes the year 1617 as the pivotal date of composition of *La estrella* and that confirms the attribution to Claramonte does so by relying upon a fashion phenomenon. I have noted in my edition the similarity between some motifs in *La estrella* and certain verses or passages from the *Fracmento a la Purísima Concepción* (*Fragment of the Immaculate Conception*), and in a note I have called attention to the reference to *arracadas* (earrings), a word that also appears in *La infelice Dorotea*: "Arracadas muy pesadas / de las orejas se cuelgan" (756–57; "Heavy earrings dangle from the ears"). This reference can be found in the *Fracmento* and is moreover developed in detail:

> *Arracada* es el sol, pendiente entre ellas
> y sus dorados rayos los pinjantes,
> y porque no haya en el defecto en nada
> hace Dios de la luna otra *arracada*.

> [The sun is an earring, hanging between them
> with its golden beams the jewels,
> and because there is no defect in it
> God makes another earring of the moon.]

As is seen, the term is repeated, and the image is quite intense for being inserted into a stellar context. The sun is an *arracada* or circular earring, and the moon is another *arracada* or curved earring.

From this analysis we can conclude that the short version of *La estrella de Sevilla*, written around 1617–18, is already the work of Claramonte. In regard to the textual re-elaborations, the analysis again confirms the hypothesis and, furthermore, makes it compatible with observations concerning the decree of 1623. Naturally, the question of authorship is open for debate; exhaustive and methodologically rigorous analysis is the only sensible approach to the problem and, given that which we have had occasion to prove, it points toward Claramonte.

Notes

1. The citations that Doña Blanca proposes as evidence are in the introduction to *Santa Juana*.

14

Staging and Polymetry

ANITA K. STOLL

THE *comedia* has been studied for most of the last three hundred years as literature to be read. Little attention was paid to these works for dramatic performance until the last two decades. In the past few years the Teatro Clásico (Classical Theater) in Madrid has brought forth several fine productions. In the United States, the Chamizal National Park has encouraged their presentation for the past seventeen years at its annual festival. Several plays have been translated and produced for English-speaking audiences, such as the performances of *Fuenteovejuna* in England in 1990 and in Washington D.C. at the Folger in 1991. The 1992 production of *El alcalde de Zalamea* (*The Mayor of Zalamea*) by the Compañía Repertorio (Repertory Company) of New York could be enjoyed in both languages. It is therefore appropriate that many Golden Age scholars have begun to look at these poetic dramas from the point of view of performance, combining knowledge of the plays as literature with historical and current studies of staging.

Patrice Pavis has provided a series of three strategies for discussing a created performance or mise en scène. These are the autotextual, the intertextual, and the ideotextual. The ideotextual approach is a concentration on the political, social, and psychological subtext, that is, opening the play to the outside world, molding it to the present day and its circumstances of reception. An example of this approach would be the metamorphosis of *Romeo and Juliet* into *West Side Story*. In contrast, the autotextual mise en scène concentrates wholly on the uniqueness and historicity of the written text, explicating "the textual mechanisms and the structure of the plot according to an internal logic, with no reference to anything beyond the text to confirm or contradict it" (1987, 98–99). This type of mise en scène would be a production of a play, perhaps in the Folger or in the corral theater in Almagro, in which nothing

was included in the staging beyond what the play text clearly indicated: no lines left out, and only the decor stated or that which
is logical historically. The third, intertextual approach, mediates
between the two, taking into account both strategies, allowing such
modifications as suit the director and perceived audience while not
losing recognition of the original text. A well-known example
would be Zeffirelli's recent filming of *Hamlet*, modified from the
original, among other ways, by the possibilities of the medium of
film itself. Another example is the production of *Fuenteovejuna* at
the National University of Mexico in 1990. The director modified
the original in only two ways: the villains wore quasi-Nazi uniforms
(while the peasants dressed in timeless peasant costumes), and
there were no intermissions. Both changes were extremely effective. All three approaches have a validity; however, for modern
productions of *comedias*, a general audience would probably be
most comfortable with the intertextual approach, which retains
recognition of historicity while adapting for the passage of intervening centuries. A careful reading of the autotextual mise en
scène, a recognition of exactly what is in the text itself, is a necessary first step to either of the other performance strategies. That
is the goal of this essay: to look at the actual stage directions
and those embedded in the dialogue, using what we know about
seventeenth-century staging to provide an autotextual mise en
scène as a preliminary step to any production.

   In order to examine the structure of the plot according to internal logic (that is, what the text clearly indicates), we must begin
with a look at the subdivisions of the acts. These are the imaginary
location and character changes that are signaled for the audience
by the departure of all of the actors from the stage and the appearance of other characters. These divisions do not necessarily correspond to those introduced by nineteenth-century editors, but
rather reflect the markings on original manuscripts, which often
had a solid line drawn across the page when the stage was completely cleared of actors (Dixon 1985, 120). These are generally
called "cuadros" by those who have written about staging history
(Varey 1985, 158). In *Estrella* we find four such divisions in act 1,
seven in act 2, and four in act 3.[1]

   Another concern in staging is to determine the location of the
action, if possible, and whether a specific location is essential to
the plot. Is there a stage direction that demands a specific location,
or scenery, or stage properties? Or is the location of the cuadro
made obvious through the dialogue itself? How much scenery is
actually required, based on the type of play and the directions in

the early manuscripts? While some types of plays required elaborate machinery, such as the *comedias de santos* (plays about saints), and decor, such as many palace productions, this type of play, a *comedia de capa y espada* (cape and sword play), required little or no scenery (Ruano 1987, 51). From Foulché-Delbosc's edition of the combined extant manuscripts, we observe that there are no stage directions in the original material regarding locations. We must therefore examine each cuadro to determine from the dialogue where the action may take place. This kind of locative material has been referred to both as "spoken scenery" (Surtz 1979, 162) and "didascalias implícitas" ("implicit stage directions") (Hermenegildo 1986, 707). On the wide and successful use of verbal geographical creation, José María Ruano comments,

> El espectador medio del siglo XVII poseía la capacidad, instigada por el actor, de imaginarse el lugar donde sucedía la acción como si fuese real. . . . Lo importante no era que lo imaginario se representase de una manera realista, sino que los actores se comportasen y lo tratasen como si fuera real. (1988, 86–87)

> [The average spectator of the seventeenth century possessed the capability, when induced by the actor, to imagine the place where the action was taking place as if it were real. . . . The important thing was not that the imaginary location was represented realistically, but rather that the actors should behave as though it were real.]

This practice underscores the primacy of words over concrete stage scenery, the auditory over the visual, as the major focal point in this drama, a matter that has produced considerable controversy (Soufas 1992; Pulice 1982, 218; Dixon 1986, 35). However, we know that locations may be indeterminate and the action can take place for the most part as though on a public street, just as in Elizabethan theater, in which the lack of locale has been termed the "open stage" (Dessen 1984, 86–87). We may also call this an "open text" after the language of the semioticians (Pavis 1987, 98).

Just as we realize the power of speech to evoke a sense of place, we also realize that the use of different meters and specific rhyme patterns also may signal emotional states, types of action, and changes in locale (Williamsen 1984, 546–56). For this reason it is useful to note the metrical changes with the cuadro changes; it is logical that they should be closely coordinated, since a stage clearing often signals a change in focus and emotional intensity as well as a possible change in the location of the action or characters involved in the action (Marín 108); see chart in appendix. Regarding the relationship between metrics and drama, J. Fernández Montesinos has observed, "La comedia está concebida de un modo, podríamos decir, musical, en que cada escena tiene una tonalidad determinada, según su índole." (1969, 13; "The comedia is conceived in a musical way, we might say, in which each scene has a determined tone, according to its nature"). Victor Dixon amplifies this idea, stating:

> The successive passages in different meters and stanza forms are indeed . . . the true building blocks of the play; the poetic structure of a *comedia* coincides with, *is* its dramatic structure, and to clarify one can only illuminate the other (1985, 121).

Therefore, along with the divisions of the acts, the logical locations of action, and stage action and plot structure conveyed through dialogue, I will include commentary on various verse forms and how they reflect the dramatic action.

While the most accessible edition of the play is that found in the anthology *Diez Comedias del Siglo de Oro* (1985), the scene divisions shown in this edition are not cuadros even though they sometimes coincide with an empty stage. Thus the important first cuadro includes the first 476 verses, which in *Diez Comedias* is divided into six scenes. The only locative phrase in these verses is the speech in which Arias speaks to the king of Busto: "En el Alcázar le vi; / veré, señor, si está allí" (210–11). While *Diez Comedias* locates the action encompassed in the first cuadro in "salón del alcázar" ("receiving room of the palace"), these two verses negate this possibility, while the conversation in this early part of act 1 suggests a much more indeterminate location that could be a public street or square, or patio, left to the imagination of the viewer. Evoked verbally also for the seventeenth-century audience is the elaborate formal reception with which kings were welcomed into cities (Strong, et al.):

> Del gasto, y recebimiento,
> del aparato en mi entrada,
> si no la dexo pagada
> no puedo quedar contento.
>
> (1.11–14)

> [If I do not leave payment
> for the expense and reception,
> of the preparation for my entrance,
> I cannot be content.]

However, none of this lavish reception need be shown on stage. The king ends the public welcome with "Yd, Sevilla, a descansar. . . . Yd con Dios" (1. 33, 50; "Go, Seville, and rest. . . . Go with God"), indicating the collective citizenry as a protagonist in the play. Now in private conversation, don Arias again comments on the sumptuousness of the king's greeting as a lead-in to the commentary on the ladies present on their balconies. One critic's analysis of the astrological symbolism of this section proposes a staging, based on an Italian model of the period, in which there was "a series of seven semi-circular grades or steps divided from left to right into seven gangways which cut vertically across the semicircles," each representing a planet (Burke 1974, 138–39). Given what we know today from recent studies of the typical corral stage, it was probably another example of verbal evocation; if they appeared on stage at all it was in the openings at the second and third levels of the back of the stage, which were frequently used when windows and balconies were needed (Ruano 1989, 2–5).[2] This private-conversation subsection of the first cuadro, occupying verses 61 to 221, leaves no doubt as to the importance of astrological symbolism in the play.

A shift from the opening *décimas,* often used to convey gravity, as in this case when the king speaks, to *redondillas* moves the topic of conversation to the petition of don Gonzalo, who, according to one of the few stage directions, is dressed in mourning, one of the many structural pairings and a visual portent of Estrella's mourning in act 3 when she says: "Una desdichada Estrella, / que sus claros rayos cubre/ deste luto" (1. 2066–68; "An unfortunate Star / which her clear rays cover / of this mourning"). The two who seek the same command, don Gonzalo de Ulloa and Fernán Pérez de Medina, initiate the important symbols "espejo" (mirror) and the related "cristal" (crystal), which are later reiterated by Busto (400, 743) and Estrella (1883–1907). These symbols relate them all to the collective group of honored citizens of Seville—as referred to in verses 25–27: "Iurados y Regidores / ofrecen con voluntad / su riqueza y su lealtad" ("Jurymen and aldermen / offer willingly / their wealth and loyalty")—in which the "riqueza" are the individual citizens Busto, Estrella, and Sancho, and also to the sundering of important pairings within the group (de Armas 1994a), presaged with verses 29 and 30; "Con condición que no sea / en daño de tu Ciudad" (29–30; "On the condition that it not be / a danger for your city").

The second cuadro, verses 477 to 692, continues in an outside location that is qualified as near Busto's house, with verse 597, as

Clarindo announces to Sancho and Estrella the arrival of Busto, who orders her: "Entrate dentro, Estrella" ("Go inside, Estrella"). The lyric tone of the conversation centered on Sancho's and Estrella's love is expressed with the italianate *estancia*. When Estrella leaves and is replaced by Busto, the lyric gives way to the more common redondilla.

Cuadro three, verses 692 to 868, continues outside, as Busto comes out to speak to the king, accompanied by don Arias, and thus tells us that they are in front of his house: "¿En mi casa Vuestra Alteza?" (697; "Your Highness in my house?"). In lines 764–68 Don Arias announces: "Essos coches llegan" ("Those coaches are arriving") and "Ya esperan / los coches" ("The coaches / are already waiting"). The audience of course does not see the carriages. A staging of this today would probably include sounds of carriage wheels and horses, while in the seventeenth century the audience could be relied upon, as established earlier, to accept such action imaginatively. When don Arias approaches Estrella on behalf of the king, her words are combined with physical action to indicate her rejection: "A tan libianos recados / da mi espalda la repuesta" (813–14; "My back gives the answer / to such lewd approaches"). The cuadro ends as Don Arias and Natilde conclude their bargain.

Cuadro four, verses 869–916, the end of act 1, is located in the Alcázar through an earlier verse, 769, in which the king orders Arias to accompany Busto in his carriage: "Guíen al alcázar," ("Drive to the palace") and through the use of a carry-on prop. The stage direction reads "Don Iñigo Osorio, Busto y Don Manuel, *con llaves doradas*" ("with gold keys"). The "llaves" remind us that the king has sent Busto to the alcázar to make him the king's chamberlain, for which he receives the keys. Busto brings up the symbolic keys in act 2 (in another pairing) when he confronts the king as he tries to enter Busto's house without a key, that is, illegally and immorally (1065, 1067). The act ends with don Arias's report to the king of the agreement with Natilde, for which he must write a "cédula" ("document"). Thus in act 1 there is little concern for specific locale and even few cases of spoken scenery; the acting company could perform on a blank stage by exiting and entering the two doors at the back of the stage.

A similar pattern emerges in act 2. Although there is no concrete indication, the audience will envision the first cuadro (917–60) on the street outside Busto's house, since the king and don Arias, bringing the "cédula," meet with Natilde there to talk of the king's entrance into Busto's house. At the beginning of the second cuadro

(961–71), Busto arrives at the same spot, announcing "Esta es mi posada" (961; "This is my dwelling") to don Manuel and don Iñigo. The stage direction indicates "vanse" ("They leave"). We may assume that all three leave and then Busto reenters, saying "Temprano me entro a acostar" (971; "I am going to bed early"), or that he remains onstage and announces his location with this statement. In either case, his words alone provide the essential locative direction for the third cuadro (971–1164). The earlier trio—don Arias, the king, and Natilde—have obviously already entered the house. As he calls for servants to light his way, Natilde and the king come on stage. Natilde, frightened, then announces her exit: "Ay Dios! yo me voy" (984; "Oh God! I am leaving"), leaving the king, disguised with his cloak, and Busto to the private encounter that causes the king to seek Busto's death. In the fourth (1165–1259), the dialogue provides a location near the alcázar, as don Arias discovers Natilde's body: "En el alcázar está / un bulto pendiente al viento" (1231–32; "There is a form on the palace / hanging in the wind"). The actors are looking toward the alcázar in the distance. It is obvious that the audience does not see the body, but rather is informed of its "presence" through the words of don Arias.

The fifth cuadro (1260–1401), in which Busto tells Estrella of his encounter with the king and of the fears that make him want her quickly married, could be on the street outside Busto's house or inside, since there is no specific indication. The use of the *romance* for the narrative sequence is usual for the comedia (Morley and Bruerton 1968, 123–25). Don Arias begins cuadro six (1402–1880) saying, "Ya en la antecámara aguarda / Sancho Ortiz de las Roelas" (1402–3; "Sancho Ortiz de las Roelas / is waiting in the antechamber"), letting the audience know that this cuadro takes place in the alcázar. The *quintillas* of the first part of the cuadro change to the more lyrical *pareados* as Clarindo brings to Sancho the message from Estrella that Busto wants their marriage to take place immediately. On receiving the message, Sancho gives Clarindo a ring to take back to Estrella. Immediately on receiving the ring, she learns of Busto's death at Sancho's hand, making the union symbolized by the ring impossible. This paradox is repeated is act 3 as the king gives her a ring with which to obtain Sancho's release from prison—again an actual and physical, yet impossible, union.

This cuadro provides an example of the fluidity of place in that, without a stage clearing, the location has to change, since Sancho kills Busto in this same cuadro (remember, Busto has never left the stage), and he surely could not be envisioned as carrying out the sentence in the alcázar. This movement is signaled verbally by Sancho—"Buscar a Busto quiero" ("I want to look for Busto")— as he begins the long monologue in which he moves figuratively (as he travels in fact) from the happy anticipation of his wedding to the horrible realization that he has agreed to kill Busto and thus to destroy all possibility of the wedding and happiness. John Varey has pointed out this type of active location change without a stage clearing in his description of the staging of *El alcalde de Zalamea* (1987, 217–226). In the first act the location changes from a dusty road to the village street outside Pedro Crespo's house to a patio inside the house to the upstairs garret, all without any· stage clearing.

The lyrical *pareados* (couplets) give way in this emotional climax to the more grave *décimas* as he opens the king's paper and learns he must kill his friend. Once the deed is done, the change to *romance* for the seventh cuadro (1881–1986) provides for the news to be carried to Estrella and, since the *romance* was the preferred form for endings, clues the audience to the end of the act. Here separations are expressed in the breaking of the mirror that Estrella drops and in the repeated image "Partida / está por medio la piedra" (1930–31; "The stone / is divided in two"). Another expression of the paradoxical union or pairing of Estrella and Sancho is the description of both in this cuadro—of Sancho as "Loco está" (1871; "He is crazy") and of Estrella in "El dolor la priva de la razón" (1972; "Pain deprives her of reason"). The logical inside location is suggested as Clarindo announces: "Ya el escalera arriba / parece que sube gente" (1941–42; "It seems that people are climbing / up the stairway now").

The first cuadro of act 3 (1987–2174) is located inside the alcázar, as implied in verse 2052, as the king, preparing for Estrella's entrance, says, "Dadme una silla y dejad / que entre ahora" (2052–53; "Give me a chair and let / her enter now"). Estrella's narration of her misfortune and request to determine the fate of her brother's killer is expressed in the somewhat unusual u-e *romance*. When the king speaks, he changes to the more ponderous *octava real*. The location of the second cuadro (2174–2555) has been prepared for us at the end of act 2 when it was announced that Sancho was "preso" (1956; "imprisoned"). A possible explanation for the presence of the musicians may be to imitate, through use of a repeated refrain, the *romances viejos* ("traditional ballads"). Such an evocation would lend authority to the poet's desire to make these tragic figures and this tragedy more than a personal one through this reference to the collective poetic tradition.[3]

The third cuadro's location is somewhere outside the prison. The stage direction: "Estrella, con manto" ("with a cloak") provides the means for Estrella's hidden identity, and an outside location makes Estrella's cloak logical (2556). They would have left the stage through one door to reappear through another. The *décimas* of this cuadro, as opposed to the lyrical Italianate forms they used earlier, lend a note of gravity to this meeting between Estrella and Sancho. Their sharing of the last two strophes repeats the earlier paradox of the rings in their simultaneous joining and parting. The stage direction at the end of this cuadro, "Vanse por distintos lados" ("They exit on opposite sides") again physically and visually carries out their definitive separation while making clear the emotional pain involved in it. The last cuadro (2646–3029) is located in the alcázar through the words of don Arias: "traeré al alcázar a Estrella. / Aquí la persuadirás" (2771–72; "I will bring Estrella to the palace / Here you will persuade her"). We find a return to the collective referent of the opening cuadro (in which don Arias stated, "la Gentilidad Romana / Seuilla en los dos celebra" (817–18; "in the two Seville celebrates / the Roman gentry") with the words, again of don Arias, "La gente desta Ciudad / obscurece la Romana" (2744–45; "The people of this city / outshine the Romans"). Then follows the individual acquiescence of the alcaldes to the king's will, only to be reversed through their observance of collective duty. There is a structural movement, then, from collective to individual in act 1 and a reversal of this movement here from individual to collective, absent the three "riquezas," or stars, of the opening words. The thrust of the repeated comparison of the population of Seville with the ancient Roman civilization is to glorify the high level of their culture and morality. The play has the typical comedia ending pattern of redondillas leading into the final *romance* (Bakker 1981, 92).

One effect achieved by the many cuadros of indeterminate location is a fast-moving pace that will keep the audience's attention; everything in this play can logically take place within the classical time precept of twenty-four hours. A distinct advantage of the blank or open stage is the ease with which it could be produced by a traveling company. Even the props are minimal; the script calls for a mirror, gold keys, paper, cloaks for Estrella and the king, and a chair. While contemporary productions are generally realistic stagings, a mise en scène similar to this one can be found in such plays of Thornton Wilder as *Our Town*. This dramatist was well-enough acquainted with Spanish *comedia* staging to write about whether the plays that called for lions used real ones or not (1953, 19–25).

To summarize, change in metrical form often relates to structural changes in the drama, such as change of location or change of emphasis in the development of the plot. In regard to the use of verse forms, the less common Italianate forms the *pareado* and *sextilla* tend to be used for lyrical passages, while the *quintillas* and *décimas* are used in situations that call for authority or gravity. The *redondilla* and *romance* are found in their well-documented uses for moving the plot forward and for endings. We must remember, as one scholar has put it, that "the metrical conventions were worn like a loose coat, not a straight jacket" (Gitlitz 1986, 24), and we can only continue to tabulate descriptive information about this important aspect of Golden Age poetic drama in order to expand our understanding of the uses of polymetry.

The outline for an autotextual staging leads to consideration of how the other types of staging could be employed for this drama. We may inquire into these by asking a series of questions. Into which category will we place the eighteenth-century refundición, *Sancho Ortiz de las Roelas?* How would either approach—the intertextual or ideotextual—deal with the single most unacceptable plot item for the contemporary world: the casual, tacitly condoned murder of Natilde? How could the central honor issue, as well as the view that all loyalty is owed the king, be dealt with today? It is my opinion that these central issues obviate the feasibility of an ideotextual production. An intertextual mise en scène, for a contemporary Hispanic audience that is becoming increasingly aware of these central issues as part of their history and attends productions of the *teatro clásico,* is the most reasonable. We can only hypothesize about these questions and wait to see what a professional director, confronted with this text, would make of it.

Notes

1. Similar structural symmetry has been noted in several of Lope de Vega's plays. See Stoll 1988, 23–30, and McGaha (1978), 451–58.

2. For a very recent consideration of the influence of the memory theater on Golden Age drama productions, see John E. Varey's essay (1991).

3. One of the features of this sojourn in hell is Clarindo's pretended double conversation, a technique pointed out by doña Blanca to ascribe the authorship of the questioned *La mujer por fuerza* to Tirso de Molina.

Appendix

The following is a summary of the cuadros correlated with metric scheme:

Act 1.

Cuadro 1:
1–476
1–220 = décimas
221–476 = redondillas

Cuadro 2:
477–598 = estancias
599–662 = redondillas
663–692 = sextillas

Cuadro 3:
693–868 = romances e-a

Cuadro 4:
869–916   redondillas which end with cuadro

Act 2.

Cuadro 1:
917–960   redondillas abba

Cuadro 2:
961–980   redondillas abba

Cuadro 3:
981–1164   redondillas

Cuadro 4:
1165–1259   quintillas which end w. cuadro

Cuadro 5:
1260–1401   romances io

Cuadro 6:
1402–1880
quintillas to 1606
pareados to 1690
décimas to 1880
romances ia to end 1986

Act 3.

Cuadro 1:
1987–2174
quintillas to 2061
romances to 2117
octavas reales to 2173

Cuadro 2:
2174–2555 romances eo

Cuadro 3:
2556–2645 décimas

Cuadro 4:
2646–end
redondillas to 2745
romances to end

Part V
Writing

15

Acts of Reading, Acts of Writing

Emilie L. Bergmann

The tragic action of *La estrella de Sevilla* evolves from failures of language: spoken and written words at odds with each other and with the characters' actions.[1] Estrella is betrayed by the written word, by letters, decrees, and contracts—*papeles* (papers)—that involve her and circulate around her. Early in the play, she is positioned as an object of the king's designs; his contracts and commands endanger her honor and deprive her of the marriage she assumed was a certainty. Her marriage contract, a document drawn up between her brother Busto Tavera and Sancho Ortiz, is rendered invalid—if not legally then in terms of honor—by the king's written command to Sancho to kill Busto. After Busto has been murdered and Sancho is imprisoned and apparently mad, Estrella represents the moral values they had upheld. Her eloquent monologues in act 3 are effective, but their function is to renounce her hopes for the future: she has lost her brother and cannot marry Sancho, since he is no longer the same man she was to marry. It is through this renunciation that she transcends the social and moral disorder wrought by the king.

The central action of the play is transferred to paper and circulates in this form on the stage during the first two acts. Estrella is excluded from the documents that will determine her fate. She has no access to the writing that moves the plot in the first two acts, and that writing nullifies hers. Her written and oral speech acts, including her silence, are equally ineffectual. Her letter to Sancho announcing that "ya ha llegado / el venturoso plazo deseado" (1649–50; "The happy day, so long desired, has come")[2] is only ancillary to Busto's official arrangements for her marriage. Furthermore, immediately after reading her good news, Sancho reads the king's note identifying Busto as his victim. Thus, her encouraging information has a different status from the commands and contracts of the male characters in the play: Estrella's writing makes nothing happen. Its information is already outdated, and the announcement is no longer valid, because the authority upon which it depends is about to be silenced. Estrella has no control over the events she attempts to report accurately to her fiancé, and this affects the status of her writing as well as the course of her life.

Estrella's speech acts are both positive and negative: confronted with don Arias's indecent proposal on behalf of the king, Estrella responds to his action with silence and the negative gesture of turning her back. In act 3, when she at last begins to speak effectively, the *papeles* have done irreparable damage. Her most significant action, that of freeing Sancho, is accomplished anonymously, at least in part: she is veiled when she arrives at the prison to take charge of the prisoner. Thus, she renounces not only her marriage but her identity, and she renounces her claim to marriage with Sancho twice: once without witnesses outside the prison, and a second time before the king.

Silences, omissions, delays in knowledge, and absences are as important to the play's discursive structure as the speech acts and written contracts. When Busto replies to the king's offer of a noble husband for his sister, he conceals his own prior commitment to Sancho Ortiz, which invalidates his expression of gratitude. In order to thank the giver, he would have to be in a position to accept the favor. Thus, Busto's omission of crucial information from an exchange initiates the series of faulty speech acts in the play, the broken contracts and promises on the part of other characters that lead from his dishonor to his death by his best friend's hand, the dramatic betrayal of a bond between equals.

The king's offer of a noble and wealthy husband for Busto's sister is clearly made in the context of bribery, (419–23), as is Arias's later offer to Estrella accompanied by flattery (807–8). The actions the king plans to carry out are those of defacing a blank page, in light of the absences and emphatic silence of Estrella in the scenes that involve the King's designs upon her. There is no dialogue of courtship; only a plan to rape a sleeping woman. The title of the play points not to the central figure but to a central absence—that of Estrella's authority for positive action—and to the erasure of inscriptions through the action of the first two acts. Burke and de Armas reveal astrological structures in this play. But a counterdiscourse, the debasing wordplay of coinage, systematically undermines the transcendent inscription of women in astrology. The king establishes the commercial context for the "divinas bellezas" ("divine beauties") of Seville by asking Arias "¿Cómo limitas y tasas / sus celajes y arreboles?" (67–68; "How do you limit and appraise their celestial radiances and rosy blushes?"; Translation mine). The mythological allusion to Phaeton's chariot and the sun is immediately devalued by the king's reference to golden "soles" ("suns") together with "blancas" ("silver coins") and "maravedíes" ("copper coins of the lowest denomination"). Estrella's exalted representation as the star of Bethlehem and as the sun is thus contaminated by the previous associations of the ostensibly absolute value of "soles" with the relative value of coinage. The king's designs on her through bribing her brother Busto inscribe her explicitly in a system of exchange.[3]

An underlying fault in the king's speech acts is revealed in these and later references to coins, and in the lines "Si tú le das y él recibe, / se obliga; y si es obligado, / pagará lo que le has dado; / que al que dan, en bronce escribe" (201–204; "For if you give and he receives, / he binds himself, and being bound, / he will repay the debt. / For whosoe'er accepts a boon, inscribes a debt in bronze.") The king and his advisor Arias do not use the term "dar" (to give) in the context of gifts but rather with reference to bribing or distracting Busto to gain access to his sister. The king intends to pay for Busto's honor, which by definition cannot be bought. "En bronce escribe" has the resonance of an inscription of eternal validity but is only the impression on a coin. The image, by its proximity to the discussion of the women in monetary terms, situates the king and his advisor Arias on the relative ground of economics rather than the exalted level of justice.

The image of the gift as an inscription in bronze seems monolithic and eternal, but it has an obverse suggested by the imagery of coins immediately preceding it.[4] The king's gift has only relative value, as do the women, on one hand compared to celestial bodies, inscribing fate indelibly in the heavens, and on the other associated with coinage as objects of exchange. This dichotomy of transcendent value and the debased coinage of the play's speech acts underscores the moral tension generated between expectations of what the king should do and his ill-advised course of action. Sancho's return to prison after Estrella has freed him, his pressure on the king to explain why he killed Busto, and Estrella's and Sancho's decision not to marry is instrumental to the exposure and rejection of that system of exchange, but the final scenes convey Estrella's and Sancho's loss and estrangement, rather than a clear affirmation of transcendent values.

Moral tension in the play begins with the two neglected *papeles* introduced in act 1, scene 4, and unread until the king, intending to ignore their contents, hands them to Busto in the next scene. They are *memoriales* ("petitions"), in this case the *curricula vitae,* of Gonzalo de Ulloa and Fernán Pérez de Medina, the two candidates for military command of Archidona. One is presented as "espejo / del cristal de mi valor" (271–72; "a mirror, fashioned of the clear crystal glass of mine own worth"), the other as "cristal / que hace mi justicia clara" (275–76; "a crystal glass, wherein the justice of my cause is clearly seen"). Busto refuses the king's unjustifiable offer of this position and instead reads the documents and makes a judgment worthy of a king's councillor. The written documents postpone and displace personal petition before the king, and they make possible a secret process of decision whose dishonesty is subject only to scrutiny of Busto, as its beneficiary. Busto treats the "espejo" and the "cristal" as if they were the persons they represent, unlike the king, who disregards people, oral agreements, and written documents equally. These apparently insignificant *papeles* establish a connection between written representation in the form of documents and contracts, and the questions of justice and honor in the play; and they establish the characters of the king and Busto.

Estrella assures Sancho Ortiz "que hechas las escrituras/ tan firmes y seguras, / el casamiento es llano" (556–59; "that now, the marriage contract / duly signed and sealed, / our union is assured"). In nearly identical terms, Busto reassures Sancho that he will convey this situation to the king: "Volviendo a informar al Rey / que están hechos los conciertos / y escrituras, serán ciertos / los contratos" (644–46; "Once I return to inform the King / that the agreement and documents have been signed, / the marriage will be certain"). And yet Busto has already tacitly accepted the king's offer, which would cancel spoken "conciertos" and written "contratos." As an emblem of this treachery and disregard for written contracts, the slave Natilde is hanged while bearing on her body— in her hand—the signs, illegible to her, that accuse and condemn her. It is important to point out that these signs change in character once she is dead: they are meant to be read by others. Her body becomes a sign in itself. The constellation of signs that the king has drawn around Estrella is equally inaccessible to her despite her social privilege and her literacy.

Representing reading and writing on stage problematizes the primary modality of the *comedia* as a spoken art form, although in the twentieth century, we experience it more often as a written text.[5] In studying *comedia* texts, we become accustomed to imagining oral performance, but in *La estrella de Sevilla,* letters, decrees, and contracts are present on stage and are important to the action. Their presence suggests a dynamic relationship between spoken and written discourse. Reading and writing are prominent in *La estrella de Sevilla,* and both are connected with the inscription of Estrella in economic and symbolic systems of exchange. Reading and writing in other plays, such as *La dama boba* (*The Lady Nitwit*), *El perro del hortelano* (*The Dog in the Manger*), and *La vengadora de las mujeres* (*The Avenger of Women*), enable women to choose some aspects of their lives; a woman is written on in *La estrella de Sevilla* and is left only with the choice to accept with dignity the disaster that writing imposes upon her.

As Elias Rivers has pointed out in "The Shame of Writing in *La estrella de Sevilla,*" the role played by written words in this play reveals one aspect of a theme that preoccupied authors in a society in transition from orality to print culture. Like Rivers's analysis of the play, mine is also indebted to the work Inés Azar has done in bringing speech act theory to the analysis of Hispanic texts (Azar 1986). Honor and writing, in this play, are both gendered problems: the problems of language involve disruptions in the community, and that disruption begins with the title role, that of the woman whose fate is not written by her own hand. Rivers discusses the conflicting obligations in the play, Busto's concealed suspicions, and Sancho's justifiable distrust of written contracts, concluding that "[t]he written contract, as a substitute speech act, destroys the honor system itself, which depends upon the non-reiterable uniqueness of the performative utterance. . . . from a traditional point of view, [a man's] signature is an inadequate substitute for the authentic oral performative utterance" (Rivers 1980, 115). Moreover, the exemplarity of Sancho's behavior is further elaborated when the king fails to fulfill his verbal obligation to protect Busto's murderer and Sancho, keeping his own promise of secrecy, is forced to remind the king of his promise.

Conflict between verbal and written contracts in the play, as Rivers has demonstrated, is played out in a moral drama of absolute and misguided power. The possible outcomes of this conflict outline a question of ideology in the literature of the Golden Age (Rivers, 115–17). For the letter to prove more durable than the spoken word, a new, "shameful" order must prevail, whereas, if the spoken word proves more binding, two traditional notions are corroborated: that the spoken word is imagined to precede the written (and the written to be no more than a debased imitation of the *logos*) and that the transcendent value of the spoken word legitimizes traditional Iberian values of honor. There is a third possible outcome, which is what happens in *La estrella de Sevilla:* neither oral nor written language can be counted on to correspond to reality, and the king fails to recognize on his own the binding force of his own word and his signature. This failure of language reflects the moral decadence in a character drawn from a turbulent moment in medieval history, as well as the transition from orality to literacy and the social and economic upheavals the *comedia* audience was experiencing. After all, the audience is witnessing an illusion made of words, in a period acutely aware of the chasm between word and referent.

In addition to reflecting the social effects of the transition from orality to literacy, the literature of the Golden Age problematizes women's literacy in particular. Juan Luis Vives, in his *Formación de la mujer cristiana* (*Instruction of a Christian Woman*, 1523), acknowledges that women of the class to which he addresses his instruction are literate and should be educated, and he concerns himself with their choice of books, favoring devotional over imaginative literature in order to ensure their chaste behavior. In understanding the role of writing in *La estrella de Sevilla,* it is important to remember that women's legal status excluded them from contractual agreements. In addition, when women wrote, even their poetry or fiction was restricted to an audience of immediate family or friends, with rare and significant exceptions.

Beyond the supposed influence of reading fictional adventures and lovers' laments in chivalric and pastoral romance, women's own writing of clandestine love letters might create occasions for dishonor. Estrella's protestation of innocence in act 2 makes this clear: "¿En las manos de algún hombre / viste algún papel escrito / de la mía?" (1288–90; "In the hands of any man / have you seen a letter written / by mine?"). In the same passage, she protests her innocence by emphasizing her chaste silence: "¿En mi boca has visto / palabras desenlazadas / del honor con que las rijo?" (1281–83; "In my mouth have you seen / any loose words released / from the honor with which I govern them?"). Estrella is well aware of the threat to her brother's honor inherent in women's uncontrolled writing or speaking. Defending herself against Busto's suspicions, she makes the strongest defense of her virtue by affirming her absence from writing, as well as from "dishonorable" speech. In other dramatic works letters between lovers might well influence the action, but they are not the decisive documents in *La estrella de Sevilla*. The papers circulating in this play belong to a masculine world of honor and legal obligations, from which Estrella is excluded. Thus, her protestations of chaste abstinence from exchanges of love letters are irrelevant. Her defense also indicates the mechanism of her downfall: she has no control over writing and speech among men, the contracts and promises from which she is excluded. When she does act through language in act 3, it is with the tragic dignity of renunciation.

A popular depiction of women reading in seventeenth-century Netherlandish paintings is pertinent to my discussion of the significance of women as subjects and objects of exchange in a culture shifting from orality to literacy. Examples of these paintings of women reading and writing, by Ter Borch, Metsu, and Vermeer are well known. Vermeer's "Woman Writing a Letter" (1666), in the National Gallery in Washington, looks boldly at the viewer; the woman with her maid in the Frick Collection is engaged in conversation. But Vermeer's depictions more often intensify the solitude of silent reading. The terms "absorption," "solitude," "self-sufficiency," "self-possession," "secrecy" are repeatedly used to describe these paintings, particularly Vermeer's Dresden "Woman Reading before a Window," (1659), and his depiction (ca. 1665) of a solitary woman in blue reading, in the Rijksmuseum, Amsterdam (Alpers 1983, 203; Pops 1979, 29–30).[6] These women do not return the viewer's objectifying gaze. They create a "double self" through the act of reading, that is, communication with an absent person, another world. Svetlana Alpers notes that, in the 1664 "Woman Reading a Letter," "Vermeer represents the absence of the letter's content as an elusiveness . . . an essential content remains inaccessible, enclosed in the privacy of the reader's or writer's absorption in the letter" (192, 203).[7]

This depiction of interiorized and private reading of secrets between lovers contrasts sharply with Estrella's lack of authority with regard to the written word. Estrella's tragedy is, in part, that she is the object of written communication, and her subjectivity is rendered ineffectual, when she is not simply excluded from acting as a writing or reading subject. The pleasure with which Sancho Ortiz receives her letter is short-lived, lasting only until the next scene when he reads the second part of the king's command. Writing in *La estrella de Sevilla* splits the social bonds of friendship, family, and marriage through treachery. The self-possession that characterizes the letter-reading Dutch women is evident in Estrella's monologues in act 3, but at this point the king's decrees have done their damage and there is nothing left to read. Estrella arrives at the prison with her face hidden, holding a jewel instead of a document. The jewel as sign of absolute royal authority matches the absolute moral value of Estrella's actions, but, as an

object that can represent exchange value as well as ideal and absolute value, the jewel embodies the contrast between Estrella's integrity and King Sancho's economy of relative values. By this point
in the play it is clear that a written decree would debase Estrella's
purpose. She takes the initiative of freeing Sancho, traveling alone
to the prison in Triana, and she also makes her own decision about
her marriage, finally able to act through her speech.

The role of women and slaves in the transition between orality
and literacy in *La estrella de Sevilla* is clarified in Eric Havelock's
discussion of the "competition and collision" between singing, reci-
tation, and speech on one hand, and reading and writing on the
other, in fifth-century Athens. There are significant differences between the role of writing in the plot of *La estrella de Sevilla* and
in that of Euripides' *Hippolytus,* the play Havelock chooses from
the "scores of examples" that depict this conflict; but the implications of the status of a written document found on a corpse are
telling:

> The plot turns on the writing of a message left by a deceased wife
> incriminating (falsely) her stepson. The presence of the tablet on which
> it is written is effectively dramatized, lying on the breast of the corpse.
> The husband arriving home discovers his bereavement, unties the tab-
> let, and reads it to himself on stage. Presumably by this time a theater
> audience could accept the fact as normal that a woman could write
> and a man could read. But as he reads, he exclaims spontaneously,
> "The tablet shouts, it cries aloud. Look, look at what I have seen in
> written letters (*en graphais*)—a song speaking aloud!" (ll. 877–880).
>
> Logically, if the message is a song or verse sung aloud, you don't
> see it. If on the other hand it is a written document, it can't sing to
> you. But the logic of either/or does not belong in these words. They
> open a window on a cultural process of transition, in which contradic-
> tion and collision are of the essence. (1986, 21–22)

Havelock explains the "stigma" attached to the written word and
the impossibility of challenging what has been falsely written "by
the truth of traditional oral testimony extracted from witnesses by
oral examination" (21–22).

The plot of *La estrella de Sevilla* does not turn on Natilde's writ
of manumission so much as on the king's written commands to
Sancho Ortiz. He refers to it as a "speaking" letter in act 3, scene
18: "Si hablara / el papel, él lo dijera; / que es cosa evidente y
clara; / mas los papeles rompidos / dan confusas las palabras"
(2935–39; "If it could tell, my lord, / 'tis clear the paper would
explain; / but papers torn and scattered / speak with most uncertain

voice"). Sancho Ortiz is reminding the king not only of the evidence that was destroyed but of his abandonment of moral responsibility. Leaving aside plot differences, it is clear that the discursive transition at work in both plays is similar, defying "the logic of either/or" and signalling the end of a traditional order. The suicide note in *Hippolytus* and the documents in *La estrella de Sevilla* have voices of their own: Phaedra's letter accuses the innocent as if it were a voice from the dead, while the letter in Natilde's hand informs the guilty, by its presence rather than its words, that his treachery is known to its intended victim, Busto. The slave Natilde, upon whose body don Arias finds the writ of manumission, has ample opportunity to explain while still alive her attempted betrayal of Estrella's (and Busto's) honor and the role of the king's promise of a monetary reward in addition to her freedom. She pays with her life for her faith in the written word, and she accuses herself by her own oral testimony. Sancho's reference to the torn letter at the end of the play speaks about speech itself: attempting to restore the order in which a man's word was his bond and shaming the king into accusing himself.

The function of letters, contracts, written promises, and commands amid the oral discourse of the *comedia* is complex, and involves on one hand social values favoring orality and on another the exigencies of performance. Unless the supposed contents of a document are read aloud by a character, neither the reader of the dramatic text nor the spectator of a play can know what is written on these objects. In addition, what an actor reads from a stage letter is not necessarily inscribed upon the paper he or she holds, nor is this an ordinary reading. Instead, it is a performance like the other lines of dialogue that reveal important information to the audience. Thus, the problem of the textual object in the dramatic space is a problem of dramatic time: the object is visible, but indecipherable until the moment at which its contents will be revealed by an actor who represents the act of reading it, or not revealed at all in reading but rather revealed through the subsequent action. This is particularly evident in act 2, scene 12 when Sancho Ortiz reads Estrella's letter silently and then again aloud, and in act 2, scene 13 when he twice reads aloud the king's written identification of the "traitor" he has agreed to kill. Clarindo observes Sancho's enjoyment in his facial expression and gestures as he silently reads Estrella's letter; the pain of reading the king's command is dramatized in his horrified declamation of each word.

The playwright's strategy of employing letters and documents on stage places the spectator, and the reader, in the position of the viewer of the Dutch paintings of women absorbed in reading letters. The letter or document on stage constitutes on one hand an enigmatic object that is an emblem of deferred meaning: we as readers or spectators can only know what it signifies through the readings of characters on stage. On the other hand, the *papel* in *La estrella de Sevilla* has a role of its own: it affects the action on stage and its words have the finality of commands or contracts, not only subject to reproduction in oral communication, but requiring it in order to participate as actors in the drama. In fact, when asked who ordered him to kill Busto, Sancho replies, "un papel" (2935). Svetlana Alpers (198) cites the Inca Garcilaso de la Vega's anecdote from his *Comentarios reales* (9:29), meant to illustrate Andean cultures' incomprehension of Europeans' written communication. According to the anecdote, two messengers sent to deliver ten melons were astonished that the list accompanying the cargo was able to communicate to the recipient the secret that they had eaten two of the melons. Alpers notes that "this fascination with letters as both a secret way of communicating and a way of communicating secrets obtains also in seventeenth-century Europe" (199). In *La estrella de Sevilla,* the letter becomes an actor on stage: perhaps the Inca's depiction of the messengers' "simplicity," their belief in the autonomous power of a written document, is not so much the response of an oral, indigenous culture to writing as it is a projection of the European cultural construction of writing in a period still haunted by the attribution of presence and authenticity to spoken communication. Another interpretation of the act of writing can be observed in the brief penultimate scene of act 1 of *La estrella de Sevilla.* Don Arias dismisses the other characters on stage: "que quiere el Rey escrebir" (902). "The king wishes to write." Does the king wish to write the past, or is he projecting the future? In fact, he has accomplished nothing worthy of note in a king's chronicles since his arrival in Seville, and in lines 909–12 it is clear that all he proposes to write is his signature on a *cédula* ("decree") granting freedom to the slave Natilde, who has promised him access to Estrella in exchange. The statement, however, carries the weight of implication that, as the king's plans have been successful so far, what he wants to write will determine the action of the play, will perhaps *be* the next two acts of the play. And yet, the king's written word will be invalid: neither he nor Natilde will be able to keep either part of the bargain after Estrella's brother Busto discovers and obstructs the king's entry into Estrella's room and hangs Natilde with the writ of manumission in her hand. The promises and failures of writing are central to the play.

Not only verbal and written contracts but gestures and silence are threatened and invalidated as speech acts in *La estrella de Sevilla*. Estrella does not appear onstage until act 1, scene 7. She communicates with the king's cynical advisor Arias by refusing to speak with him: she turns her back on Arias in answer to his indecent proposal in act 1: "¿Qué respondo? / Lo que ves . . . A tan livianos recados / da mi espalda la respuesta" (811–14; "What is my answer? / What you see . . . To such a ribald message, sir, / my back is my sole answer"). Where Phaedra's letter and Natilde's *cédula* are significantly attached to their bodies, Estrella's answer is enunciated by her body, or rather her back—now personified as speaker—which signifies a refusal to engage in this negotiation in which Estrella would be the object of exchange. Her back is not the negative of her identity; it signifies the obverse of her speaking countenance, like a coin's, and her refusal to dignify Arias's proposal with her face.

When Estrella speaks to Sancho in act 3, she is veiled; thus the authority of her identity and that of her speech are split. In act 1, her presence, her voice, and her silence are affirmed, but they are shown to lack the authority to protect Estrella's honor and her plans for her future with Sancho Ortiz. In act 3, she is able to use her authority to set Sancho free, but at the same time she renounces the future she had planned and dissolves the marriage obligation, the only contract to which her agreement was necessary for it to be valid. In addition, seeing and hearing relatively little of Estrella herself in the first two acts is an effective dramatic strategy for representing her inviolable virtue: public exposure and discourse can only be detrimental to a woman's honor.

Silence, rather than speech or written documents, signifies honor. The broken mirror in act 2, scene 17, is a "verdadera cifra" ("true sign"), misinterpreted by Estrella and her maid. It serves as an emblem and a foreshadowing of shattered honor and the disruption of identity in Sancho's mad dialogue with Clarindo in act 3. Sancho seems to have forgotten who he is and to have lost faith in language as "espejo." Sancho is disillusioned with the honor valued by his peers, and true honor is too fragile to keep:

> *Sancho.* . . . el verdadero honor
> consiste en no tenerlo. . . .
> Dinero, amigo, buscad;
> que el honor es el dinero.

> (2482–83; 2486–87)

[Sancho. True honor consists in not having it. . . . Money, my friend, is what you should seek, for honor is money. (Translation mine)].

Honor appears now to have exchange value rather than the absolute value Busto and Sancho had attributed to it. Sancho's identity is defined by renunciation and absence after he is brought back with magical words from Hell to the prison of Seville: he gives up his right to marry Estrella as certified in a signed document and as reward for murdering Busto. In the imagery of the play, coinage and mirrors are only apparently opposing views of identity and value, since the mirror of honor can be broken down into small change. The two sides of the *papel,* the document and the king's role that commanded and authorized Sancho to kill Busto, are revealed to be equally invalid. The play illustrates the fragility of honor as a social value invested with transcendence, and the fragility of social identity that goes with it, in a world in which written and spoken language has become a medium of exchange in a system of relative values.

The question of identity suggested in the "espejo" and "cristal" of Gonzalo de Ulloa's and Fernán Pérez de Medina's petitions in act 1 is echoed in the variations on "yo soy quien soy" ("I am who I am") that, in the course of the play, begin to ring false: Busto assures Sancho that the king's authority will protect the signed contract of his marriage to Estrella: "el Rey es Rey" (661; "The King is King"); Sancho, rejecting the king's offer of a written immunity, says, "Yo soy quien soy. . . . Quien es quien es, haga obrando / como quien es" (2340; 2344–45; "I am who I am. . . . He who is who he is, would act according to who he is"; translation mine). Estrella, in defending herself from her brother's suspicions when King Sancho appears at their house, says, "¿No me conoces? ¿No sabes / quién soy?" (1279–80; "Don't you know me? Don't you know who I am?"; (translation mine).

In *La estrella de Sevilla,* Sancho's and Estrella's unequivocal gestures of rejection of the king's manipulations and aggressive acts do not suffice to protect their marriage vows from the disruption of speech acts and written contracts. Estrella's most emphatic speech act is silence, but, as Sor Juana points out in her response to Sor Filotea, silence requires both an explicating and an authorizing voice to enable it to be effective in the symbolic order. Estrella is inscribed as an object in the symbolic systems that determine her fate, but she is simultaneously inscribed in and excluded from the systems of exchange that move around her. She is described in mercantile terms, and those terms are connected through writing with the symbolic order. Excluded from language, Estrella loses both her brother and her fiancé. Her most meaningful actions and words, the ones that reaffirm the traditional values of honor in an oral society, constitute her renunciation. The fragile *papeles* that move about the stage of *La Estrella de Sevilla* affect the plot as if they were characters, but require other characters to give them a voice. Writing in both plays is instrumental to the plot, but it also reflects upon the social order and inscription of women in systems of exchange that belie the discourses of absolute value precariously entrusted to language in the social context of honor.

Notes

1. Earlier versions of this essay were read at the Renaissance Society of America Annual Meeting, Harvard University, 30 March 1989; the Eleventh Louisiana Conference on Hispanic Languages and Literatures, Louisiana State University, Baton Rouge, 23 February 1990; and the International Symposium on *La estrella de Sevilla*, Pennsylvania State University, 2–5 April 1992. I thank Professor Inés Azar for her helpful critical comments.

2. Unless otherwise indicated, translations are from *The Star of Seville: A Drama in Three Acts and in Verse Attributed to Lope de Vega*, trans. Henry Thomas (Newtown, Montgomeryshire, Wales: Gregynog Press, 1935).

3. Sancho Ortiz also speaks of love in monetary terms: "¿Cuándo seré tu dueño / sacando deste empeño / las ansias que te envío?" (478–80; "When will you be mine, / enabling me to redeem from pawn / my longings for you?"; translation mine). He proceeds to create a verbal portrait of Estrella, another form of "ownership."

4. Although she does not specifically address *La estrella de Sevilla*, Yvonne Yarbro-Bejarano's analysis of this aspect of the *comedia* aptly brings together Gayle Rubin's model of the "traffic in women" with the imagery of coinage in English Restoration drama cited by Eve Kosofsky Sedgwick (Yarbro-Bejarano 1987, 624–25, Sedgwick 1985, 50–55).

5. For the reader of the *comedia* as text, however, the expectation of the text's reproduction of another text inscribed on an object is exemplified in lines 241–48 of Garcilaso's *Egloga* 3, in which the words carved on a tree are both described and transcribed: " . . . que hablavan ansí por parte della: / 'Elisa soy . . . '" Garcilaso's reproduction of prosopopeia involves a new set of problems, but illustrates the expectation that, with the presence of a written text in a fictional world, its substance may be expected to be known to the reader.

6. Martin Pops paraphrases Gaston Bachelard's *Poetics of Space* in his discussion:

> The woman in [*Woman Reading at a Window*, ca. 1657–59] is more formidably barricaded than anyone else in [Vermeer's] *oeuvre*. Her corner is an enclave, and Vermeer denies its merely quotidian aspect. . . . The woman reads a letter from without which draws her further within.
> "This painting is Vermeer's first essay on reflection. The woman who reads generates a second self, the woman absorbed in what she reads. In the set of reading, the reader is doubled: one self inhabits the sensuous world, the other a transparent reach beyond the

bars of the reflecting glass. The self which migrates into the world of the text is seduced by language and held captive. . . . [In paintings of the Annunciation] the Virgin's book is the attribute of her interiority. Reading is a type of parthenogenetic fertilization, magic doubling. The woman reading gives birth to her second self. (Martin Pops, "The *Woman Reading at a Window*," *Salmagundi* 44–45 (1979): 29–30)

7. Alpers points out (196–200) that "the relationship between surface presence and inner inaccessibility" is "thematized in the viewer's relationship to the woman. . . . What is suggested is not the content of the letters . . . but rather the letter as an object of visual attention, a surface to be looked at," as well as the letter's "ability to close distances, to make something present, to communicate secretly." To read a document aloud on stage places it in two worlds: the reader's private and personal gaze and privilege of interpretation, and the public world on stage in which the document's words become a verbal rather than a written act. Alpers's study, however, is concerned with distinguishing the Dutch pictorial tradition from the Italian narrative tradition in painting, a tradition to which the function of letters in the *comedia,* and the semiotics of the *comedia* itself, more appropriately belong.

16

Writing the *Saturnalia*

JAMES F. BURKE

IF one is to judge from evidence in the play, graphic writing and the documents that it produces do not appear to bear much credibility in *La estrella de Sevilla*.[1] From the beginning of the drama it becomes obvious that it is actions and not written evidence, at least that type consigned to paper, that provide the paradigm for the shaping of future events. Don Arias makes this clear in the advice he gives to the King to help him to secure Busto's acquiescence to his pursuit of the lovely Estrella. "Si tú le das y él recibe, / se obliga; y si es obligado, / pagará lo que le has dado; / que al que dan, en bronce escribe" (201–4; "If you give him something and he accepts it, he owes something; and if he is obliged, he will repay the favor; since when something is given to someone, the act is inscribed in bronze"). The allusion to the writing in bronze not only implies a more durable script than that which could be secured on paper but also brings to mind the entire context of stirring historical deeds and activities for which the city of Seville had become famous. Such activities are referred to, of course, at many junctures throughout the work.

The play then continues with a long series of references that subtly undermine the validity and worth of documentary writing. Near the beginning are the written petitions from don Gonzalo de Ulloa and Fernán Pérez de Medina that substantiate their respective claims to the position of Captain General for the frontier of Archidona (337–56). The king, already blinded by his desire for Estrella, has no intention of adjudicating the claims. The same is true in regard to the *escrituras* ("writings") that seemingly establish in law the bethrothal of Estrella and Sancho Ortiz de las Roelas (555–57). Busto expects that such a contract can remain valid despite royal desires to the contrary, but such is scarcely the case. "Volviendo a informar al Rey / que están hechos los conciertos /

235

y escrituras, serán ciertos / los contratos; que su ley / no ha de atropellar lo justo" (643–47; "By informing the King again that the agreements and written documents have been executed, the contracts will be assured—since his law should not come into conflict with that which is just").

The importance of such *escrituras* is constantly challenged, as Sancho has already inferred, by the unending change that affects the human condition. ". . . ¿cómo en tanta mudanza / podré tener del tiempo confianza?" (586–87; "How in the midst of so much change, shall I be able to have confidence in time?").

The king's very position itself has been brought into question by Papal Bulls which imply that his nephew's candidacy for the throne may have validity (678–80 and again at 2692–93). The *cédula* ("royal certificate") the king gives to Natilde (845–47), granting her freedom in exchange for having facilitated his entry into Busto's house, is of no protection to her against her irate master and she is found by the king and don Arias hanged, with the document in her hands (1240–41).

The theme of the written guarantee reappears a short time later when the king summons Sancho to his presence (1402). In his hands he holds two papers, one bearing the name of the individual whom Sancho must kill; the other is another guarantee, stating that it was he, the king, who made the decision to take the life of Busto Tavera. Sancho, of course, will agree to kill Busto, since the king accuses him of lèse majesté (1512–13), but he will refuse to utilize the paper in his own defense—eventually forcing the king to admit verbally his own responsibility.

Other references in *La estrella de Sevilla* that question the worth of writing are the humorous ones that come forth during Sancho and Clarindo's imagined journey to hell. There are no *escribanos* ("scribes") in the underworld because the demons appear to realize that their presence there would certainly occasion lawsuits. And the playwright has even attacked the very profession from which he draws his livelihood. "¡Válgame Dios! Saber quiero / quién es aquél de la pluma" (2449–50; "By Jove! I want to know who that one with the pen is"), exclaims Clarindo. Sancho's indentification includes some of the finest writers in the classical tradition—Homer, Virgil, Horace, Lucan, and Ovid. The fate of these writers seems to stand in stark constrast with the fame of those active heroes whose deeds and accomplishments provide a kind of backdrop against which the present life of Seville always seems to be measured in the drama. The grounds for such comparison are established at the beginning of the play when Don Arias says in regard to the city: "El adorno y sus grandezas / de las calles, no sé yo / si Augusto en Roma las vió, / ni creo tantas riquezas" (61–64; "I don't know whether Augustus saw such adornment and grandeur in the streets of Rome, nor do I believe that he saw such richness").

What the work seems to proclaim in one way, then, is the kind of tension between the written and the oral that Derrida has studied in *Of Grammatology*. One has to understand the "oral" here to encompass the entire sphere of that which is active and alive, the spirit, in contrast to that which has been consigned to the memorial, the letter. This antagonism of the active to the passive, presented in terms of writing, is strongly drawn in Sancho's outburst when it is discovered that he has killed Busto and don Arias asks what has happened: "Decidle al Rey mi señor / que tienen los sevillanos / las palabras en las manos, / como lo veis, pues por ellas / atropellan las Estrellas y no hacen caso de hermanos" (1845–50; "Tell the King my lord that the Sevillians bear their words in their hands, and because of them the Stars collide with one another and pay no attention to brothers").

La estrella de Sevilla is, of course, a drama, a work composed to be played, to be presented actively before the eyes of an audience. A wider definition of writing, writing as genus of which the graphic variety is species, implies a process in which a selection is constantly made among possibilities on a paradigmatic axis as one moves along a syntagmatic axis. What happens in most instances is that a number of choices are involved on both planes. One important thing that the literary work accomplishes is to select from the variety and focus the attention of the reader or spectator upon the ones chosen, thereby excluding a multitude of additional possibilities.

In a play such as *La estrella de Sevilla* the syntagmatic axis is the ordered chronological line along which the actions of the work take place. The characters, actions, scenes, and settings are themselves elected from all those that are potentially available to form the ordered content of the work. As the drama unfolds, the totality of its meaning is, as it were, "rewritten" in space and time to be "read" by the onlookers. The words of Sancho just quoted, "las palabras en las manos" ("their words in their hands") suggest that such a reading is supposed as accomplished by the characters within the confines of the play itself while the phrase ". . . pues por ellas / atropellan las Estrellas" ("and because of them, the stars collide") would suggest that the effect of such actions are felt even in the macrocosm, that even the stars "read" and assimilate the message sculptured into reality by the deeds of the "sevillanos."

Of course the usual interpretation of astrology in ancient times was that the effect of the movement of the planets and the stars produced an effect in the sublunary world. What was written in the stars was thought to be imprinted upon the raw material of human life and experience. The message, then, that an audience viewing *La estrella de Sevilla* could have been expected to receive, "to read," would have been at least threefold. First, there is the one that comes from the glorious history and tradition of the city and its previous inhabitants. Second, there would have been the astrological script, the one presented in the play in terms of characters who are constantly portrayed as representing heavenly bodies. And there also would have been the actions of the characters themselves, partially informed and shaped in all instances by the previous two texts. Is there further the possibility of a fourth text, one of a more general nature that would have supported and furthered the message inherent in the first three?

Julio Caro Baroja has studied the Roman feast of the *Saturnalia* as a possible model for a whole series of "fiestas de invierno" ("festivals of winter") in Spain such as that of the "obispillo de San Nicolás," ("the boy bishop of Saint Nicholas"), the "Rey de la Faba" ("the King of the Bean"), and the "reyes y alcaldes de Inocentes" ("kings and mayors of the Day of the Holy Innocents"), as well as for Carnival itself. These are often festivals of reversal in which the roles of the mighty and powerful are temporarily taken by the most humble members of society. The purpose of such inversion is to signal that elementary principle of semiotics which says that a rule is most strongly affirmed by the signalling of its contrary. Caro Baroja also quotes such late medieval and renaissance writers as Hernando de Talavera and Bartolomé de las Casas to demonstrate that the Roman *Saturnalia,* the great classical example of this idea, was known in Spain during the period (304).[2]

The figure of Saturn had been associated with themes of prosperity and progress in Spain during the Middle Ages, as is made clear in the *General estoria* (*General History*) of Alfonso el Sabio:

Saturno . . . e fue princep derechero, e começo muchos derechos en la tierra: vender las cosas a medida e a peso, et fazer por los buenos logares mercados pregonados e coteados, a que se acogiessen los omnes a vender e a comprar, et mando tomar metales en precio de las otras cosas segund valiessen, et fazie las yentes sin toda contienda e a cada uno en lo suyo, e tenie la tierra en paz, en justicia e abondada. (1: 156)

[Saturn . . . and he was a just prince, and he initiated many good practices in the land: the selling of things by weight and by measure, and the establishing of well-known markets with regulated prices in good places where people could go to buy and to sell, and he ordered that metals be accepted in exchange for other things according to value, and he erased contention between people and gave to each his own, and he caused the land to be in peace, justice and abundance.]

The last sentence in this quote makes clear the place that the ruler would have in that scheme of things which would establish this realm of harmony and justice upon the earth.

The importance of the "rey saturnalicio" (Saturnalian king) has been amply studied and commented upon by Caro Baroja as a figure that parodies the true ruler and thereby serves to reinforce the relevance of the role the monarch plays in society (290). In the context of the Saturnalian celebrations, the feigned sacrifice of the pretended king took on great importance if the real ruler was thought to have become weakened, corrupt, or enervated. For the social group the *Saturnalia* with its masks and games could serve to evoke the process of renovation and regeneration periodically necessary for its well-being and survival.

In an article written several years ago (1974) I suggested that the lovely Estrella represents not as might be expected the planet named for the goddess of love, Venus, but the seventh planet, Saturn.[3] Such is implied by the description the king gives of her as a kind of black star whose light is able to eclipse that of even the sun (141–50) and also by Sancho Ortiz de las Roelas when he associates her metaphorically with the last planet: "¿Cuándo, alegre y dichoso, / me llamaré tu esposo / a pesar de los tiempos que detienes, / que en perezoso turno / caminan con las plantas de Saturno?" (505–9; "When, happy and favored, shall I call myself your husband, this despite the hours which you delay, hours which in slow turn, proceed at the pace of Saturn?").

Estrella is the last of a group of women whom the king has seen at the beginning of the play as his procession winds through the streets of Seville. Later he inquires as to who the women are, and don Arias obliges by telling him. Don Arias mentions seven women before reaching Estrella but two of these are sisters and might be taken symbolically as one. I also suggested that the women might represent the seven planets and that the theatrical technique used here could be similar to that employed in the memory theater of the renaissance thinker Guilio Camillo. This construction was a series of seven semicircular grades divided into seven pathways that cut vertically across the semicircles. At the top of each pathway was a symbol to represent one of the seven planets. On each step of the pathway below were images that alluded to the various and sundry positive attributes of the planets. The onlooker could, as Frances Yates so well put it, "read off at one glance . . . the whole contents of the universe" (1966, 155).

Don Arias and the king also may be said to "read" the attributes of the women whom they observe along the route of the procession, but the interpretation they derive is one that has to do with matters of love. My suggestion is that what they find written there is also a description of the seven planets and that it is the final one which will be of great importance for the king in the play. Estrella describes herself to Sancho as "Estrella . . . que te guía" (2594; "a Star . . . that guides you"), and I think that she will act in a similar manner for the king as he learns to accept the behavior and manner appropriate for a ruler.

If Estrella is to be taken as representing a positive Saturn whose influence exercises a beneficial effect upon King Sancho, can her role be understood as functioning within a dramatic sphere that may be seen as symbolically supporting her function? I think that it can and that this mode is that of a literary *Saturnalia* conceived in the main to convey, within the confines of the theater, a message similar to the one conveyed by the festival to the public in the streets. This *Saturnalia* is the fourth text that incorporates and unites the three referred to previously.

It is not immediately clear why the action and setting of the play might be identified with that of the *Saturnalia* or with one of its theoretical descendants in Spain, as described by Caro Baroja. The work does begin, of course, with the festive circumstance of an *adventus regis* (triumphal entry of a king), and there is almost immediately an indication of role reversal. Don Arias refers to the richness of Seville and the glory of its history (61–64), but the king shows little interest. "Y las divinas bellezas, / ¿por qué en silencio las pasas?" (65–66; "And the divine beauties, why do you pass over them in silence?"). The king is consumed by lust and will immediately direct his energy and that of his courtiers toward the achievement of a goal scarcely associated with his royal mission of good government, the administration of justice, and the pursuit of the Reconquest. The role of the king in the play is precisely the reverse of what it should be.

The proper course of action in *La estrella de Sevilla* is demonstrated by Busto Tavera, Sancho Ortiz de las Roelas, and of course by Estrella herself. In effect the play sets up "mock rulers" who, instead of giving a ridiculous rendering of the circumstances of the king or bishop, as in the ceremonies of the Feast of Fools or the Boy-bishop, present the correct paradigm in contrast to that effected by the true monarch.

When the king goes to Busto's house after bribing the slave Natilde and is confronted by Busto, he immediately covers himself to conceal his identity, symbolically donning the mask traditional in the festivals of reversal (982). But thus disguised and obviously intent upon a purpose that so little pertains to the royal rank and dignity, he cannot merit the respect due to the regal office, and Busto is more than willing to challenge him: ". . . que sacras y humanas leyes / condenan a culpa estrecha / al que imagina o sospecha / cosa indigna de los reyes" (1037–40; ". . . both sacred and human laws condemn with harsh blame anyone who imagines or suspects an unworthy action on the part of a king").

Estrella, when she goes to give Sancho his liberty, also covers her face in order initially to disguise herself from the young man (2556–2645). It is significant that she reveals her identity just before uttering the line previously alluded to "Estrella soy que te guía" (2594; "I am a star that will guide you").

Thérèse Malachy has studied the theme of Carnival in the works of Molière and has pointed out that, in the French playwright's drama *Dom Juan,* as well as in its prototype *El burlador de Sevilla* (*The Trickster of Seville*), Don Juan effectively stands the system of social codes upon its head and thereby creates for himself a personal Carnival within the context of organized society (1987, 53). But, as she succinctly puts it (50), "Le carnaval solitaire est proscrit" ("A personal Carnival is prohibited"). And how could it be otherwise if society is to maintain itself and the integrity of its collective functions?

The figure that restores order in both plays, of course, is the statue of the dead Commendador, which implies in the Lacanian, Kristevan scheme of things the return of the law, the re-imposition of the "non(m) du père" ("the 'no'/'name' of the father"). In *La estrella de Sevilla* the king, in attempting to allow himself sexual license, behaves in a manner characteristic of a *Saturnalia* or Carnival in that his conduct will resemble that manifested in the reversals of role often permitted in these celebrations. He abandons his own private carnival not because he himself is destroyed but because of the death of Busto and the actions of Sancho and Estrella. One of the three "mock rulers" is sacrificed in the manner traditional for the *Saturnalia* in order to facilitate a personal anagnorisis on the part of the king. The other two, while remaining alive, face a personal loss that bears a very high price indeed.

If it is the statute of the dead father that reestablishes patriarchal order in the plays that deal with Don Juan, what symbol or nexus of themes is there that accomplishes a similar function in *La estrella de Sevilla?* Busto, Sancho, and Estrella can surely not be seen as signifying in and of themselves the series of codes that modern critics term the "law of the father." Rather, the actions of the three seem to evoke, to recall, the patterns of virtuous behavior and conduct implicit in the positively cast symbolic domain.

Jacques Bril in his study of the mask and its relevance in society has explained such facial coverings and the festivals within which they are used as metaphorizations of the mechanisms that organize a group (1983, 43). The mask suggests the primordial Father understood as the structuring figure inherent in the social order. But it also implies much more. It refers to the spirits, ancestors, and heroes who provide the affirming mythic and historical foundation upon which the society is grounded (1983, 41). Not only the mask but also a whole series of objects accorded a particular significance in a given culture can serve as symbols to evoke the basic principles of structure that the group employs to order itself: ". . . masques, statues ou crucifix—seraient les effecteurs et les médiateurs" (199; ". . . masks, statues or crucifix—these would be the agents of change and the mediators").

The time of the year when such artefacts assume the greatest importance is during the festivals of reversal, when there is a kind of feigned return to primoridal chaos with ensuing implications of re-creation and renewal. But, of course, for most societies, and certainly in Europe before the Enlightenment, re-creation always meant the revival of, or reinvigoration of, certain basic paradigms and ways of doing things that had been established in some variety of hypothetical golden age. The figures utilized during the festivals of reversal were ones that could evoke the positive patriarchal archetypes associated with those principles supposedly established during the lost epoch of harmony. "Mais, essentiellement, le roi de carton du Carnaval et ses acolytes masqués ne sont qu'un seul et même personnage . . . et le représentant totémique du Père end eviendra à n'être plus qu'un symbole, parmi d'autres, de la culture des fils" (135; "But, essentially, the cardboard king of Carnival and his masked acolytes are but one and the same thing . . . the totemic representative of the Father, which become nothing more than a symbol, among others, of the culture of the son").

For Bril the importance of the historical forbears of a group is that they act as a kind of tutor for those having to decide upon a course of action in the present. The masks utilized during certain festivals of reversal are the images that help symbolically to transmit this ancestral knowledge and experience into terms accessible to the group: "Les ancêstres . . . jouent pour les sociétés le même rôle que les parents pour l'enfant. . . . Nous avons insisté sur le rôle joué par les masques d'intermedaires entre l'espace réel des vivants et le domain fantastique des morts. . . . Les mascarades sacrées, même laïcisées en carnivals, relèvent clairement de ce registre médian et médiateur" (159; "Ancestors . . . serve for societies the same role as parents for the child. . . . We have insisted upon the role played by masks as intermediaries between the real space of the living and the fantasy domain of the dead. . . . Sacred mascarades, even when laicized in Carnivals, demonstrate clearly this intermediate and mediating register").

In *La estrella de Sevilla* there is a long series of both implied and direct identications of Seville with the grandeur and glory of imperial Rome, which is clearly depicted in the play as the patriarchal forbear of the city and its noble inhabitants. As previously noted, don Arias at the beginning of the play compares the decorations in the streets to those of Augustan Rome (61–64). Later Don Arias associates the King with Augustus Caesar: "El Rey Don Sancho, a quien llaman / por su invicta fortaleza / *el Bravo* el vulgo, y los moros, / porque de su nombre tiemblan, / el Fuerte, y sus altas obras / el Sacro y Augusto César, / que los laureles romanos / con sus hazañas afrenta" (781–87; "The common people call King Don Sancho 'The Fierce One' because of his unvanquished strength and the Moors, because they tremble at his name, [call him] 'The Strong One' and because of his exalted works, the Sacred and August Caesar since he, with his deeds, challenges the Roman laurels of victory").

The very next line don Arias utters, however, demonstrates that the king intends something which will be at great variance with the role such comparisons would imply: ". . . esa divina hermosura / vió en un balcón, competencia / de los palacios del alba" (789–91; ". . . he saw on a balcony that divine beauty who [gives] competition to the palaces of the dawn").

Busto refers to a Roman precedent for his being forced to hang Natilde: ". . . que quiero que el Rey conozca / que hay Brutos contra Tarquinos / en Sevilla" (1374–76; ". . . I want the King to know that there are Brutuses against the Tarquinii in Seville"). Later, toward the end of the play when the king and don Arias are amazed by the refusal of Sancho to declare that he had been ordered to kill Busto by the king, don Arias demonstrates to what degree the Sevillians adhere to the paradigms of behavior bequeathed to them by their classical forbears: "La gente desta ciudad / oscurece la romana" (2744–45; "The people of this city obscures the Romans").

The king himself suggests the kind of concrete reminders mentioned by Bril in giving voice to his astonishment at the courage and virtuous behavior of the Sevillian authorities: "No he visto gente / más gentil ni más cristiana / que la desta ciudad: callen / bronces, mármoles y estatuas" (2774–76; "I have never seen people more virtuous nor more Christian than that of this city. Be silent bronzes, [works sculptured in] marble and statues").

With these images the king invokes not only the Roman heritage of the city but also the precepts and teachings of Christianity as implied and suggested to the faithful by statues of Christ, the Virgin, and the saints. He has thus called forth the entire range of positive, civilized examples that would support correct and proper modes of conduct both at a personal and a more general level. It is these models, made present for him in the behavior of Busto, Sancho, and Estrella, that will finally force him to accept the role traditional for the ruler: "Admirado me ha dejado / la nobleza sevillana" (2982–83; "The Sevillian nobility has left me amazed").

But, of course, it is the happenings in the play, actualized within the context of the drama, that provide the example for the audience. I suggest that these events are "written," inscribed upon the face of reality in terms of a literary *Saturnalia*. Within the context of the drama, these happenings focus the attention of the onlookers upon the correct course of action by alluding to the historical grandeur of the city's past, and by holding up as mirror for the aberrant king the three characters in the play who re-enact the correct paradigms in the present.

Notes

1. Elias Rivers has produced very perceptive comments on the function of writing in the play and sees it as related to the opposition that exists between honor and shame as a binary pair which orders a traditional society (1983, 85).

2. Bermejo Barrera also points out that the fertility of the fields was associated with Saturn in the Spanish Golden Age (1982, 27).

3. This identification has been accepted by de Armas (1979; 1980) who has given further insights as to the role and function of Saturn in the play.

17

Shame, Writing, and Morality

CHARLES ORIEL

THE implications of writing and inscription have received increasing attention from critics and theorists alike, due in large part to the relentless critique of the metaphysical tradition offered by Jacques Derrida and his "assorted and surly" cohorts. Coming from a very different viewpoint, Walter J. Ong (1977; 1982) has contrasted speaking and writing in the following way: while the spoken word occurs within a context of mutual presence of "sender" and "receiver," writing presupposes their mutual absence. The written word is thus often thought of as a temporary but necessary substitute for face-to-face, oral communication. This way of thinking is reinforced by the fact that writing appears to be secondary—a sign that is twice removed from the reality that it ostensibly represents: the graphic indicator of an oral sign. Derrida (1967) has variously described this privileging of orality over writing, using such terms as *metaphysics of presence* and *logocentrism*.

One of my basic contentions throughout this paper is that the metaphysics of presence is literalized and championed by the action of *La estrella de Sevilla* (1623), for King Sancho effectively dishonors the citizens of Seville by way of the so-called *supplement* to oral communication, that absential and mediated means: written texts. The written word's inherent absence enables him to function in secrecy and to subordinate his social role as monarch to personal desires. As Elias Rivers has pointed out in his seminal article on "The Shame of Writing in *La Estrella de Sevilla*" (1980)—an article to which this essay's title makes obvious reference—the written word implicitly threatens the code of honor:

> The written contract, as a substitute speech-act, destroys the honor system itself, which depends upon the non-reiterable uniqueness of the performative utterance. A man may sign his name after he raises his right hand and swears; but, from a traditional point of view, that signa-

245

ture is an inadequate substitute for the authentic oral performative
utterance, pronounced face to face. . . . Notaries are invented as witnesses to supplement with their signatures the written traces of a
speech act, but what remains is only paper . . . without the honor
identified with the unique act and presence of flesh and blood. When
a man is judged in terms of a fixed written law code, we can safely say
that the traditional oral system of personal honor is dead. (115–16)

Rivers's study conceives *La estrella de Sevilla* as a dramatization
of conflicts engendered by the traditional code of personal honor.
This code governs all sexual and social relations and is dependent
upon presence, which is the necessary prerequisite to oral communication: "Feelings of honor and shame function only when people
can face and talk to one another orally; only under such circumstances of physical presence are there genuine speech acts, honorable obligations, or shameful losses of face" (1980, 115). It follows
that written communication tends to subvert the traditional honor
code, for it functions by way of absence: the act of writing is always
private, spatially and temporally removed from the equally private
act of reading and, in that respect, "liberates" the author from
responsibility for its contents.

One of the first references to writing in *La estrella* is when Estrella Tavera attempts to ease Sancho Ortiz's concern about possible obstacles to their marriage. She assures him that: "hechas las
escrituras / tan firmes y seguras, / el casamiento es llano" (556–58;
"such firm and binding contracts ensure that the wedding will take
place"). Sancho nevertheless remains uneasy, for he cannot bring
himself to believe in written words as a guarantee. This is, of
course, only the beginning of a sustained criticism of written communication by Sancho Ortiz.

Another important written text is the document with which the
king bribes the slave girl Natilde: an order declaring her freedom.
Written orders issued by a king have immediate and public effects,
for all the weight of officialdom and royal authority is behind them.
But because the motivations for issuing this order are private
rather than public, and dishonorable rather than honorable, it is
issued in secrecy. By acting secretly in this way, the king not only
subverts the social order that is conventionally maintained by such
documents; he also implicitly undercuts the institutional functioning of all such written documents.

Despite its conventionally public function, this document is the
private contradiction of a previously established wedding contract:
those "escrituras . . . firmes y seguras" ("firm and binding con-

tracts") that publicly guarantee the wedding between Sancho and Estrella. The king's order is not motivated by institutional desire for the public good, but by personal, that is, sexual desire. Symbolized by the contradiction of these two written texts—one of which actually appears on stage and the other merely referred to—is that tension which is inherent in any monarchy between the king's "two bodies": between the office and the man (Kantorowicz 1957). The king's moral corruption has been made clear by the illicit methods he uses to attempt to seduce Estrella, but the written order constitutes material evidence that is there for Busto Tavera (and all the inhabitants of Seville, after him) to see.

By using written texts, the king maintains himself in absence and thereby temporarily avoids owning up to his acts; the drama thus draws an insistent connection between presence and moral responsibility. Paradoxically, the king remains absent in this moral sense even when he is physically present. When he enters Busto's house, for example, he does so secretly (at night), hiding his identity under a cape and making sure beforehand that Busto will be absent. When Busto comes home unexpectedly and confronts him, the king insists that he has entered Busto's house in order to honor him. Busto, of course, denies this claim:

> . . . si mi honor procuráis,
> ¿cómo embozado venís?
> Honrándome ¿os encubrís?
> Dándome honor ¿os tapáis?
>
> (1009–12)

[. . . if you strive to do me honor, why come hidden by a cloak? Honoring me, you cover yourself up? Giving me honor, you hide yourself?]

Busto argues that true honor consists in the responsibility implied by open and public presence. His words throughout this scene serve, in fact, to emphasize that the intruder's absential and secretive manner is radically opposed to the self-consciously public manner of a true king. The king's "disembodied" voice forcefully illustrates the dynamic play of presence and absence in this scene.

When Busto finds out about Natilde's involvement in the king's illicit entry, he executes her by hanging her outside of the palace walls and leaving her body there suspended, with the king's written order of her freedom in her hand. Busto's reaction is a direct refutation of the king's written order and, at the same time, a raising of the stakes from the private realm to the public one. The king has already dishonored Busto by the very act of entering his house without permission. He has thereby transgressed the principle of the inviolability of personal domain, just as he did by bribing Busto's slave (yet another piece of personal property) and by attempting the seduction of his sister, a woman he knows to be promised to another man in marriage. The king has thus denied Busto's personal integrity, his status, and his authority as an individual: he has, in short, denied him his honor.

By putting the written order in the hand of the dead Natilde, Busto has radically changed its original communicative context (to say the least). Instead of the liberty that the document purports to guarantee, Natilde receives nothing other than death. Busto's unwritten communication is a forcefully expressed refutation of the king's abuse of authority and a public exposure of his unlawful and unjust mode of ruling: the king's written orders, Busto implies, are nothing more than "dead letter."

The hanged slave manifests the conflict between the king and Busto, between moral absence and moral presence. Earlier, when his advisor don Arias had informed him of the preparations made to facilitate his seduction of Estrella, the king praised Natilde by claiming that "Castilla / estatuas la ha de labrar" (907–8; "Castile will erect statues in her honor"). His words constitute an ironic anticipation of her fate: Busto converts her into a figurative statue, one that testifies neither to Natilde nor to the greatness of the king, but rather to the moral corruption of both.

In assessing this situation, J. L. Brooks (1955) correctly observes that "Busto, by publicly executing Natilde for her part in allowing the king to enter his house, makes no effort to prevent possible gossip and, in fact, attracts attention to himself in the cause of pure justice" (12). But this observation contradicts Brooks's own earlier judgment that Busto does not care about public opinion (12); on the contrary, he *does* care about it and attempts, in fact, to utilize it to force the king to act with honor. What is important here, however, is that Busto's unwritten communication is open and public, while nearly all of the king's communications throughout are closed and secret. Busto's openness and the king's secrecy together constitute an inversion of the modes by which king and subject conventionally operate, for Busto acts as a king ought to act—publicly and with honor—while King Sancho acts like a private citizen, that is, privately and guided by personal motives and desires.

This is exemplified most clearly in the king's first conversation with Sancho Ortiz. When the monarch tells Sancho that there is a certain man that he wants executed, he insists upon total secrecy, something that Sancho argues vehemently against:

> Pues, ¿cómo muerte en secreto
> a un culpado se le da?
> Poner su muerte en efeto
> públicamente podrá
>   vuestra justicia, sin dalle
> muerte en secreto; que así
> vos os culpáis en culpalle,
> pues dais a entender que aquí
> sin culpa mandáis matalle.
>   Y dalle muerte, señor,
> sin culpa, no es justa ley,
> sino bárbaro rigor;
> y un rey, sólo por ser rey,
> se ha de respetar mejor.

(1478–91)

[Why should a criminal be executed secretly? As administrator of Justice, you can effect this death publicly, not in secrecy; by acting in secrecy you incriminate yourself when you accuse him, because you create the impression that you are executing him unjustly. And to execute an innocent man is not justice, it is mere barbarity. A king, simply because he is king, should have more respect for himself."]

Sancho's words are true with a vengeance. The king can exercise "mere barbarity" only because it is secret (no one else is to know about it) and because it is mediated (the king himself will not execute Busto: Sancho will enact it). According to Sancho, the very secrecy that the king proposes will make the execution suspect. Like Busto before him, Sancho explicitly emphasizes the importance of authorizing one's acts with a sense of full presence and moral responsibility, and the consequent necessity—especially in the case of a king—of acting openly and publicly.

The king orders Busto's execution by way of two written documents. One of them names the so-called traitor who is to be executed, and the other contains a pardon that Sancho is to use to clear himself, once the order has been carried out. Harlan and Sara Sturm (1970, 288) have pointed out how the ambivalence of the word *papel* (meaning both "paper" and "role") is utilized in this scene to emphasize Sancho's personal dilemma:

When the King approaches Sancho to give him the assignment, he carries two *papeles*. The dramatist thus takes advantage of the double meaning associated with the word *papel:* Sancho el Bravo is, in effect, imposing on Sancho Ortiz a role consistent with the monarch's own distorted values but totally in opposition to the noble's sense of honor.

Sancho rejects the "role" that the king has assigned to him, that of secret and anonymous executioner. He cannot willingly absent himself in this way; he can only be himself, acting with full responsibility. But he also rejects a *papel* in the literal sense, for he refuses to accept the king's written pardon, claiming that he trusts completely in his spoken promise:

> Estoy admirado
> de que tan poco conceto
> tenga de mí Vuestra Alteza.
> ¡Yo cédula! ¡Yo papel!
> Tratadme con más llaneza,
> que más en vos que no en él
> confía aquí mi nobleza.
> Si vuestras palabras cobran
> valor que los montes labra,
> y ellas cuanto dicen obran,
> dándome aquí la palabra,
> señor, los papeles sobran.
> A la palabra remito
> la cédula que me dais,
> con que a vengaros me incito,
> porque donde vos estáis
> es excusado lo escrito.
> Rompeldo, porque sin él
> la muerte le solicita
> mejor, señor, que con él;
> que en parte desacredita
> vuestra palabra el papel.
> Sin papel, señor, aquí
> nos obligamos los dos,
> y prometemos así,
> yo de vengaros a vos
> y vos de librarme a mí.
>
> 1555–81)

[I'm amazed that you could have so low an image of me! A written order—for me? Have more respect for my honor, which depends much more upon you personally than upon any piece of paper. If your words have power to move mountains, and if they do what they say, then merely by giving me your word here and now, any paper is unnecessary.

Your spoken word, which incites me to perform your justice, is worth more than any written order, because wherever you are present, writing is unnecessary. Rip up the written order, because without it, the execution will be more efficiently carried than with it; a written order actually undermines your spoken words. Without papers, then, here and now, we commit ourselves to one another, and thus we promise: I, to effect your justice, and you, to pardon and free me.]

As Rivers (1980, 115) has noted, this is the drama's most powerful indictment of written texts. Sancho is shocked to see that the king could have so low an opinion of him as to offer him a written guarantee of freedom. He trusts much more in the king's actual presence, the flesh-and-blood person, than he could in any mere piece of paper. He emphasizes the absolute authority of the king's spoken words by appealing to their institutionally performative nature ("cuanto dicen *obran*" ["they do what they say"]) that is dependent on a radical sense of presence ("dándome *aquí* la palabra, / señor, los papeles sobran ["giving me your word *here,* papers are unnecessary"] . . . *donde vos estáis* / es excusado lo escrito" ["*wherever you are,* writing is unneeded"]). According to Sancho, true honor lies in the conformity between one's words and one's deeds, and thus there is no need of a written guarantee; he therefore rips up the pardon. It is an act that resonates with meaning in reference to Natilde's written order of freedom, for this is the second time that a promise of liberty, written by the hand of the king, has been denied efficacy.

Immediately following this exchange, Sancho receives a letter from Estrella, informing him of their imminent marriage. He then reads the king's order and finds out that Estrella's brother Busto is the "traitor" whom he must kill. The two written documents represent a torturous decision that he must make, for they are inherently contradictory insofar as Sancho himself is concerned. Killing Estrella's brother, in accordance with the king's written order and as he himself has promised, will eliminate any possibility of his marrying her. Besides this, the king's insistence upon secrecy has made Sancho suspect that the execution will be anything but an act of justice. Sancho does finally keep his promise to the king and kills Busto: he can do no other than embody the simple principle that a man is as good as his word.

By killing Busto in such a public and open way, Sancho provokes his own immediate imprisonment by the authorities. Under questioning, Sancho refuses to go back on his promise of secrecy to the king, even when questioned by the monarch himself:

> *Rey.*   ¿Quién te mandó darle muerte?
> *Sancho.*   Un papel.
> *Rey.*   ¿De quién?
> *Sancho.*   Si hablara
> el papel, él lo dijera;
> que es cosa evidente y clara;
> mas los papeles rompidos
> dan confusas las palabras.
>
> (2934–39)
>
> *King.*   Who ordered you to execute him?
> *Sancho.*   A paper.
> *King.*   From whom?
> *Sancho.*   If the paper could speak, it would say
> who—this is clear and obvious—but torn-up papers present
> mixed-up words.

Sancho reiterates his distrust of the written text, which liberates and distances its producer from responsibility for its contents. The only thing left of the writer is his or her traces: the inscribed words, which cannot, in any case, be held accountable. Sancho implicitly denies the authority of the written word by describing its communicative power in terms of (what else?) orality: "Si hablara / el papel, él lo dijera" ("If the paper could speak, it would tell who"). He bitterly implies that even a written-upon piece of paper seems to have more of a sense of presence, integrity, and self-consistency than does this king, who—at least thus far—has not honorably lived up to his word by freeing him. Sancho, however, remains steadfast: he had accepted only the orally spoken words of the king as a promise of pardon and he will accept only spoken words as the pardon itself.

The final written text in *La estrella* is Sancho's death-sentence issued by the town council of Seville, whose integrity—like that of Sancho before them—is tested by the king's behavior. The monarch speaks separately to two councilmen and requests that Sancho be sentenced to exile rather than death. This is, of course, consistent with the king's essential *modus operandi*. He approaches the councilmen in absence from one another and from all other witnesses so as to continue operating privately: he wishes to spare Sancho's life without publicly admitting responsibility for Busto's death. He hopes to influence privately the decision that they will make in their public roles as upholders of the law. But in such roles they are guided by their vision of public justice: they see Sancho as guilty and sentence him accordingly, regardless of the king's privately manifested desire. When the monarch reads

the sentence and demands to know why they did not comply with
his privately manifested request, one of them responds thusly:

> Como a vasallos nos manda,
> mas como alcaldes mayores,
> no pidas injustas causas;
> que aquello es estar sin ellas
> y aquesto es estar con varas,
> y el Cabildo de Sevilla
> es quien es.
>
> (2915–21)

[You may command us as your loyal vassals, but as council members,
do not force unjust causes upon us; as vassals, we act without the
wands of justice, but as administrators of justice, we act with them:
the Council of Seville is what it is.]

The councilman clearly distinguishes his individual status as a private citizen from his public capacity that is symbolized by the wand
of justice. His final words are perhaps the strongest indictment of
the king's behavior throughout. Contrary to the king, who has
effectively absented himself from public responsibility, the town
council is thoroughly present and integral, in all of the moral and
public senses those words have: "es quien es" ("It is what it is").
This phrase echoes Sancho Ortiz's earlier refusal to reveal all that
he knows about Busto's death:

> Yo soy quien soy,
> y siendo quien soy me venzo
> a mí mismo con callar,
> y a alguno que calla afrento. . . .
> *Quien es quien es, haga obrando*
> *como quien es; y con esto,*
> de aquesta suerte los dos
> *como quien somos haremos.*
>
> (2340–47)

[*I am who I am, and being who I am, I both control myself* by remaining silent and accuse one who remains silent. . . . *Whoever is himself, let him act as he is in his own essence;* and in this way, the two
of us *as we are, so shall we act.*]

Sancho insists that essential presence is manifested by one's own
acts and that those acts—verbal and otherwise—help to constitute
the responsible, individual self. It is Sancho's and the councilmen's

honorable integrity, their utter sense of self in this regard, that forces the king to live up, finally, to his public responsibility.

The monarch's final public admission that he was behind Busto's death may be considered his first truly responsible act—his first completely public and oral utterance as a king. But it is not an independent one, for he does not utter a single word until he sees that there is no way of escaping this public admission other than by allowing Sancho Ortiz to die. In desperation, therefore, he turns to his counselor and asks him what he should do. Don Arias's one-word response, "Hablad" (2968; "Speak") shows that his control over the king continues until the very end of the drama, that is, that no true moral conversion has taken place. The one term that should most indicate the king's public presence and responsibility—by way of an emphatic orality ("Hablad")—ironically serves here to manifest his continuing ethical absence.

Interestingly, most of the king's oral communication throughout *La estrella* partakes of absence, that is, the absence of any third-party witnesses. His conversations are for the most part private and one-to-one; he tends to speak to individuals, not to groups. The king talks individually, for example, to the councilmen near the end of the drama, and he most often speaks secretly to Arias in asides, which serve functionally to absent all others.

What is the relation between honor and morality in this play and how does that relation function? In many Golden Age dramas, the king is represented as the source of all honor. *La estrella* dramatizes a clear exception to this rule, for, although the verb *honrar* ("to honor") is most frequently associated with King Sancho, this association is always highly ironic. As part of a consistent pattern of linguistic and social subversion, his public act of *honrar* inevitably translates into *deshonrar* ("to dishonor") on the personal level. In contrast to the king's subversive *honrar,* the word *honor* is most frequently associated with Busto Tavera and, later on, with Sancho Ortiz. The drama thus appears insistently to oppose two types of honor: an essentially *social* honor that has to do with the public perception of a given individual, and a more *personal* honor that may be identified with an individual's own sense of achievement, integrity, and virtue. In his essay on *La estrella,* Brooks (1955, 11–12) explicitly distinguishes these two types of honor by calling them, respectively, *honra* and *honor:*

> In the play, as in the *comedia* in general, of course, the two words are used indiscriminately to express the concept of *honor* as it was used by the dramatists, but there seems to be a clear cut distinction between

the two ideas. Whereas to the king the outward—*lo que dirán* ("what others will say")—in other words, *honra,* is what matters, to Busto and Sancho it is virtue, the inner quality of goodness, or *honor* that is important.

Brooks conceives of *honra* in *La estrella* as exterior and social; *honor,* on the other hand, is interior, personal, and has a specifically moral basis: "the inner quality of goodness."

The contrast between these two types of honor has actually already been exemplified by the very first written documents that appear in the play. Early in act 1, the King receives petitions from two men who are competing for the position of general on the frontier of Archidona. The first, written in prose (between verses 336 and 337), is from Gonzalo de Ulloa, who bases his appeal on the fact that his father had served in this position for more than fourteen years. The second petition, in verse (340–56), is from Fernán Pérez de Medina and appeals to its author's own twenty years of service as a soldier. The first petition represents social (exterior) honor that may been gained through inheritance, while the second represents honor that is based upon individual endeavor, morality, and personal accomplishment.

This second, morally based concept of honor is clearly related to Alexander A. Parker's well-known application of the principle of *poetic justice* to the *comedia* (1970, 687), that is, "that wrongdoing should not go unpunished and that virtue should not go unrewarded." Within the context of *poetic justice,* the two types of honor *do* have a specifically moral value: *honra* is the "just" reward—the outer and social recognition—of one who lives and acts with inner, personal *honor.* In Saussurean terms, this relation might be described by saying that *honra* is a type of motivated "signifier" to *honor,* its "signified." It is clear, however, that *La estrella*'s King Sancho consistently utilizes public *honra* in order to subvert personal *honor,* both his own and that of his subjects. The play dramatizes, therefore, a radical problematizing of this ideally motivated relation between *honra* and *honor,* and it is precisely from this problem that *La estrella* derives much of its tragic force. This postulated ideal relation between *honra* and *honor* might also be described—in Derridean terms—as a kind of "metaphysics of honor," according to which *honra* is the outer sign and therefore the potentially distorting *supplement* of "pure" *honor.* The relation between *honra* and *honor* thereby reiterates that which apparently exists between written and spoken communication.

To summarize: King Sancho is the author of various written

texts throughout that enable him to give orders *in absentia*. In this way, the play dramatizes the tragic consequences of a moral and civic absence that undercuts the code of personal honor. We may see now in retrospect that the drama's written texts are organized in pairs whose members are mutually contradictory. The two written petitions presented to the king at the beginning of the drama contradict one another in that they are mutually exclusive: the king can award the military post to only one of the two petitioners. The written order of freedom with which the king bribes Natilde is the secret contradiction of those "escrituras / tan firmes y seguras" ("firm and binding contracts") that ostensibly guarantee Estrella's honorable wedding to Sancho Ortiz. Finally, the king's written order to kill Busto Tavera contradicts the letter that Sancho receives soon after, from Estrella, announcing to him their imminent marriage: Sancho's carrying out of the first will make the second an impossibility.

By portraying written texts in this way (that is, as mutually contradictory), *La estrella* reveals how their fragile authority is ultimately derived from and dependent upon that which inheres in those "authentic oral performative utterance[s]" of which they are mere inscribed reminders (Rivers 1980, 115). The only written text in the drama that is not paired up with its own written contradiction is Sancho's death sentence. *Its* contradiction is the king's final and fully performative oral admission of responsibility. This is intelligible in terms of the dichotomy of writing and speaking that is established throughout: the king's pattern of absential subversion, effected largely by way of written documents, can be stopped only by the presence that is implicit in oral communication. *La estrella de Sevilla* dramatizes the age-old conflict between personal desire and public duty, and manifests it in the opposition between written and oral communication, an opposition that is resolved when the king is forced, finally, to speak in presence—a presence that is both physical *and* metaphysical.

Nevertheless, *La estrella* remains an elusive and suggestive drama, despite efforts to examine it according to the various oppositions described throughout this essay. Despite the seeming clarity of such oppositions as self/other, presence/absence, desire/justice, writing/orality, private/public, and *honra/honor,* the drama problematizes all of them by showing that these terms are not independent or absolute, but rather mutually defining and dependent. (One clear example of this has been discussed above: both Sancho Ortiz and Busto, despite their inclination toward personal *honor* that is based upon morality, *do* care about social *honra*. Even that

SHAME, WRITING, AND MORALITY

seeming ideological absolute, *honor* based upon *presence,* is shown to be yet one more form of cultural—if not literal—inscription.) At the center of *La estrella* is thus a radical questioning of the institutions that define and delimit society itself: institutions such as honor and justice. Even the *self,* posited metaphysically as a given and unitary essence, becomes part of the dialectic, a open-ended process rather than a finished product. *La estrella* continues to fascinate us because of this essential duality—because it looks back nostalgically at a lost metaphysics while at the same time acknowledging that *différance* has irremediably invaded the world.

18

The Shame of Writing

Elias L. Rivers

[I deeply appreciate the editor's invitation to reprint this old essay in the present collection. It was first published in a special issue of *Folio,* no. 12, June 1980, entitled "Studies in the Sixteenth and Seventeenth Century Theatre of the Iberian Peninsula" and edited by Michael J. Ruggerio; I thank the General Editor, Martha O'Nan, for permission to reprint, with translations of the Spanish now added.

In the past ten years progress has been made in the understanding of speech-act theory and of its possible applications to the analysis of literature in general and of drama in particular; see especially *The Semiotics of Theatre and Drama* (London: Methuen, 1980) by Keir Elam and *Speech Acts and Literary Theory* (New York: Routledge, 1990) by Sandy Petrey, who discusses the important article on Austin by Jacques Derrida, "Signature Event Context," *Glyph* 1 (1977): 172–97. See also a collective volume, which I have edited, entitled *Things Done with Words: Speech Acts in Hispanic Drama* (Newark, DE: Juan de la Cuesta, 1986). Within this context, it is possible that my old essay may still be of some interest.]

Anthropologists, who tend to specialize in illiterate cultures, have found male honor and female modesty to be almost as universal as the prehistoric taboo on incest. This fundamental taboo, which is not a biological trait common to animals, but a specifically human cultural phenomenon, insures a minimal degree of exogamy, that is, an exchange of women between patriarchal groups. The father, or a father-substitute, is usually held responsible for protecting the virginity of a girl until she is handed over, intact, to her husband; from that point on, the husband is responsible for protecting his own exclusive rights. The male honor of father, father-substitute (e.g., brother), or husband depends upon the female shame, modesty, or chaste submissiveness of the daughter, sister, wife; she must always obey only one man, who in turn protects her from rape or seduction. Her social value as a woman, and his as a man, depend upon the public fidelity of this mutual relationship.[1]

But male honor is not only defensive: it is also aggressive and grows with the rape or seduction of other men's women, outside one's own patriarchal family. Hence extended families and political loyalties tend to ramify the rules of incest, honor, and shame, with a growing network of honorable obligations. We see this, for example, in Lope de Vega's *Fuenteovejuna* (1619): the Comendador should be obeyed, as the village's feudal lord and father-figure, even to the point of his exercising the *droit du seigneur* as part of a premarital rite; but he must respect the incest taboo protecting his "daughters" against personal sexual advances having nothing to do with providing a proper husband. Like a father, he may give his "daughters" away in marriage, but only if he can guarantee that they have not been sexually shameless. The rules of courtship and of courtesy, of family love and honor, restrain male aggressiveness and female shamelessness; social justice and harmony are the ideal results. When the unmarried Comendador ignores these rules, by raping and seducing the village's women without providing them with proper husbands, he is killed by his own subjects and is replaced by the Catholic King and Queen, Ferdinand and Isabella, who thereby become the father and mother of the village; their legitimate succession and marriage guarantee symbolically, not only fertility, but also a universal *limpieza de sangre* ("blood purity") and social harmony, that is, every man's honor and every woman's virtue. The family is thus extended from village to nation. *Fuenteovejuna* is a celebration of this Spanish extension of the honor system, with the elimination of intermediate treason and corruption.

We can see the Spanish *comedia,* especially in the hands of Lope de Vega, as a social institution designed to celebrate the anthropological roots of Spanish honor, courtesy, and national unity: closest to these roots are the illiterate *cristianos viejos* (old Christians, not recent converts) of the villages, whose pastoral innocence and racial sense of honor are protected and upheld by the Catholic monarchy. In Auerbach's words (332), the so-called realism of the Spanish *comedia*

> is extremely colorful, poetic, and illusionistic. It brightens everyday reality with ceremonious forms of social intercourse, with choice and

precious turns of phrase, with the emotional force of chivalric ideals, and with all the inner and outer enchantment of Baroque and Counter-Reformation piety. It turns the world into a magic stage. And on that magic stage . . . a fixed order reigns, despite all the elements of adventure and miracle. . . . There are passions and conflicts, but there are no problems. God, King, honor and love . . . are immutable and undoubted.

But what if this closed system of honor fails at the level of the king himself? Barring the direct intervention of God, there is no higher court of appeal: the king, unlike a Comendador, can hardly be killed and replaced by a superior political authority. In *La estrella de Sevilla* (1623) the king does fail, but he is taught a lesson in honor by his noble subjects in the city of Seville. The play is a tragedy in that the death of one character constitutes an irreparable damage[2] to two survivors; but there are never any doubts about the system of honor itself, to which the king finally subordinates his own passions, apparently gaining wisdom through suffering, or at least through acute embarrassment or shame. Without the harmonious Neoplatonic overtones of *Fuenteovejuna*, *La estrella de Sevilla* teaches a similar lesson: that a subject's sexual honor, within his immediate family or social group, is a more fundamental value than the ramifications of political obligation.

The sexual attractiveness of Seville's women, and the responsiveness of men to this attractiveness, are basic to the action of our play: not only the king but also Estrella's own brother Busto devote themselves to courting those "divinas bellezas" (406; "divine beauties"). Thus we see that, even though Busto as father-substitute is "wedded" to his sister's honor ("soy de una hermana marido" [406; "I am a sister's husband"]—a phrase which, despite its incestuous implications, means that he will not get married himself until she is safely married), he nevertheless is involved in amorous adventures every night, leaving his sister alone with the servants.

The king's first move in his campaign to deflower Estrella, intending no doubt to provide her eventually with dowry and husband, is to shower favors upon her brother Busto: a well-known principle among honorable Spaniards is that the acceptance of favors obliges one to reciprocate. It is the king's adviser don Arias who proposes cynically to make use of this principle as a tactic:

Si tú le das y él recibe,
se obliga; y si es obligado,

pagará lo que le has dado;
que al que dan, en bronce escribe.

201–4

If you give and he accepts,
he's obliged; and if obliged,
he'll pay for what you've given;
for the receiver inscribes in bronze.

He who inscribes something in bronze, at least figuratively, cannot forget it, even if he wants to. Busto is wary of such brazen inscriptions, that is, of the dangers incurred by accepting favors; by refusing them as undeserved, he shames the king for the first time, early in the play:

Rey.   Basta; que me avergonzáis
           con vuestros buenos consejos.
Busto.   Son mis verdades espejos;
           y así, en ellas os miráis.

397–400

King.   Enough, for you shame me
           with your good advice.
Busto.   My truth is a mirror;
           and in it you see yourself.

The king's insistence makes Busto secretly (that is, courteously) suspicious from the outset:

Busto.   Tanto favor . . .

(Aparte.)   No puedo entender por qué.
            Sospechoso voy: quererme,
           y sin conocerme honrarme . . .
           El rey quiere sobornarme
           de algún mal que piensa hacerme.

439–44

Busto.   So great a favor . . .

(aside)   I cannot understand why.
           I'm suspicious: loving and
           honoring me without knowing me . . .

The King wants to bribe me
for some evil he plans to do me.

In two subsequent encounters with the king, who continues his
campaign to possess Estrella by entering her brother's house, with
his consent or without it, Busto shames the king again and again.
To shame a man means essentially to accuse him of being without
honor, to impugn his manhood. The king, though an outsider in
Seville and hence without an inner sense of obligation to the local
bonds of honor, understands perfectly well how the system works
and is quite aware of Busto's indirect insults to him.

The skirmishes of honor are fascinating dramatic scenes in which
courtesy cannot fully disguise the underlying sexual violence of
two men fighting over a woman. There are two such major scenes
in our play: one at the end of act 1, and the other at the beginning
of act 2. The question in both cases is whether the king has the
right to enter Busto's house, an act that in itself subtly implies the
exercise of the *droit du seigneur*. This question has been broached
indirectly in the first encounter, at the Alcazar, or royal palace,
between the king and Bustos:

> ¿Sois casado?
>
> *Busto.*   Gran señor,
> soy de una hermana marido,
> y casarme no he querido
> hasta dársele.
>
> *Rey.*   Mejor,
> yo, Busto, se le daré.
> ¿Es su nombre?
>
> *Busto.* Doña Estrella.
>
> *Rey.* A estrella tan clara y bella,
> no sé qué esposo le dé
> si no es el sol.
>
> *Busto.*   Sólo un hombre,
> señor, para Estrella anhelo;
> que no es estrella del cielo.
>
> *Rey.* Y la casaré, en mi nombre,
> con hombre que la merezca.
>
> *Busto.* Por ello los pies te pido.
>
> *Rey.* Daréla, Busto, marido
> que a su igual no desmerezca.
> Y decidle que he de ser
> padrino y casamentero,
> y que yo dotarla quiero.

405–23

         Are you married?
Busto.   My lord,
         I am a sister's husband,
         and I have kept from getting married
         until giving her a husband.
King.   A better one
         I, Busto, will give her.
         What's her name?
Busto.   Lady Star.
King.   To so bright and fair a star
         I know not what husband to give
            unless it be the sun.
Busto.   Only a man,
         sire, do I want for Star;
         she's not a star in the sky.
King.   And I'll marry her off, in my name,
         to a man that deserves her.
Busto. Thank you for such a favor!
King.   I'll give her, Busto, a husband
         not unworthy of such as she.
         And tell her that I'm to be
         sponsor and marriage broker,
         and that I want to dower her.

Here it is Busto's courtesy that keeps him from telling the king that his sister is already engaged: he must show that he appreciates the favor ("Por ello los pies te pido," literally, "For that I kiss your feet") that the king is doing him by offering to find a husband for Estrella. But there is already the implication that the king would like to replace Busto as father-substitute, and consequently, perhaps, impose his *pernada,* his right to the first night with her. And we, as audience or readers, know that Estrella has already caught the king's eye: in a scene reminiscent of *Fuenteovejuna,* after a triumphant public reception by the municipality, the king at once begins to review privately, with his secretary, the local women available to him, and don Arias makes a promise: "Yo esta Estrella te daré," (216; "I will give you this Star.")

Busto's deference to the king implies that the marriage contract that he has already signed is less binding than the face-to-face offer of favor that the king makes. Sancho Ortiz, the fiancé, does not trust the durability of written contracts:

Sancho.   ¿Qué dice al fin tu hermano?
Estrella. Que hechas las escrituras
            tan firmes y seguras,

> el casamiento es llano,
> y que el darte la mano
> unos días dilate
> hasta que él se prevenga.

Sancho. Mi amor quiere que tenga
mísero fin; el tiempo le combate.
Hoy casarme querría;
que da el tiempo mil vueltas cada día.

555–65

Sancho.   What is your brother's final word?
Estrella. That with signed documents
so firm and solid,
marriage is obvious,
and that I should put off for a few days
giving you my hand
until he can get ready.
Sancho.   He wants my love to reach
a wretched end; time's against it.
I would prefer to get married right now;
time takes a thousand turns each day.

When Busto tells him of the king's offer, Sancho protests:

> Mas no cumples con la ley
>   de amistad, porque debías
> decirle al Rey que ya estaba
> casada tu hermana.
Busto.   Andaba
entre tantas demasías
   turbado mi entendimiento
que lugar no me dio allí
a decirlo.
Sancho.   Siendo así,
   ¿no se hará mi casamiento?
Busto.   Volviendo a informar al Rey
que están hechos los conciertos
y escrituras, serán ciertos
los contratos; que su ley
   no ha de atropellar lo justo.
Sancho. Si el Rey la quiere torcer,
   ¿quién fuerza le podrá hacer,
habiendo interés o gusto?

> But you break the law
>   of friendship, for you should

have told the King that already
your sister was married.
Busto.   My mind
was wandering in confusion
among so many extremes
that I had no chance at that point
to say so.
Sancho.   This being so,
will my marriage not take place?
Busto.   By informing the King again
that the agreements and documents
have been drawn up, our contract
will take effect; for his law
   will not violate what is right.
Sancho. If the King wants to twist things,
who can force him otherwise,
against his benefit or pleasure?

During the first real skirmish of honor at the doorway of his
house, Busto does tell the king that his sister is already promised:

Busto.   Son casas de un escudero.
Rey.   Entremos.
Busto.   Señor, son hechas
para mi humildad, y vos
no podéis caber en ellas;
que para tan gran señor
se cortaron muy estrechas,
y no os vendrán bien sus salas,
que son, gran señor, pequeñas,
porque su mucha humildad
no aspira a tanta soberbia.
Fuera, señor, de que en casa
tengo una hermosa doncella
solamente, que la caso
ya con escrituras hechas,
y no sonará muy bien
en Sevilla cuando sepan
que a visitarla venís.
Rey.   No vengo, Busto, por ella;
por vos vengo.
Sancho.   Gran señor,
notable merced es ésta;
y si aquí por mí venís,
no es justo que os obedezca;
que será descortesía
que a visitar su rey venga

al vasallo, y que el vasallo
lo permita y lo consienta.

705–30

Busto.   This is the house of a simple squire.
King.   Let's enter.
Busto.   Sire, it is built
for my humility, and you
are too big for it;
for such a great lord
it was made too narrow,
and its rooms won't suit you,
for, great lord, they are small,
because their low humility
does not aspire to such pride.
Besides, sire, at home
I have a lovely maiden
only, whom I am marrying off
with wedding contract signed,
and it will not sound good
in Seville for people to know
that you come to visit her.
King.   I'm not coming, Busto, for her
but for you.
Busto.   Great lord,
this is an enormous favor;
and if you come here for me,
it's not right for me to obey;
it will be discourteous
for the king to come to visit
his vassal and for the vassal
to consent and permit it.

We can see very clearly in this scene how courtesy is used as a curtain to conceal violence; the vassal's only defense against his lord is to outdo him in courtesy. This face-to-face oral encounter is very close to the reality of physical, political, and economic violence; this is clear in don Arias's aside to the king:

Rey.   Habla paso, no te entienda,
que tiene todo su honor
este necio en las orejas.
Arias.   Arracadas muy pesadas
de las orejas se cuelgan;
el peso las romperá.

754–59

King. Speak softly, let him not hear you,
for this fool keeps
all his honor in his ears.
Arias. Very heavy jewels
are hung from one's ears;
their weight will break them.

Busto's honor depends on his sister's reputation in Seville, on what people say ("el qué dirán" of line 737), on what is heard in the community's supreme court of oral gossip.

Physical violence comes fully to the surface in the second skirmish between Busto and the king, when Busto pretends to be too courteous to believe that the king himself would enter his house alone and secretly at night. By pretending to refuse to believe the words of the man in disguise, that he is the king, Busto is in fact calling the king a liar, in a virtual face-to-face situation giving him the lie, which is the ultimate attack on a man's honor. The king thereupon draws his sword to fight; when servants arrive, he flees to avoid recognition by witnesses, leading inevitably to lèse majesté, but he expects to take vengeance:

> Escaparme quiero
> antes de ser conocido.
> De este villano ofendido
> voy, pero vengarme espero.
>
> 1101–4

> I want to escape
> before being recognized.
> I've been offended by this
> peasant, but I will have revenge.

The climax of Busto's "courteous" insults centers around the bribing, and the consequent death, of the slave girl Natilde. Don Arias had approached her with these words:

¿Eres criada de casa?
Natilde. Criada soy, mas por fuerza.
Arias. ¿Cómo por fuerza?
Natilde.   Que soy
esclava.
Arias.   ¿Esclava?
Natilde.   Y sujeta,
sin la santa libertad,
a muerte y prisión perpetua.

Arias.   Pues yo haré que el Rey te libre,
               y mil ducados de renta
               con la libertad te dé,
               si en su servicio te empleas.
Natilde.   Por la libertad y el oro
               no habrá maldad que no emprenda;
               mira lo que puedo hacer,
               que lo haré como yo pueda.
Arias.   Tú has de dar al Rey entrada
               en casa esta noche.
Natilde.   Abiertas
               todas las puertas tendrá,
               como cumplas la promesa.
Arias.   Una cédula del Rey
               con su firma y de su letra
               antes que entre te daré.
Natilde.   Pues yo le pondré en la mesma
               cama de Estrella esta noche.
Arias.   ¿A qué hora Busto se acuesta?
Natilde.   Al alba viene a acostarse.
               Todas las noches requiebra;
               que este descuido en los hombres
               infinitas honras cuesta.

                                                        827–54

               Are you a house servant?
Natilde.   I am a servant under duress.
Arias.   How, under duress?
Natilde.   I am
               a slave.
Arias.   A slave?
Natilde.   And subject,
               without sweet liberty,
               to death and life imprisonment.
Arias.   Well, I will have the King free you
               and give you a thousand ducats
               income, along with liberty,
               if you will enter his service.
Natilde.   For liberty and gold
               there is no evil I won't commit;
               tell me what I can do,
               and I'll do it if I can.
Arias.   You are to give the King entrance
               into this house tonight.
Natilde.   Wide open
               he'll have all the doors,
               provided you keep your promise.

Arias.   A paper from the King
           signed by his own hand
           I'll give you before he enters.
Natilde.   Then I'll put him in Estrella's
           very own bed tonight.
Arias.   At what time does Busto retire?
Natilde.   At dawn he comes to bed.
           He spends every night courting,
           a carelessness that costs men
           their honor time and again.

In order to seduce the women of other men whose honor he is
under no obligation to protect, Busto leaves his own sister's honor
at the mercy of a slave girl; and a slave, deprived of all liberty, is
not bound by honor to anyone. Nor does anyone consider himself
bound by his word to a slave: the written promise of the king is
Natilde's only security. Slavery, money, and written promises, or
contracts, all contribute to the corruption of honor. In Natilde's
own words:

> El oro ha sido en el mundo
> el que los males engendra,
> porque, si él faltara, es claro
> no hubiera infamias ni afrentas.
>
> 865–68

> In this world gold has been
> that which engenders evils,
> for, without gold, it is obvious
> there would be no infamy or insults.

The king realizes that, in a society based on the mutual obligations of honor, a written contract would not be necessary; as he
himself says to Natilde:

> Aunque decillo bastaba,
> éste es, mujer, el papel,
> con la libertad en él;
> que yo le daré otra esclava.
>
> 921–24

> Though it would suffice to say so,
> here, woman, you have my paper
> with your freedom on it;
> I'll give him another slave girl.

After his encounter with the disguised king, Busto's suspicions about his slave Natilde are fully confirmed when he sees this written document. He then says to her:

> Ven conmigo.
> Natilde.   ¿Dónde voy?
> Busto.   Vas a que te vea el Rey.

> 1157–58

> Come with me.
> Natilde.   Where am I going?
> Busto.   You're going for the King to see you.

We realize a little later that the king will see her, not alive, but hanged, and with that shameful written document in her dead hand. This is what finally makes the king swear vengeance.

Writing in itself—and this is the point of my essay—threatens the honor system; among the most honorable men in Lope's comedies are illiterate peasants. When Busto accuses his sister Estrella of having abetted the king's assault on his honor, she defends herself indignantly:

> ¿No me conoces? ¿No sabes
> quién soy? ¿En mi boca has visto
> palabras desenlazadas
> del honor con que las rijo?
> ¿Has visto alegres mis ojos
> de la cárcel de sus vidrios
> desatar rayos al aire,
> lisonjeros y lascivos?
> ¿En las manos de algún hombre
> viste algún papel escrito
> de la mía?

> 1280–90

> Don't you recognize me? Don't you know
> who I am? On my lips have you ever
> heard words unbound by the honor
> with which I rule them?
> Have you ever seen my eyes gaily,
> from within their glassy prisons,
> firing lightning into the air
> with lascivious flattery?
> Have you seen in the hands
> of any man a piece of paper
> written by my hand?

She has rigorously controlled the evanescent words of her mouth and glances of her eyes, that is, the signs of face-to-face communication. An even greater threat to her modesty would be words written by her hand and held in the hand of a man; but she has scrupulously avoided writing any such permanent incriminating evidence.

The king is not so careful about written contracts. Besides his signature held by the dead slave girl's hand, in his plan to have Busto killed he writes two documents:

> . . . en este papel sellado
> traigo su nombre y su muerte,
> y en éste, que yo he mandado
> matalle: y de aquesta suerte
> él quedará disculpado.
>
> 1407–11

> . . . on this sealed piece of paper
> I have written his name and death,
> and on this other piece, that it is I
> who have ordered his death; in this way
> he will be freed of guilt.

The "he" is of course Sancho, Estrella's fiancé, who will be commissioned by the king to kill Estrella's brother. The king sends out of the room don Arias, whose presence as a witness might make for a feeling of shame; but Sancho is much more sensitive than the king to the delicate oral nature of true honor, and indignantly refuses to accept a written promise from him:

Rey.   Matalde como queráis;
        que este papel para abono
        de mí firmado lleváis,
        por donde, Sancho, os perdono
        cualquier delito que hagáis.
          Referidlo. (*Dale el papel.*)
Sancho.   Dice así:
(Lee.)   "Al que ese papel advierte,
        Sancho Ortiz, luego por mí,
        y en mi nombre, dalde muerte,
        que yo por vos salgo aquí;
         y si os halláis en aprieto,
        por este papel firmado
        sacaros dél os prometo.
        Yo el Rey."—Estoy admirado

de que tan poco conceto
　　tenga de mí Vuestra Alteza.
¡Yo cédula, yo papel!
Tratadme con más llaneza,
que más en vos que no en él
confía aquí mi nobleza.

　　Si vuestras palabras cobran
valor que los montes labra,
y ellas cuanto dicen obran,
dándome aquí la palabra,
señor, los papeles sobran.

　　A la palabra remito
la cédula que me dais,
con que vengaros me incito,
porque donde vos estáis
es excusado lo escrito.

　　Rompeldo, porque sin él
la muerte le solicita
mejor, señor, que con él;
que en parte desacredita
vuestra palabra el papel. (*Rómpele.*)

　　Sin papel, señor, aquí
nos obligamos los dos
y prometemos así:
yo de vengaros a vos,
y vos de librarme a mí.

　　Si es así, no hay que hacer
cédulas, que estorbo han sido.

1542–83

King.　　Kill him however you wish;
I give you this paper
as a guarantee signed by me,
whereby, Sancho, I pardon you
for any crime you may commit.
　　Read it. (*He gives him the paper.*)
"It reads:

Sancho.　The man mentioned in the other paper,
you, Sancho Ortiz, forthwith are to kill
for me and in my name;
I hereby defend you;
　　and if you find yourself accused,
by this signed paper
I promise to deliver you.
I the King." I'm amazed
that Your Highness has
　　so low an opinion of me.

For me, documents and papers!
Treat me more simply,
for my nobility has greater
trust in you than in paper.
    If your words have power
to move and shape mountains,
and if they bring about everything they say,
if you here give me your word,
sire, papers are superfluous.
    To your word I remit
the document you give me,
with which I'm incited to avenge you,
for where you are present
there is no need for writing.
    Tear it up, for without it
death will seek him out
more surely than with it,
for in a sense the document
discredits your word. (*Tears it up.*)
    Without paper, sire, we hereby
oblige ourselves to one another
and promise as follows:
I to take vengeance for you,
and you to liberate me.
    If this is so, there is no need
for documents, which have been obstacles.

In this passage we have the fullest indictment of writing as shameful.

Previous critics have mentioned the dramatic function of written messages in this play, but so far as I know only Leo Spitzer has glimpsed the opposition between writing and a certain Renaissance concept of natural law, what I have defined as the anthropological concept of honor. Most of the third act depends on Sancho's insistence that the king has an unwritten obligation to come to his defense orally and in public. Sancho's moral victory shames the king without provoking more violence; it humbles him in a politically positive way.

I think perhaps some recent ideas of linguistic philosophers such as Austin and Searle[3] about the importance of illocutionary speech acts and performative utterances can help us to understand the difference between an oral society's system of honor and shame, and modern society's dependence upon written documents as substitutes for speech acts. An oral promise is in itself performative: I obligate myself to you, under proper circumstances, simply by the act of saying to you that I will do something. According to a traditional saying, "a man's word is his bond"; from the more radically traditional point of view expressed in our play, a man's speech act is not merely equal to, but takes absolute precedence over, any written bond. Conversely, the greatest insult in the code of honor is to give the lie, that is, to impugn the validity of another man's word by saying "mentís" ("you lie") to him, face to face. Feelings of honor and shame function only when people can face and talk to one another orally; only under such circumstances of physical presence are there genuine speech acts, honorable obligations, or shameful losses of face.

The written contract, as a substitute speech act, destroys the honor system itself, which depends on the nonreiterable uniqueness of the performative utterance. A man may sign his name after he raises his right hand and swears; but, from a traditional point of view, that signature is an inadequate substitute for the authentic oral performative utterance, pronounced face to face. In fact, as Sancho implies, it may actually weaken the speech act by pretending to repeat it: a man of honor does not repeat his promise, because that would imply that his first word was somehow deficient. Notaries are invented as witnesses to supplement with their signatures the written traces of a speech act, but what remains is only paper, "que lo aguanta todo, that can be made to say anything," without the honor identified with the unique act and presence of flesh and blood. When a man is judged in terms of a fixed written law code, we can safely say that the traditional oral system of personal honor is dead. Modern political, mercantile, and industrial societies could not exist without written laws, contracts, corporations, and lawyers; but an intimate moral alienation is the price that is paid. *La estrella de Sevilla* is a moving dramatic defense of the traditional system of personal honor; only a poor slave girl, a person who can be bought and sold within a mercantile system, is eager to have a written contract, a substitute utterance, and she is killed without mercy.

In the curtain scene the king receives his final lesson. He tries to get Sancho and Estrella to marry one another, as they had promised, but they now courteously refuse, absolving one another of their mutual promises:

Rey.   ¿Qué os falta?
Sancho.   La conformidad.
Estrella.   Pues ésa
          jamás podremos hallarla

	viviendo juntos.
Sancho.	Lo mesmo digo yo, y por esta causa de la palabra te absuelvo.
Estrella.	Yo te absuelvo la palabra; que ver siempre al homicida de mi hermano en mesa y cama me ha de dar pena.
Sancho.	Y a mí estar siempre con la hermana del que maté injustamente, queriéndolo como al alma.
Estrella.	¿Pues libres quedamos?
Sancho.	Sí.
Estrella.	Pues, adiós.
Sancho.	Adiós.
Rey.	Aguarda.
Estrella.	Señor, no ha de ser mi esposo hombre que a mi hermano mata, aunque le quiero y le adoro. (*Vase.*)
Sancho.	Y yo, señor, por amarla, no es justicia que lo sea. (*Vase.*)

2999–3018

King.	What do you lack?
Sancho.	Agreement.
Estrella.	And that we will never be able to reach living together.
Sancho.	The same say I, and for this reason I absolve you of your word.
Estrella.	Of your word I absolve you; always to see the murderer of my brother at table and in bed would cause me to suffer.
Sancho.	The same for me to be always with the sister of the man I killed unjustly, while loving him as myself.
Estrella.	Then we're free?
Sancho.	Yes.
Estrella.	Well, goodby.
Sancho.	Goodby.
King.	Wait.
Estrella.	Sire, he cannot be my husband who has killed my brother,

>   though I love and adore him. (*Exit.*)
> *Sancho.* And, sire, since I love her,
>   it isn't right for me to be her husband. (*Exit.*)

According to Ruth Lee Kennedy, this lesson of subordinating personal desire to the honor code was the playwright's message to the youthful Philip IV: he was "holding up a mirror (one that was both positive and negative) to his sensual young king and to that astute mentor who stood behind him. . . . This play catches up, as though on a sounding board, most of the gossip that was floating about Madrid between early 1621 and late 1623" (Kennedy 408). But, in addition to this narrowly historical or topical message, the play speaks to us today, more profoundly, about Spain's quixotic attempt to maintain a prehistoric system of social justice, one that antedates by millennia any written promises, including the Magna Carta, the *fueros* or local Spanish written law, and constitutional monarchy. For history itself did not come into existence until the invention of writing, that is, of literature.

Notes

1. See, for example, Peristiany's collection of anthropological studies dealing with Spain, Greece, and the Arab world. More sociological and historical is Maravall's essay on the function of honor in traditional society.

2. See Brooks's essay and the basic studies by Anibal.

3. I cannot at this point do more than refer to the recent proliferation of work in the area of applying speech-act theory to the study of literature; see, for example, the article by Stanley E. Fish, the book by Mary Louise Pratt, and the review of this book by Michael Hancher. Pratt uses sociolinguistic concepts from William Labov. Also essential to an eventually adequate theory would be certain essays by Emile Benveniste. In this context, *La estrella de Sevilla* not only contains, like Shakespeare's *Coriolanus*, direct comments on the social validity of speech acts, and the dramatic enactment of many fictitious illocutionary acts, but also provides, as a seventeenth-century Spanish theatrical performance, an example of the sociolinguistic function of a literary text within a political context.

Works Cited

Abellán, José Luis. 1979. *Historia crítica del pensamiento español 2, La edad de Oro (Siglo XVI)*. Madrid: Espasa-Calpe.

————. 1988. *Historia crítica del pensamiento español 3, Del Barroco a La Ilustración (Siglos XVII y XVIII)*. Madrid: Espasa-Calpe.

Aguilar Piñal, F. 1987. *Un escritor ilustrado: Cándido María Trigueros*. Madrid: Consejo Superior de Investigaciones Científicas.

Alfonso X. *General Estoria*. 1930. Vol. 1. Edited by A. G. Solalinde. Madrid: Junta para Ampliación de Estudios e Investigaciones Científicas. Centro de Estudios Históricos.

Alpern, Hymen. 1923. "Jealousy as a Dramatic Motive in the Spanish *Comedia*." *Romanic Review* 14: 276–85.

————. 1926. "A Note on Guillén de Castro." *MLN* 41: 391–92.

Alpern, H. and J. Martel. 1935. *Aventuras de Don Quijote by Miguel de Cervantes*. New York: Houghton Mifflin.

————. 1939. *Diez comedias del Siglo de Oro*. New York: Harper and Row.

Alpers, Svetlana. 1983. *The Art of Describing: Dutch Art in the Seventeenth Century*. Chicago: University of Chicago Press.

Anglo, Sydney. 1969. *Machiavelli: A Dissection*. London: Victor Gollanz.

Angulo Iñiguez, Diego. 1952. *La mitología y el arte español del Renacimiento*. Madrid: Editorial Maestre.

Aníbal, C. E. 1934. "Observations on *La estrella de Sevilla*." *Hispanic Review* 2.1: 1–38.

Antología del Teatro del Siglo de Oro. 1989. Edited by Eugenio Suárez-Galbán Guerra. Madrid: Orígenes.

Arguijo, Juan de. "Cuentos mui mal escritos." Biblioteca Nacional, Madrid, MS.

Aristotle. 1943. *Politics*. Translated by Benjamin Jowett. New York: Random House.

Asín Palacios, Miguel. 1919. *La escatología musulmana en la "Divina Comedia."* Madrid: Imprenta de Estanislao Maestre.

Auerbach, Erich. 1953. *Mimesis: The Representation of Reality in Western Literature*. Princeton: Princeton University Press.

Augustine. 1952. *The Confessions; The City of God. Selections in Great Books of the Western World*. Vol. 18. Edited by Maynard Hutchins. Chicago: Encyclopedia Britannica.

Austin, J. L. 1962. *How to Do Things with Words*. Oxford: Oxford University Press.

Azar, Inés. 1986. "Self, Responsibility, Discourse: An Introduction to Speech Act

Theory." In *Things Done with Words: Speech Acts in Hispanic Drama*, edited by Elias L. Rivers, 1–14. Newark, Del.: Juan de la Cuesta.

Bakker, Jan. 1981. "Versificación y estructura de la comedia de Lope." In *Diálogos hispánicos de Amsterdam No. 2: Las constantes estéticas de la 'comedia' en el Siglo de Oro*, 93–102. Amsterdam: Rodopi.

Baudin, Maurice. 1941. *The Profession of the King in Seventeenth Century French Drama*. Baltimore: Johns Hopkins University Press.

Bennassar, Bartolomé. 1979. *The Spanish Character*. Berkeley: University of California Press.

Benveniste, Emile. 1966–74. *Problemes de linguistique générale*. 2 vols. Paris: Gallimard.

Berman, Paul. 1992. *Debating P.C.: The Controversy over Political Correctness on College Campuses*. New York: Dell.

Bermejo Barrera, José C. 1982. *Mitología y mitos de la Hispania prerromana*. Madrid: Akal bolsillo.

Bradbury, Malcolm. 1987. *Mensonge*. London: André Deutsch.

Bril, Jacques. 1983. *Le Masque, ou le père ambigu*. Paris: Payot.

Brooks, John. 1928. "Slavery and the Slave in the Works of Lope de Vega." *Romanic Review* 19: 231–43.

———. 1955. "*La estrella de Sevilla*: 'Admirable y famosa tragedia.'" *Bulletin of Hispanic Studies* 32: 8–20.

Brown, Jonathan and J. H. Elliott. 1989. *A Palace for a King*. New Haven: Yale University Press.

Bunés Ibarra, Miguel de. 1989. *La imagen de los musulmanes y del norte de Africa en la España de los siglos XVI y XVII*. Madrid: Consejo Superior de Investigaciones Científicas.

Burckhardt, Jacob. 1990. *The Civilization of the Renaissance in Italy*. Translated by S. G. C. Middlemore. Introduction by Peter Burke. Notes by Peter Murray. London: Penguin Books.

Burke, James F. 1974. "*The estrella de Sevilla* and the Tradition of Saturnine Melancholy." *Bulletin of Hispanic Studies* 51: 137–56.

Caldera, Ermanno. 1974. *Il dramma romantico in Spagna*. Pisa: Università di Pisa.

Caro Baroja, Julio. 1965. *El carnaval (análisis histórico-cultural)*. Madrid: Taurus.

Carrasco-Urgoiti, María Soledad. 1976. *The Moorish Novel*. Boston: G. K. Hall.

Casa, Frank P. 1983. "Conflicto y jerarquía de valores en el teatro del Siglo de Oro." In *Estudios sobre el Siglo de Oro: homenaje a Raymond R. MacCurdy*, edited by A. González, T. Halzapfel, A. Rodríguez, 15–24. Madrid: Cátedra.

———. 1986. "The Use of the Royal Audiencia in Golden Age Drama." *Segismundo* 43–44: 63–79.

———. 1987. "The Duality of the King in Golden Age Drama." In *La Chispa '87 Selected Proceedings*, edited by G. Paolini, 51–59. New Orleans: Tulane University.

———. 1988. "La responsiblidad de la belleza." *Les Cahiers Scientifiques* (University of Ottawa), *Sección Hispánica* 1: 31–40.

Cascardi, Anthony J. 1988. "Don Juan and the Discourse of Modernism." In *Tirso's Don Juan: The Metamorphosis of a Theme*, edited by Josep M. Solé-

Solé and George E. Gingras, 151–63. Washington, D.C.: Catholic University of America Press.

Castiglione, Baldassarre. 1960. *Il Cortigiano*. Edited by Giulio Preti. Torino: Einaudi.

Castigos y documentos del rey don Sancho 1952. In *Escritores en prosa anteriores al siglo XV* 51: 79–228. Madrid: *Biblioteca de autores españoles*.

Castro, Guillén de. 1925–27. *Obras de Guillén de Castro*. Edited Eduardo Juliá Martínez. 3 vols. Madrid: Real Academia Española.

Cervantes Saavedra, Miguel de. 1962. *Novelas ejemplares*. Edited by Francisco Rodríguez Marín. Madrid: Clásicos Castellanos.

Chejne, Anwar G. 1983. *Islam and the West. The Moriscos*. Albany: State University of New York Press.

Claramonte, Andrés de. 1991. *La estrella de Sevilla*. Edited by Alfredo Rodríguez López-Vázquez. Madrid: Cátedra.

———. 1988. *La infelice Dorotea*. Edited by Charles Ganelin. London: Tamesis.

Cotarelo y Mori, Emilio. 1930. "*La estrella de Sevilla* es de Lope de Vega." *Revista de la Biblioteca, Archivo y Museo del Ayuntamiento de Madrid* 7: 12–24.

Covarrubias, Sebastián de. 1610 (1979). *Tesoro de la lengua castellana o española*. Madrid: Ediciones Turner.

Craddock, Jerry. 1986. "Dynasty in Dispute: Alfonso el Sabio and the Successon to the Throne of Castile and León in History and Legend." *Viator* 17: 197–219.

Crapotta, James. 1984. *Kingship and Tyranny in the Theater of Guillén de Castro*. London: Tamesis Books.

Crawford, J. P. W. 1930. "An Early Nineteenth Century English Version of *La estrella de Sevilla*." In *Estudios eruditos in memoriam de Adolfo Bonilla y San Martín (1875–1926)* 2: 495–505. Madrid: J. Rates.

Daniel, Norman. 1958. *Islam and the West*. Edinburgh: Edinburgh University Press.

———. 1975. *The Arabs and Medieval Europe*. London: Longman.

de Armas, Frederick A. 1979. "The Apples of Colchis: Key to an Interpretation of *La estrella de Sevilla*." *Forum for Modern Language Studies* 15: 1–13.

———. 1980. "The Hunter and the Twins: Astrological Imagery in *La estrella de Sevilla*." *Bulletin of the Comediantes* 32: 11–20.

———. 1991. "Fashioning a New World: Lope de Vega and Claramonte's *El nuevo rey Gallinato*." In *Critical Essays on the Literatures of Spain and Spanish America*, edited by Luis T. Gonzalez-del-Valle and Julio Baena, 1–10. Boulder, Col.: Society of Spanish and Spanish-American Studies.

———. 1994a. "Splitting Gemini: Plato, Girard and *La estrella de Sevilla*." *Hispanófila* 111: 17–32.

———. 1994b. "Un nuevo Hércules y un nuevo Sol: la presencia de Felipe IV en *La estrella de Sevilla*." *Actas del XI Congreso de la Asociación Internacional de Hispanistas*, edited by Juan Villegas.

de Lauretis, Teresa. 1983. *Alice Doesn't: Feminism, Semiotics, Cinema*. Bloomington and Indianapolis: University of Indiana Press.

de Man, Paul. 1986a. "The Resistance to Theory." In *The Resistance to Theory*, edited by Wlad Godzich, 320. Minneapolis: University of Minnesota Press.

————. 1986b. "The Return to Philology." In *The Resistance to Theory,* edited by Wlad Godzich, 21–26. Minneapolis: University of Minnesota Press.

Derrida, Jacques. 1967. *Of Grammatology.* 1976. Translated by Gayatri Chakravorty Spivak. Baltimore: Johns Hopkins University Press.

Dessen, Allen C. 1984. *Elizabethan Stage Conventions and Modern Interpreters.* Cambridge: Cambridge University Press.

Deyermond, Alan D. 1984. *La edad media española. Historia de la literatura española.* Vol. 1. Barcelona: Ariel.

Diez Borque, José María. 1978. *Sociedad y teatro en la España de Lope de Vega.* Barcelona: Antoni Bosch.

Diez comedias del siglo de oro. 1939. Edited by José Martel and Hymen Alpern. New York:Harper and Row.

Diez comedias del siglo de oro. 1968. 2d. ed. Edited by José Martel and Hymen Alpern, revised by Leonard Mades. New York: Harper and Row.

Diez comedias del siglo de oro. 1968, 1985. New York: Harper and Row. Reprinted by Waveland Press: Prospect Heights, Ill.

Dixon, Victor. 1985. "The Uses of Polymetry: An Approach to Editing the *Comedia* as Verse Drama." In *Editing the Comedia I,* edited by Michael McGaha and Frank P. Casa, 104–25. Ann Arbor: Michigan Romance Studies.

————. 1986. "La comedia de corral de Lope como género visual." *Edad de oro* 5: 35–58.

Doane, Mary Ann. 1989. "Veiling over Desire: Close-ups of the Woman." In *Feminism and Psychoanalysis,* edited by Richard Feldstein and Judith Roof, 205–241. Ithaca, N.Y.: Cornell University Press.

Dolan, Jill. 1988. *The Feminist Spectator as Critic.* Ann Arbor: University of Michigan Press.

Domínguez, Frank. 1979. *The Medieval Argonautica.* Potomac, Md.: Studia Humanitatis.

Domínguez Ortiz, Antonio. 1971. *The Golden Age of Spain 1516–1659.* Translated by James Casey. New York: Basic Books.

Dumont, Louis. 1980. *Homo Hierarchicus.* Translated by Mark Sainsbury, Louis Dumont, and Basia Gulati. Chicago/London: University of Chicago Press. First published as *Homo Hierarchicus. Essai sur le système des castes.* Paris 1966, rev. 1979.

Dunn, Peter. 1960. "Honour and the Christian Background in Calderón." *Bulletin of Hispanic Studies* 37: 75–105.

Dutton, Brian. 1991. *Cancionero del siglo XV. c. 1360–1520* Vol. 3 Salamanca: Universidad de Salamanca.

Elam, Keir. 1980. *The Semiotics of Theatre and Drama.* London and New York: Methuen.

Elliott, J. H. *Imperial Spain: 1469–1716.* 1963. New York: The New American Library.

————. 1986. *The Count-duke of Olivares: The Statesman in an Age of Decline.* New Haven: Yale University Press.

Ellis, John M. 1989. *Against Deconstruction.* Princeton: Princeton University Press.

Erasmus. 1964. *The Essential Erasmus.* Translated by John P. Dolan. New York: Mentor-Omega.

La estrella de Sevilla. 1920. Edited by R. Foulche-Delbosc. *Revue hispanique* 48, 114: 497–678.

———. 1939. Edited by Frank Otis Reed and Esther M. Dixon. Introduction by John M. Hill. Boston and New York: D. C. Heath and Co.

———. 1968. ed. J. Martel, H. Alpern, L. Mades in *Diez Comedias del Siglo de Oro.* New York: Harper and Row.

Eulogio Palacios, Leopoldo. 1957. *La prudencia política.* Madrid: Rialp.

Fernández de Moratín, Leandro. 1982. *La comedia nueva. El sí de las niñas.* Edited by J. Dowling and René Andioc. Clásicos Castalia 5. 2d ed. Madrid: Castalia.

Fernández-Santamaría, J. A. 1983. *Reason of State and Statecraft in Spanish Political Thought, 1595–1640.* Lanham, Md.: University Press of America.

Fischer, Susan L. 1979. "Reader-Response Criticism and the *Comedia:* Creation of Meaning in Calderón's *La cisma de Ingalaterra.*" *Bulletin of the Comediantes* 31: 109–25. Reprinted in *Approaches to Teaching Spanish Golden Age Drama* (1989), edited by Everett W. Hesse, 92–111. York, S.C.: Spanish Literature Publications.

Fish, Stanley. 1976. "How to Do Things with Austin and Searle: Speech Act Theory and Literary Criticism." *MLN* 91: 983–1025.

———. 1980. *Is There a Text in This Class? The Authority of Interpretive Communities.* Cambridge: Harvard University Press.

Fitzpatrick, Tim. 1990. "Models of Visual and Auditory Interaction in Performance." *Gestos* 9: 9–22.

Forastieri Braschi, Eduardo. 1976. *Aproximación estructural al teatro de Lope de Vega.* Madrid: Hispánica.

Foulché-Delbosc, R. 1920. "*La estrella de Sevilla.*" *Revue Hispanique* 48: 497–678.

Fowler, Alastair. 1982. *Kinds of Literature: An Introduction to the Theory of Genres and Modes.* Cambridge: Harvard University Press.

Fox, Dian. 1986. *Kings in Calderón: a Study in Characterization and Political Theory.* London: Tamesis Books.

Freedman, Barbara. 1988. "Frame-Up: Feminism, Psychoanalysis, Theater." *Theatre Journal* 40: 375–97.

———. 1991. *Staging the Gaze: Postmodernism, Psychoanalysis, and Shakespearean Comedy.* Ithaca, N.Y.: Cornell University Press.

Freund, Elizabeth. 1987. *The Return of the Reader: Reader-Response Criticism.* London and New York: Methuen.

Gaibrois de Ballesteros, Mercedes. 1936 (1967). *María de Molina: Tres Veces Reina.* Madrid: Espasa Calpe.

———. 1922. *Historia del reinado de Sancho IV de Castilla.* Madrid.

Ganelin, Charles. 1994. *Rewriting Theatre: The Nineteenth Century "Refundiciones" and the Comedia.* Lewisburg, Pa.: Bucknell University Press.

García-Varela, Jesús. "El discurso del loco en la obra dramática de Lope de Vega." Kentucky Foreign Language Conference. Lexington, 25 April 1991.

Garver, Eugene. 1987. *Machiavelli and the History of Prudence.* Madison: Wisconsin University Press.

Gates, Henry Louis, Jr. 1992. *Loose Canons: Notes on the Culture Wars.* Oxford: Oxford University Press.

Gitlitz, David M. 1986. "Which Comes First: The Sentence or the Verse?" *Revista de estudios hispánicos* 20, 1: 15–26.

González-Marcos, Máximo. 1982. "El antiabsolutismo de *La estrella de Sevilla*." *Hispanófila* 74: 1–24.

Grant, Helen. 1972. "El mundo al revés." In *Hispanic Studies in Honour of Joseph Manson*, 119–37. Oxford: Dolphin Book Co.

Grassi, Ernesto, and Maristella Lorch. 1986. *Folly and Insanity in Renaissance Literature*. Binghamton, N.Y.: Medieval and Renaissance Texts and Studies.

Gravdal, Katherine. 1991. *Ravishing Maidens*. Philadelphia: University of Pennsylvania Press.

Guillory, John. 1990. "Canon." In *Critical Terms for Literary Study*, edited by Frank Lentricchia and Thomas McLaughlin. Chicago: University of Chicago Press.

Hamilton, Bernice. 1963. *Political Thought in Sixteenth-Century Spain*. Oxford: Clarendon Press.

Hancher, Michael. 1977. "Beyond a Speech-Act Theory of Literary Discourse." *MLN* 92: 1081–98.

Hartsock, Nancy C. M. 1983. *Money, Sex, and Power: Toward a Feminist Historical Materialism*. New York: Longman.

Havelock, Eric. 1986. *The Muse Learns to Write*. New Haven: Yale University Press.

Hays, H. R. 1964. *The Dangerous Sex: The Myth of Feminine Evil*. New York: G. P. Putnam's.

Hermenegildo, Alfredo. 1986. "Acercamiento al estudio de las didascalias del teatro castellano primitivo: Lucas Fernández." In *Actas de VIII Congreso de la Asociación Internacional de Hispanistas*, edited by David A. Kossoff et al., 1: 709–27. Madrid: Istmo.

Hernández Valcárcel, Carmen. Forthcoming. *La historia de América y España en el teatro de Lope de Vega*. Publication of the Quinto Centenario.

Hill, John M. 1939. "Introduction." *La estrella de Sevilla*. Edited by Frank Otis Reed and Esther M. Dixon. New York: D. C. Heath and Co.

Historia General de España. 1893. Madrid: El Progreso Editorial.

Holland, Norman H. 1968. *The Dynamics of Literary Response*. New York: Oxford University Press.

Hollis, Martin J., and Edward J. Nell. 1975. *Rational Economic Man: A Philosophical Critique of Neo-Classical Economics*. London: Cambridge University Press.

Holub, Robert C. 1984. *Reception Theory: A Critical Introduction*. Methuen: New York and London.

Howard, Jean E. 1986. "Scholarship, Theory, and More New Readings: Shakespeare for the 1990s." In *Shakespeare Study Today*, edited by Georgianna Ziegler, 127–51. New York: AMS Press.

Howarth, W. D. 1975. *Sublime and Grotesque. A Study of French Romantic Drama*. London: Harrad.

Iser, Wolfgang. 1974. "The Reading Process: A Phenomenological Approach." In *The Implied Reader: Patters of Communication in Prose Fiction from Bunyan to Beckett*, 274–94. Baltimore and London: The Johns Hopkins University

Press. Also published in *New Directions in Literary History* (1974), edited by Ralph Cohen, 125–45. Baltimore: Johns Hopkins University Press.

———. 1978. *The Act of Reading: A Theory of Aesthetic Response.* Baltimore and London: Johns Hopkins University Press.

Jakobson, Roman. 1960. "Closing Statement: Linguistics and Poetics." In *Style and Language,* edited by Thomas A. Sebeok, 350–57. Cambridge: MIT Press.

Jardine, Lisa. 1983. *Still Harping on Daughters: Women and Drama in the Age of Shakespeare.* New York: Columbia University Press.

Jed, Stephanie. 1989. *Chaste Thinking: The Rape of Lucretia and the Birth of Humanism.* Bloomington: Indiana University Press.

Joucl-Ruau, André. 1977. *Le Tacitisme de Saavedra Fajardo.* Paris: Editions Hispaniques.

Kamen, Henry. 1980. *Spain in the Later Seventeenth Century, 1665–1700.* London: Longman.

Kantorowicz, Ernst H. 1957. *The King's Two Bodies: A Study in Mediaeval Political Theology.* Princeton: Princeton University Press.

Kennedy, Ruth L. 1974. *Studies in Tirso 1.* Chapel Hill: North Carolina Studies in the Romance Languages.

———. 1975. "*La estrella de Sevilla,* Reinterpreted." *Revista de Archivos, Bibliotecas y Museos* 78: 385–408.

———. 1993. "*La estrella de Sevilla* as a Mirror of the Courtly Scene—and of its Anonymous Dramatist (Luis Velez?)." *Bulletin of the Comediantes* 45: 104–43.

Knapp, Steven, and Walter Benn Michaels. 1985. "Against Theory." In *Against Theory: Literary Studies and the New Pragmatism,* edited by W. J. T. Mitchell, 11–30. Chicago: University of Chicago Press.

Lacan, Jacques. 1981. *The Four Fundamental Concepts of Psycho-Analysis.* Translated by Alan Sheridan. New York: Norton.

Lafond, Jean, and Agustin Redondo. 1979. *L'Image du monde renversé et ses représentations littéraires et para-littéraires de la fin du XVIe siècle au milieu du XVIIe.* Paris: Librairie Philosophique J. Vrain.

Larson, Donald R. 1977. *The Honor Plays of Lope de Vega.* Cambridge: Harvard University Press.

Lauer, Robert. 1987. *Tyrannicide in Drama.* Stuttgart: Franz Steiner.

Leavitt, Sturgis E. 1930. "Apples of Hesperides in *La estrella de Sevilla.*" *MLN* 45: 314.

———. 1931a. "Apples of Hesperides Again." *MLN* 46: 33–34.

———. 1931b. *The Estrella de Sevilla and Claramonte.* Cambridge: Cambridge University Press.

Lévi-Strauss, Claude. 1966. *The Savage Mind.* Chicago: University of Chicago Press.

———. 1969. *The Elementary Structure of Kinship.* Rev. ed. Translated by James Harle Bell and John Richard von Sturmer. Edited by Rodney Needham. Boston: Beacon Press.

Lida de Malkiel, María Rosa. 1960. "El moro en las letras castellanas." *Hispanic Review* 28: 350–58.

Lynch, John. 1981. *Spain Under the Habsburgs.* Vol. 1. New York: Oxford University Press.

Lyon, John. 1983. *The Theater of Valle-Inclán*. Cambridge: Cambridge University Press.

MacCurdy, Raymond R., ed. 1971. *Spanish Drama of the Golden Age*. New York: Appleton.

MacDonald, Robert A. 1965. "Alfonso the Learned and Succession: A Father's Dilemma." *Speculum* 40: 647–53.

———. 1990. "Introducción." *Espéculo. Texto jurídico atribuido al Rey de Castilla Don Alfonso X, el Sabio,* xxxvii-lix. Madison: Hispanic Seminary of Medieval Studies.

Machiavelli, Niccolo. 1984. *Discorsi sopra la prima deca de Tito Livio*. Milano: Rizzoli.

———. 1988. *Il Principe*. Edited by Quentin Skinner and Russell Price. *Cambridge Texts in the History of Political Thought*. Cambridge: Cambridge University Press.

Maitland, F. W. 1936. "The Crown as Corporation". In *Selected Essays*. Cambridge: Cambridge University Press.

Malachy, Thérèse. 1987. *Molière: Les Métamorphoses du Carnaval*. Paris: A. Nizet.

Mandrell, James. 1992. *Don Juan and the Point of Honor: Seduction, Patriarchal Society, and Literary Tradition*. Penn State Studies in Romance Literatures. University Park: Pennsylvania State University Press.

Maravall, J. A. 1944. *La teoría española del Estado en el siglo XVII*. Madrid: Instituto de Estudios Políticos.

———. 1975. *Estudios de historia del pensamiento español. Siglo XVII*. Madrid: Ediciones Cultura Hispánica.

———. 1978. "La función del honor en la sociedad tradicional." *Ideologies and Literature* 2: 9–27.

———. 1981. *La cultura del Barroco*. Barcelona: Ariel.

Mariana, P. Juan de. 1930. *Del rey y de la institución de la dignidad real*. Translated by E. Barriobero y Herrán. Madrid: Mundo Latino.

Marín, Diego. 1982. "Función dramática de la versificación en el teatro de Calderón." *Segismundo* 167: 95–113.

Marinis, Marco de. 1984. *L'esperienza dello spettatore: Fondamenti per una semiotica della recezione teatrale*. Urbino: Centro Internazionale di Semiotica e di Linguistica.

———. 1986. "Problemas de semiótica teatral: La relación espectáculo-espectador." *Gestos* 9: 11–24.

Mariscal, George. 1991. *Contradictory Subjects: Quevedo, Cervantes, and Seventeenth-Century Spanish Culture*. Ithaca, N.Y.: Cornell University Press.

Márquez Villanueva, Francisco. 1975. *Personajes y temas del "Quijote."* Madrid: Taurus.

———. 1984. "El problema historiográfico de los moriscos." *Bulletin Hispanique* 86. 1–2: 61–135.

———. 1985. "Literatura bufonesca o del 'loco.'" *Nueva Revista de Filología Hispánica* 34: 501–8.

Martín Gaite, Carmen. 1987. *Usos amorosos del dieciocho en España*. Barcelona: Anagrama.

Martínez Kleiser, Luis. 1978. *Refranero general ideológico español*. Madrid: Editorial Hernando.

Marx, Karl. 1967. *Capital: A Critique of Political Economy*. Translated by Samuel Moore and Edward Aveling. Edited by Frederick Engels. 3 vols. New York: International Publishers.

Mauss, Marcel. 1967. *The Gift: Forms and Functions of Exchange in Archaic Societies*. Translated by Ian Cunnison. New York: Norton.

McCrary, William C. 1971. "Ritual Action and Form in *La estrella de Sevilla*." In *Homenaje a William L. Fichter: Estudios sobre el teatro antiguo hispánico y otros ensayos,* edited by A. David Kossoff and José Amor y Vázquez, 505–13. Madrid: Castalia.

McGaha, Michael D. 1978. "The Structure of *El caballero de Olmedo*." *Hispania* 61: 451–58.

———. 1990. "Antonio Enríquez Gómez and the Count-Duke of Olivares." In *Texto y espectáculo: Nuevas dimensiones críticas de la comedia,* edited by Arturo Pérez-Pisonero. El Paso: University of Texas at El Paso.

McGuire, Philip C. 1985. *Speechless Dialect: Shakespeare's Open Silences*. Berkeley and Los Angeles: University of California Press.

McKendrick, Melveena. 1974. *Woman and Society in the Spanish Drama of the Golden Age: A Study of the 'mujer varonil.'* London: Cambridge University Press.

———. 1984. "Celebration or Subversion?: *Los comendadores de Córdoba* Reconsidered." *Bulletin of Hispanic Studies* 61: 352–60.

———. 1992. Letter to Frederick A. de Armas. 4 December 1992.

Mechoulan, Henry. 1977. *Mateo López Bravo. Un socialista español del siglo XVII*. Madrid: Editora Nacional.

Menéndez y Pelayo, Marcelino. 1949. *Estudios sobre el teatro de Lope de Vega* 4: 173–244. Madrid: CSIC.

Megill, Allan. 1985. *Prophets of Extremity: Nietzsche, Heidegger, Foucault, Derrida*. Berkeley: University of California Press.

Mondragón, Jerónimo de. 1953. *Censura de la locura humana y excelencias della*. Edited by Antonio Vilanova. Barcelona: Selecciones Bibliófilas.

Montemayor, Jorge de. 1970. *Los siete libros de la Diana*. Edited by Francisco López Estrada. Madrid: Espasa-Calpe.

Montesinos, J. Fernández. 1969. "La paradoja del 'arte nuevo.'" In *Estudios sobre Lope de Vega*. Salamanca: Anaya.

Morley, S. Griswold, and Courtney Bruerton. 1968. *Cronología de las comedias de Lope de Vega*. Madrid: Gredos.

Morrison, Toni. 1989. "Unspeakable Things Unspoken: The Afro-American Presence in American Literature." *Michigan Quarterly Review* 28: 1–34.

Mulvey, Laura. 1975. "Visual Pleasure and Narrative Cinema." *Screen* 16: 6–16.

———. 1989. *Visual and Other Pleasures*. Bloomington and Indianapolis: University of Indiana Press.

Newman, Karen. 1990. "Directing Traffic: Subjects, Objects, and the Politics of Exchange." *Differences* 2. 2: 41–54.

O'Callaghan, Joseph F. 1975. *A History of Medieval Spain*. Ithaca, N.Y.: Cornell University Press.

Ong, Walter J. 1977. *Interfaces of the Word*. Ithaca: Cornell University Press.

———. 1982. *Orality and Literacy: The Technologizing of the Word*. New York: Methuen.

Oriel, Charles. 1993. *Writing and Inscription in Golden Age Drama*. West Lafayette, Ind.: Purdue University Press.

Parker, Alexander, A. 1959. "The Approach to the Spanish Drama of the Golden Age." *Tulane Drama Review* 4: 42–59.

———. 1962. "Towards a Definition of Calderonian Tragedy." *Bulletin of Hispanic Studies* 39: 222–37.

———. 1970. "The Spanish Drama of the Golden Age: A Method of Analysis and Interpretation." In *The Great Playwrights*, edited by Eric Bentley, 1: 679–707. New York: Doubleday.

Parr, James A. 1990. "La Crítica Conflictiva." In *Confrontaciones Calladas: El Crítico frente al Clásico*, 9–17. Madrid: Orígenes.

———. 1991a. "Criticism and the Comedia: 20 Years Later." In *After Its Kind: Approaches to the Comedia*, edited by Matthew Stroud, Anne Pasero, and Amy Williamsen, 137–59. Kassel: Reichenberger.

———. 1991b. "Method as Medium and Message: Technique and Its Discontents." In *After Its Kind: Approaches to the Comedia*, edited by Matthew Stroud, Anne Pasero, and Amy Williamsen, 107–17. Kassel: Reichenberger.

———. 1992. "Canons for the *Comedia*: Interrelations, Instrumental Value, Interpretive Communities, Textuality." *Gestos* 7: 95–104.

Pavis, Patrice. 1987. "From Text to Performance." In *Performing Texts*, edited by Michael Issacharoff and Robin F. Jones, 86–100. Philadelphia: University of Pennsylvania Press.

Peristiany, J. G. 1966. *Honour and Shame: The Values of Mediterranean Society*. Chicago: University of Chicago Press.

Pitt-Rivers, Julian. 1966. "Honour and Social Status." In *Honour and Shame: The Values of Mediterranean Society*, edited by J. G. Peristany, 19–77. Chicago: University of Chicago Press.

———. 1977. *The Fate of Shechem or The Politics of Sex: Essays in the Anthropology of the Mediterranean*. Cambridge: Cambridge University Press.

Pops, Martin. 1979. "The *Woman Reading at a Window*." *Salmagundi* 44–45: 29–30.

Pratt, Mary Louise. 1977. *Toward a Speech Act Theory of Literary Discourse*. Bloomington: Indiana University Press.

Pring-Mill, R. D. F. 1962. "Sententiousness in *Fuenteovejuna*." *Tulane Drama Review* 7: 5–37.

Pulice de Amadei, Alicia. 1982. "El *stile rapprasentativo* en la comedia de teatro de Calderón." In *Approaches to the Theater of Calderón*, edited by Michael D. McGaha, 215–29. Washington, D.C.: University Press of America.

Quevedo, Francisco de. 1958. *Obras completas 1: Obras en prosa*. Madrid: Aguilar.

———. 1966. *Política de Dios y gobierno de Cristo*. Edited by J. O. Crosby. Madrid: Castalia.

Read, Jan. 1974. *The Moors in Spain and Portugal*. London: Faber and Faber.

Read, Malcolm. 1990. *Visions in Exile: The Body in Spanish Literature and Linguistics, 1500–1800*. Amsterdam/Philadelphia: John Benjamins/PUMRL.

Rivadeneyra, P. Pedro de. 1868. *Obras escogidas. Biblioteca de Autores Españoles.* Vol. 60. Madrid.

Rivers, Elias L. 1980. "The Shame of Writing in *La Estrella de Sevilla.*" *Folio: Essays on Foreign Lanuages and Literatures* 12: 105–28.

———. 1983. *Quixotic Scriptures: Essays on the Textuality of Hispanic Literature.* Bloomington: Indiana University Press.

Rodríguez López-Vázquez, Alfredo. 1984 "*La estrella de Sevilla* y *Deste agua no beberé:* ¿el mismo autor?" *Bulletin of the Comediantes* 36: 83–100.

———. 1991. "Introducción." Andrés de Claramonte. *La estrella de Sevilla.* Madrid: Cátedra.

Romancero General o Colección de romances castellanos. 1945. Edited by Agustín Durán. *Biblioteca de autores españoles* 16. Madrid.

Ruano de la Haza, José. 1987. "The Staging of Calderón's *La vida es sueño* and *La dama duende.*" *Bulletin of Hispanic Studies* 64: 51–63.

———. 1988. "La puesta en escena en los teatros comerciales." *Criticón* 42: 81–102.

———. 1989. "Actores, decorados, y accesorios escénicos en los teatro comerciales del siglo de oro." In *Actas del Congreso Internacional sobre el actor y técnica de representación en el teatro clásico español del Siglo de Oro a hoy,* edited by José María Díez Borque, 1–20. London: Tamesis.

Rubin, Gayle. 1975. "The Traffic in Women." In *Toward an Anthropology of Women,* edited by Rayna R. Reiter, 157–210. New York: Monthly Review Press.

Rubio, Julián María, et al. 1970. *Gran historia general de los pueblos hispanos.* Vol. 3. Barcelona: Instituto Gallach.

Saavedra Fajardo, Diego de. 1947. *Idea de un príncipe político-cristiano representada en cien empresas: Obras de don Diego de Saavedra Fajardo. Biblioteca de Autores Españoles* 25.

Said, Edward W. 1979. *Orientalism.* New York: Vintage Books.

———. 1985. "Orientalism Reconsidered." *Race & Class* 27. 2: 5–15.

Salazar, Fray Juan de. 1945. *Política española.* Madrid: Instituto de Estudios Políticos.

Sanmartín Boncompte, Francisco. 1951. *Tácito en España.* Barcelona.

Scoles, Robert. 1992. "Canonicity and Textuality." In *Introduction to Scholarship in Modern Languages and Literatures,* 2d ed., edited by Joseph Gibaldi, 138–58. New York: MLA.

Searie, John R. 1969. *Speech Acts: An Essay in the Philosophy of Language.* Cambridge: Cambridge University Press.

Sedgwick, Eve Kosofsky. 1985. *Between Men: English Literature and Male Homosocial Desire.* New York: Columbia University Press.

Selden, Raman. 1989. *A Reader's Guide to Contemporary Literary Theory.* 2d ed. Lexington: University Press of Kentucky.

Selección de Comedias del Siglo de Oro Español. 1973. Edited by Alva V. Ebersole. Madrid: Castalia.

Shakespeare, William. 1972. *The Pelican Shakespeare: Twelfth Night.* Edited by Charles T. Prouty. New York: Penguin.

Sieber, Harry. 1994. "Cloaked History: Power and Politics in *La estrella de Sevilla,*" *Gestos* 17: 98–109.

Silverman, Kaja. 1983. *The Subject of Semiotics*. Oxford: Oxford University Press.

Skinner, Quentin. 1978. *The Foundations of Modern Political Thought*. Vol.1, *The Renaissance*. Vol.2, *The Age of Reformation*. Cambridge: Cambridge University Press.

Snow, Edward. 1979. "The Head of a Young Girl." *Salmagundi* 44–45: 122–41.

Soufas, Teresa S. 1990. *Melancholy and the Secular Mind in Spanish Golden Age Literature*. Columbia: University of Missouri.

———. 1992. "The Receptive Circuit and the *Mise en scène* in/of La Estrella de Sevilla." *MLN* 107: 220–35.

Southern, R. W. 1962. *Western Views of Islam in the Middle Ages*. Cambridge: Harvard University Press.

Spitzer, Leo. 1934. "Die *Estrella de Sevilla* und Claramonte." *Zeitschrift für romanische philologie* 54: 533–88.

Stoll, Anita K. 1988. *A Study and Critical Edition of Lope de Vega's "La noche de San Juan."* Kassel, Germany: Edition Reichenberger.

Stradling, R. A. 1988. *Philip IV and the Government of Spain, 1621–65*. Cambridge: Cambridge University Press.

Strong, Roy. 1973. *Splendor at Court: Renaissance Spectacle and the Theater of Power*. Boston: Houghton Mifflin.

Stroud, Matthew D. 1990. *Fatal Union: A Pluralistic Approach to the Spanish Wife-Murder Comedias*. Lewisburg, Pa: Bucknell University Press.

Sturm, H., and S. Sturm. 1969. "The Astronomical Metaphor in *La Estrella de Sevilla*." *Hispania* 52: 193–97.

———. 1970. "The Two Sanchos in *La Estrella de Sevilla*." *Romanistisches Jahrbuch* 21: 285–93.

Sullivan, Henry. 1990. "Lacan and Calderón: Spanish Classical Drama in the Light of Psychoanalytic Theory." *Gestos* 10: 39–55.

Surtz, Ronald E. 1979. *The Birth of a Theater*. Madrid: Editorial Castalia.

Swift Lenz, Carolyn Ruth, et al., eds. 1980. *The Woman's Part: Feminist Criticism of Shakespeare*. Urbana and Chicago: University of Illinois Press.

Tate, Robert B. 1954. "Mythology in Spanish Historiography of the Middle Ages and the Renaissance." *Hispanic Review* 22: 1–18.

Thomas, H., ed. 1923. *La Estrella de Sevilla*. Oxford: Oxford University Press.

Thucydides. 1931. *The Peloponnesian War*. Translated by Charles Foster Smith. Vol. 3. London: Heinemann.

Tierno Galván, E. 1971. "El tacitismo en las doctrinas políticas del Siglo de Oro Español." In *Escritos (1950–60)*. Madrid: Ed. Tecnos.

Tirso de Molina. 1946–59. *Obras completas*. Edited by Blanca de los Ríos Lampérez. 3 vols. Madrid: Aguilar.

Trigueros, Cándido María. 1800. *Sancho Ortiz de las Roelas*. Madrid: Imprenta de Sancha.

Unamuno, Miguel de. 1960. "Mi Religión." In *Obras Selectas*, edited by Julián Marías, 255–60. Madrid: Plenitud.

Valesio, Paolo. 1971. "The Language of Madness in the Renaissance." *Yearbook of Italian Studies* 11: 199–234.

Varey, John. 1985. "Staging and Stage Directions." In *Editing the Comedia*, edited by Michael D. McGaha and Frank P. Casa, 148–161. Ann Arbor, Michigan: Michigan Romance Studies.

———. 1987. *Cosmovisión y escénografía: El teatro español en el siglo de oro.* Madrid: Editorial Castalia.

———. 1991. "Memory Theaters, Playhouses, and *Corrales de Comedias.*" In *Parallel Lives: Spanish and English National Drama 1580–1680,* edited by Louise and Peter Fothergill-Payne. Lewisbury, Pa: Bucknell University Press.

Vázquez, Luis, ed. 1989. Tirso de Molina. *El burlador de Sevilla y convidado de piedra.* Madrid: Estudios.

Vega Carpio, Lope de. 1890–1913. *Los comendadores de Córdoba.* In *Obras de Lope de Vega,* vol. 11, edited by Marcelino Menéndez y Pelayo. Madrid: Real Academia Española.

Velasco, Recaredo F. de. 1925. *Referencias y transcripciones para la historia de la literatura política en España.* Madrid: Editorial Reus.

Villamediana, Conde de. 1990. *Poesía impresa completa.* Edited by José Francisco Ruiz Casanova. Madrid: Cátedra.

von Hallberg, Robert, ed. 1984. *Canons.* Chicago: University of Chicago Press.

Wardropper, Bruce W., ed. 1970. *Teatro Español del Siglo de Oro.* New York: Scribner's.

———., ed. 1983. *Siglos de oro: Barroco.* In *Historia y crítica de la literatura española,* vol. 3, edited by Francisco Rico. Barcelona: Editorial Crítica.

Weiner, Jack. 1981. "Zeus y la metamorfosis de Sancho IV en *La Estrella de Sevilla.*" *Explicación de textos literarios* 10: 63–67.

Wilder, Thornton. 1953. "Lope, Pinedo, Some Child Actors and a Lion." *Romance Philology* 7: 19–25.

Williamsen, Vern. 1977. "La función estructural del verso en la comedia del siglo de oro." In *Actas del Quinto Congreso Internacional de Hispanistas,* 883–91. Bordeaux, France: University of Bordeaux, Instución de Estudios Iberos e Iberoromanos.

———. 1984. "Rhyme as an Audible 'Sign' in Two Calderonian Plays." *Neophilologus* 68: 546–56.

———. 1989. "La asonancia como señal auditiva en el teatro de Tirso de Molina." In *Actas del IX Congreso de la Asociación Internacional de Hispanistas,* 687–94. Frankfurt am Main: Verwuert Verlag.

Yarbro-Bejarano, Yvonne. 1987. "Hacia un análisis feminista del drama de honor de Lope." *La Torre, Revista de la Universidad de Puerto Rico* n.s. 1, 3–4: 615–32.

Yates, Frances A. *The Art of Memory.* 1972. London: Routledge & Kegan Paul.

Young, Richard A. 1979. *La figura del rey y la institución real en la comedia lopesca.* Madrid: Porría.

Index